30-DAYS TO
CHRISTIAN
MEDITATION

Journey Into Christian Mysticism To Discover Your Authentic New Life In Christ

STEVEN J. SMITH

Copyright © 2020 by Steven J. Smith

All rights reserved.

No part of this book may be reproduced, stored in a retrieval system, or transmitted in any form or by any means—electronic, mechanical, digital, photocopy, recording, or any other—except for brief quotations in critical reviews and certain other noncommercial uses permitted by copyright law, without the prior permission of the author.

Scripture texts in this work are typically from the New American Bible, revised edition © 2010, 1991, 1986, 1970 Confraternity of Christian Doctrine, Washington, D.C. and are used by permission of the copyright owner. All Rights Reserved. No part of the New American Bible may be reproduced in any form without permission in writing from the copyright owner.

https://interiorlife.app

ISBN: 978-1-7358184-0-5

30-days to Christian Meditation – Table of Contents

Acknowledgements and Dedication v
Preface vii
The Landscape of this Book xv
Introduction 1
Day 1: Retreat Opening 5
Week 1: The Giant World of Christian Mysticism 19
(each session followed by 5 minutes of silent prayer)
    Day 2: Mental Prayer – *What* is it and *Why* is it indispensable? ... 21
    Day 3: *How* We Learn About Mental Prayer - Catholic
        Spiritual Tradition 31
    Day 4: The *Who* of Mental Prayer part 1 - Our Role and What
        It Means to be Human 49
    Day 5: The *Who* of Mental Prayer part 2 – God's Role and the
        Life of the Trinity 70
    Day 6: The Interior Life is Necessary to Sustain the Active Life 84
    Day 7: The Three Ages of the Interior Life 98
    Day 8: Week 1 – Putting It All Together – What is your *Why*? 115

Week 2: Meditation Dispositions and Principles 129
(each session followed by 7 minutes of silent prayer)
    Day 9: Dispositions and Principles vs Technique and Method ... 131
    Day 10: Dispositions Part 1 – Faith and Trust as the Basis for
        Mental Prayer 143
    Day 11: Dispositions Part II – Purity of Intention and Humility 155
    Day 12: Dispositions Part III – Fortitude 167
    Day 13: Principles Part I – Primacy of God's Action and Love 176
    Day 14: Principles Part II – The Humanity of Jesus and
        Indwelling of the Spirit 185
    Day 15: Week 2 – Putting It All Together with Asceticism 197

Week 3: Meditation, Our Starting Point 211
(each session followed by 10 minutes of meditation)
    Day 16: Meditation – Into the Silence, To Know God and
        Listen to Him 213
    Day 17: Christian Meditation Step 1 - Recollection 226

    Day 18: Christian Meditation Steps 2 and 3 – Read and Reflect . . 236
    Day 19: Christian Meditation Steps 4 and 5 – Relate and Resolve 246
    Day 20: Dealing with Distraction – Immediate Responses 260
    Day 21: Remote Preparation for Prayer 276
    Day 22: Week 3 – Putting It All Together – Keeping it Simple. . . . 296

Week 4: Put Out into the Deep 309
(each session followed by 15 minutes of silent prayer)
    Day 23: Consolation, Desolation and Spiritual Combat 311
    Day 24: Growing in Virtue and Conquering Your Root Sin 324
    Day 25: Grace and Gifts of the Spirit 336
    Day 26: Discernment of Spirits – An Ignatian Approach 347
    Day 27: Spiritual Direction 360
    Day 28: The Sacramental Life and Mary, Our Blessed Mother . . . 369
    Day 29: Week 4 – Putting It All Together, Fruits of the Holy
             Spirit and Beatitude 379

Day 30: Retreat Closing 396
Appendix: Recommended Resources and References 411
About the Author 415

ACKNOWLEDGEMENTS AND DEDICATION

Like countless others, our Blessed Mother was instrumental in bringing me home to her Son. This book and apostolate were borne out of that motherly love which brought me to the redeeming love of Jesus Christ.

I am very grateful to my spiritual directors, Fr. Jim and Fr. Erik, the Spiritual Mentorship program (Apostles of the Interior Life and Holy Family School of Faith), ACTS Ministries, and many others, for generously sharing their gifts of formation.

God has richly blessed me through close friends and family - I give thanks for that to God, and each of you. In particular I thank the intrepid band who went through the trial version of this retreat (Tim, Nora, Marcela, Tom, Larry, Brad, Mike and Kevin) – at the risk of over-stepping my bounds, I predict time off in purgatory for each of you.

And I especially thank God for my beautiful wife and best friend, Karen, and equally-beautiful daughters Annie and Kalie – to whom this work is dedicated.

PREFACE

"'You are Simon the son of John.' Jesus was calling him specifically to become someone else while still remaining himself." (Dom Lepori, *Simon, Called Peter*)

We all have the sense at different points in life that something is out of order. Either we are not living the life we are supposed to live. Or, we're not the person we're supposed to be living our life. Or, we're living our life, but there's something we're missing, something we're not doing that we should, so that we would be living our life at the highest level we can. Somehow, we should still be ourself, but we should be made new at the same time.

Christian meditation is the key to how Christ makes us new, right in the midst of our "ordinary" life. And there is no substitute for it. There is no other path, no other way, no other technique, no other discipline - the only way to genuine, lasting transformation in this life is through Christian meditation.

Or, perhaps, you once had a profound spiritual or conversion experience and came away filled with energy and realization of God's love in a way that changed how you looked at life. But over time it seems that conversion has stalled, and the initial experience is an ever more distant memory. Here again, Christian meditation is the key to how we are spiritually renewed each day.

And yet Christian meditation is almost completely unknown

in our time. Like a priceless work of art stored away in an attic and forgotten amid the churning and relentless current of time.

But there seems to be an awakening.

This book (please God) is a small part of the Holy Spirit's larger response to the spiritual challenges of our time in history.

More on that in a moment.

This book is also written with the hope to break that cycle of yearning for "something more." A cycle we all know too well. We do something for our spiritual growth, there is an initial burst of energy, but it quickly dwindles and all-too-soon we return to searching for *that next thing*. This book is based on *the one thing* that must underly all our other good spiritual endeavors, and endeavors in general, for them to truly take root and bear fruit.

And, more on that in a moment.

To begin at the beginning, this book was born out of a lifetime of prayer.

Strike that. This book was born out of a lifetime of "praying." Not a lifetime of genuine *prayer*. For the opening acts of my life (spanning decades) the praying was primarily prayer of intercession (mostly in desperation "Lord I *need* this. *Now*"). From time to time there would arise a prayer of thanksgiving ("Well done, God. Thanks for seeing things my way"), and a certain type of contrition ("God, I wish I hadn't done that"). Rarer still, a prayer of adoration. In all this praying the communication was basically one way, and you can tell which way.

On the rarest occasion I might have made the attempt to listen to Him. But mostly it was all talking, no listening. How well does that work in other relationships? Exactly. It was no different in this situation. I wasn't making room for God to do His work in my life.

A one-way relationship, isn't. Period. It exists no more than a one ended walking stick. There is no "relating" involved in a one-way relationship. I was never trying to get to know God. I was just talking at Him and trying to get Him to know me on my terms - what I wanted and what I needed. I never asked about Him, pondered Him, asked what I could do for Him. I never asked Him what He desired for me nor what He desired to do for others through me.

By God's grace, and through a string of providential happenings and encounters, I finally came to understand the Truth known to so many others - that we were made for a real relationship with God. "Whoever loves me will keep my word, and my Father will love him, and we will come to him and make our dwelling with him." (Jn 14:23)

This led to many years of praying to God in earnest, coming to know Him, and learning to listen to His voice.

This apostolate, *Interior Life*, was born from that experience, years of spiritual direction, intensive reading, studying, retreats, formation, and most importantly, daily holy hours. I have endeavored to put all of this into real-life practice. How does an average person live out the mystical and ascetical tradition of the Church amid everyday life? How do we come to recognize the interplay of our interior and exterior life? How do we discern God's will for our life? As with so many other faithful Christians around the world and throughout history, I've delved into the well-established answers to these questions as part of my journey of living a very "ordinary" life in the world and in my vocation as a husband and father (a very blessed husband and father I should add!).

Once I started catching on, again and again I'd find myself thinking "how have I gone all this time and not known ... about the Church's tradition for how to have a real, living relationship with Christ .... about the movements of consolation and desolation ... how to hear God speaking to me ... how to discern God's will for my life ... what spiritual combat is all about ... how suffering is transformed into grace ... the real fruit of asceticism ... what it really means to be human ...

how to master my emotions ... how to overcome my flaws and wounds ... " and on, and on.

The reason, of course, was mostly me. I was bound and determined to live life on my terms. That didn't leave much room nor opportunity to give my will over to God's and learn His ways.

But it is also the case that the Church's beautiful and powerful mystical and ascetical tradition had gone mostly underground. Even once I had a hunger to follow that path it took no small amount of work to find and uncover it (with the help of outstanding spiritual directors and guides).

Our true Interior Life grows and flows from our relationship with God. A key component of that, where we all start and grow, is Christian meditation. The two most important things that happen in Christian meditation are that we get to know Jesus Christ and we learn to listen to Him.

Additionally, we certainly get to pour our heart out to Him - and we come to learn that we really don't know our own hearts, not in the full.

How we come to know Jesus and listen to Him, through Christian meditation, is what this book and the *30 Days to Christian Meditation* retreat are all about.

And it goes beyond that - our interior life is meant to grow and envelop and sanctify all that we do: our vocations, our relationships, our service work, our occupations, our leisure time, our personal growth and all our other spiritual endeavors like consecrations, novenas and scripture studies.

Everything we do is enriched through our interior life.

This brings us back to the "Seek-Hope-Despair" cycle:

We all have a deep, unfulfilled longing. St. Augustine says, "Our hearts are restless." Inevitably we come upon something that we hope will fill that void (ranging from worldly distractions, to self-help methods, to good Christian devotions). We dive in with hope and optimism and for a time, perhaps, the void seems filled. But it isn't. Because our void is God-sized. Anything we put in the void smaller than God will ultimately get swallowed up (even our closest human relationships). And when the "next great thing" ceases to satisfy, we become discouraged and give up on it. We again find ourselves face-to-face with the emptiness and start seeking anew.

Nothing will satisfy our longing until we commit ourselves to the one *the one thing* that must underly all our other good endeavors, spiritual or otherwise. And the one thing that makes everything else take root and bear fruit is a deep, meaningful relationship with Jesus Christ through Christian meditation.

Jesus' own words and example, the lives of the apostles, the testimony of the Saints and the teaching of all the great mystics and spiritual masters is that nothing else will suffice for Christian meditation. Nothing.

So, wherever you are in life, I hope there is something in this retreat for you, because we can always go deeper in our relationship with Christ – and going deeper in that relationship always results in becoming more fully who we were created to be.

And to be clear – this retreat is not "Steve Smith on prayer." To the best of my ability, I am simply distilling the ancient Christian tradition that has been passed on to all of us. To the extent that there is anything in this book that helps you grow closer to God and neighbor, and to become more fully who you were created to be, it's because I succeeded in not getting in the way of passing on the wisdom given to us by Christ and passed on through His Church and her many great Saints, mystics and spiritual masters.

As I noted at the outset, this book is also a response to the Spirit of the times.

We're not talking about the "eat, drink and be merry" worldly spirit of the times, but the true Spirit of the times – how the Holy Spirit is moving through our current world at this time in history.

The Spirit is always adapting to the needs of the times. In the Counter Reformation, the movement of the Spirit was just that – Reform. In the 1960's and 70's, the rebellion of the sexual revolution was very bold and outward. So too was the response of the Spirit in the charismatic renewal.

Today, the rebellion is ever more inward – in our interior. We don't need God's blessing and providence; we have science and technology. We don't need God's peace; we have yoga, entertainment, home gyms and pharmaceuticals galore. We don't need God's eternal, absolute Truth; we have our own personal truth and a ready supply of internet voices to tell us whatever we most want to hear.

This is the interior rebellion. And just so, you can sense the movement of the Spirit, to awaken us to a true interior life.

None of us, especially none of us living in the first world, are immune to this interior battle, this marginalization of God. It creeps and slithers into our lives from all angles, through any crack or crevice it can find.

As I write this, the world is hurtling toward an unknown future, turned upside down first by the Chinese coronavirus pandemonium and then by the racial protests turned to agitated riots and activism. For the moment most everyone is coming to the realization that their exterior sources of security and control (jobs, savings accounts, health care systems, governments, communities) can all come crashing down in a heartbeat.

It's a stark reminder that all control and security in this world is an illusion. Our only bedrock and safe harbor is Christ Jesus.

Did God "ordain" these trials as a response to our rebellion? I don't know. Will He work through them to draw us to Himself? Absolutely.

And we can see how the enemy is also working through all the current chaos to bend events, as well as our thoughts and actions, to his twisted purpose. Which is the destruction of souls.

There we have it, as it has always been. The battle for souls. God calls us to join that battle, which is what living is really all about.

Jesus tells us, "I came that they may have life, and have it abundantly."

First and foremost, Jesus is speaking of our Interior Life. Which is where much of the battle plays out. It is also where we are transformed into who we were created to be so we can live the life we were meant to live.

And it all starts with Christian meditation.

Steven J. Smith

West Friendship, MD

June 14, 2020 (Solemnity of the Body and Blood of Christ)

THE LANDSCAPE OF THIS BOOK

THIS RETREAT IS best experienced in combination with the video sessions and guided meditations provided in the *Interior Life* mobile app (in your app store or www.interiorlife.app).

Color versions of charts and graphics in this book are available in the ebook and video version of this retreat.

Each day of the 30-day retreat is a separate chapter of the book.

Each week is dedicated to a specific theme.

The end of each chapter includes a summary of the key points from that day for easy future reference – these entries are referred to as "Pearls".

There is open space at the end of each chapter for you to write down your thoughts and insights (your own pearls).

The postscript for Day 1 presents important recommendations for getting the most out of this retreat.

You will also find this book uses an allegory of traveling through a jungle. Each day starts with an entry from this allegory. Please note this truly is an allegory. It is meant to illustrate a key point from that day – it is in no way meant to be a rigorous theological representation of the nature of God and man.

Why does this book equate your spiritual journey with a mission through a jungle? See for yourself...

INTRODUCTION

You are lost in a jungle.

It's dark. Dense. Hot and humid.

Everything is strange. Everything *looks* dangerous. Everything *sounds* dangerous.

Should you remain still? Should you stay right where you are? But what happens when night comes?

Should you start moving in the hope of finding someplace safer?

If you try moving somewhere else, which way should you go? You can barely see the sky through the thick canopy. You can barely see in front of you through the thick undergrowth. As bad as things are now, how do you know if you start walking one way or another it won't go from bad to worse?

And which way to start walking when each direction looks treacherous?

Maybe to the right? It looks like the way is a little easier to the right. You move some thick branches out of the way so you can see a little better. It's dark ahead, full of bushes and vines, but maybe not as bad as other directions. You slowly move forward. But within a few paces you've walked into a web. It's stuck to your face. And you get a look at the spider that made it. Large and covered with bright markings. What happens if one of *those* bites you?

Introduction

You instinctively back away, one foot behind the other, eyes glued to that awful spider. And you back right into more bushes and vines (more spiders?). You quickly twist away from them and try to get back to your starting point. Going to the right was no good. Maybe to the left is the better way to go. But wait a minute, which way is left? Are you even back at your starting point?

You look wildly around. Left. Right. Up. Down. That's when it catches your eye. Almost invisible in the moss and growth of the jungle floor. But there it is. Slithering toward you. Dark, green, thick, long and almost silent. You're paralyzed with fear.

All you can do is stare. Powerful coils steadily pushing it toward you. Closing in on you. Dead eyes fixed on you.

And then from nowhere a foot comes down on its head. Crushing it into the ground.

The person standing before you is peaceful and at ease. Perfectly in control even amid these terrible surroundings. His gaze is fixed on you. His gaze full of life; full of concern for you.

You are so amazed you barely hear His words to you:

If you want to live, follow me.

These are Jesus' words to each one of us: "If any man will come after me, let him deny himself, and take up his cross daily, *and follow me.*" (Lk 9:23) Whether we know it or not, we are traveling through a spiritual jungle. It is treacherous. The only safe way through, to happiness in this life and eternity with God in the next, is to follow Christ.

How do we follow Him? How do we live each day with a genuinely real, meaningful, transforming relationship with Christ? That is the purpose of Christian mental prayer (meditation and contemplation).

Countless saints, mystics, spiritual masters and people of good will of all stripe have followed this path. Because it is the path that Christ himself shows us.

Even if you've never heard the term "mental prayer" (these days, few have), have no doubt or concern. You were literally created by God to have relationship with him through mental prayer. By your birth and baptism you were given the physical and spiritual equipment necessary for it.

This 30-Day retreat will walk you through this millennia-old tradition so you can continue on a life-long adventure with Christ.

DAY 1: RETREAT OPENING

> Welcome to Day 1 of our retreat! We're going on a spiritual adventure covering a great deal of ground: what you're made of, what the life of God is like, how to hear God speaking to you, how to tell God's voice from imposters, and that's just for starters. How do we get started? Really, there's no other way than to just jump in. Here we go.

Let's open with prayer:

Come Holy Spirit, make of me a fitting dwelling place for the Lord.

Our opening prayer, based on Ephesians 2:22, calls to mind that God is present with us at this very moment. We are going to comment again and again in this retreat that these are not empty, sentimental words. God is truly present right now. If it does not *feel* that way to you, then you have come to the right place - by the end of this retreat you will have a much better awareness of God's presence and how it relates to our feelings.

It is also an all-important starting point for this 30-day journey that we call to mind that God created us, God loves us, God desires a relationship with us and God wants us to be happy in this life and spend eternity with Him in Heaven. To guide us to that home, God became man, dwelled among us, and left us his Spirit so that He could continue to dwell with us.

St. Teresa of Avila was a towering mystic of the counter reformation (the Catholic Church reforming herself in response to Martin Luther's Protestant reformation). Instructing her Carmelite sisters, St. Teresa taught them (and us) "Now if we think carefully over this, sisters, the soul of the righteous man is nothing but a paradise, in which, God tells us, He takes His delight." She has this on good account from Proverbs 8:31 and, for that matter, the entirety of scripture and salvation history.

God dwells in us. God delights in us.

So, how do we share in that? How do we make these more than just nice sounding words? How do we take them to heart? This is the goal of our retreat – to make those words as real to you as you are to yourself (and in time even more real than that). We are going to spend these next 30 days together learning how God speaks with us, particularly through mental prayer. That statement is perfectly accurate. God speaks to you. In fact, He desires to speak *with* you.

A Little About Me and You

My name is Steve Smith. I am the founder of *Interior Life* and am so happy that you are making this retreat. A little about me - I was raised a "cradle Catholic" in a loving home with wonderful parents and a great sister. But I also spent many years in spiritual mediocrity, going through the motions. At a certain point God made His move and began actively drawing me to Him. First, during life's challenges, which we all encounter in one form or another, and through our blessed mother. And then I had a providential encounter with my future spiritual director in an airport which led me on a journey through Ignatian and Carmelite spirituality. This entailed years of spiritual direction, many retreats, careful study and internalization of the writings of dozens of spiritual masters, training as a spiritual mentor and, most importantly, countless hours with the Lord in mental prayer. All of this renewed my life in the Church and the world around me, bringing many wonderful new relationships and opportunities to serve, and enriching my relationship with my lovely wife and daughters.

Most fundamentally, that journey brought me into a genuine relationship with God. All of that transpired while I was living an "ordinary life" in the world as a husband and father and working in the field of forensic engineering. I learned that living a contemplative life does not have to be at odds with living in the world, but in fact the contemplative life elevates and perfects all the other facets of life. Everything I do now, including *Interior Life* and this retreat, is a response to God's goodness and sharing that as best as I can with others.

That's me. How about you?

It is quite likely that part of why you are here is that you have a deep desire for fulfillment – everyone does. It is written into us. Fulfillment in developing your own special gifts and abilities. Fulfillment in relationships. Fulfillment in carrying out your vocation, most likely with your family. And, fulfillment in your relationship with God. All of scripture (New Testament and Old), all of the examples of the Saints, all of the great spiritual masters and theologians, unanimously proclaim that the closer we get to God the more we become fully ourselves, fully who we were created to be - *fully*, as in fulfillment.

Everything else flows from our relationship with God: peace, joy, kindness, accomplishing great things, every bit of it. The key is growing close to God. Mental prayer – silent personal prayer – is the foundation of this relationship. As with all relationships, our relationship with God must have other facets as well – most importantly living out our vocation and growing in love for our neighbor – but the time we spend alone with God, speaking with Him and listening to Him, is the foundation.

Our Destination

While on the subject of speaking with God, let's turn for a moment to God speaking to us in sacred scripture, where he often invokes mountains. Mountains have a powerful effect on us. Looking up at them we sense nature's immensity. Looking down from them we feel part of that immensity, in the clouds above and the earth spread out below us. Much of the drama of scripture plays out on mountains. Noah disembarks and repopulates the earth from Mount Ararat. Abraham demonstrates his faith in God on Mount Moriah. Moses sees and hears God in the burning bush on Mount Sinai. Elijah hears God's whisper on Mount Carmel. The City of David is founded on Mount Zion. Jesus is transfigured on Mount Tabor. Jesus sweats drops of blood on the Mount of Olives. Jesus sacrifices His life for you and me on Mount Moriah. And there is more than that. Prophets were often led to mountains. Jesus' greatest sermon was delivered on the Mount. And yet, with faith the size of a mustard seed we can tell the mountain to "move from here to there, and it will move." (Mt 17:20)

Mountains have much to do with seeing what lies before us, growing close to God and growing strong in faith. This is a good place to start our 30-day journey in mental prayer; ascending a virtual mountain top to gaze outward and gain perspective on where we are headed.

Perspective is critical in life. Everyday wisdom tells us that any important undertaking should begin with the end in mind. When cooking an intricate recipe, the best approach is to read through the entire recipe to make sure the right ingredients are at hand, to be familiar with all of the steps of the preparation and to know what the finished dish should be like: its look, smell, texture and taste. Or to use another analogy appropriate to the matter at hand, consider driving to a far off and unfamiliar destination.

You could just get in the car, pull up the GPS and go.

That's my method, by the way, and I've tested it out enough to know it's not great, or even very good.

Better (especially when you are traveling with wife and children) is to first know a few things like: How far is it? How long will it take? Is there likely to be heavy traffic? Where might be good places for a rest stop? How will you recognize the destination (it's a blue house, third on the left...)? How can you avoid adding 2 hours to a 5-hour trip by accidentally taking the scenic route through Pennsylvania (I'll never live that down)? As you may have guessed – this *better way*, of looking ahead, is how my wife does things.

Back to our mountain top and gazing outward, we'll see our desired destination is an even higher peak, off in the distance – Heaven, "In the last days the mountain of the LORD's temple will be established as the highest of the mountains; it will be exalted above the hills, and all nations will stream to it." (Is 2:2) The goal of *this* life is to spend the *next* life (eternity) in Heaven, with God and the angels and saints.

There is a complimentary part of this goal, which is to participate in getting others to Heaven (first and foremost our families and the people God has specifically entrusted to us). The two great commandments are to love God with all our heart, mind, and strength and to love our neighbor as our self. If we love God as best as we are able, we will naturally want to be in Heaven with Him. And if we love our neighbor as best as we are able, we will desire and work for the highest and best things for them – and the highest and best thing we can desire for anyone is Heaven – in fact to be ahead of us in line!

What's your starting point on this journey? This very moment. This is your starting point. Right here and now, in this momentary slice of reality. Wherever you are right now is your personal starting line.

Between you and that far-off mountain is a deep and dense jungle. Traveling unaided through a jungle it is easy to become lost and turned around. And, end up in dark and dangerous places. We will discuss in

Week 4 why a jungle really is an appropriate analogy for the spiritual life. But there is a ribbon of a path that winds from where you are to that far-off mountain top, if you can find it and stay on it. And with the right guides, the jungle can also be a place of breathtaking beauty and thrilling adventure. Christian prayer, with God as our Guide, is how we find our way along that tricky jungle path. It is our spiritual GPS if you will.

What is your personal path to Heaven? I have no idea! No person on Earth knows your individual path to that far-off mountain top, to Heaven. Only God knows, and He is keeping it a secret all to himself. No, He's not. He very much desires to show you your path to Heaven. But he wants you to participate in its unfolding. One of the things we will talk about is that God connects with us here, in this moment. He is not in the past. And He is also not giving away the future – like going to see a movie with someone who tells you the ending before it even begins. He is arranging a beautiful future for you, but you must choose to travel with Him to that destination, and that happens moment by moment. St. Catherine of Sienna tells us "the two most important moments of our life are now and the hour of our death." And in the Hail Mary we ask her to pray for us "now and at the hour of our death." Aside from the moment when we depart this earthly life, right now, "this magic moment," is the single most important moment of our life.

That is not to say that God doesn't sometimes give us glimpses and encouragements and answer our questions. In fact, there is an entire aspect of spirituality called *discernment* that we will talk about as well – discerning Spirits and discerning God's will for our life. This is going to be such a fantastic 30 days – we have been given so many pearls to uncover. But the immediate point is this - there is a particular path you are meant to travel. Yes, we should all be striving to follow the same *way* (which is Christ), but there are aspects of your particular journey that are uniquely yours. God desires to accompany you, help you and care for you along your path. Prayer is how you communicate with God so that he can lead you home.

The Way We Will Follow

This 30-day retreat is focused on a form of prayer known as *mental prayer*. Mental prayer is silent, meditative prayer and is uniquely ordered to conversation with God - to God speaking with us in our heart. These aren't just sentimental words. There is nothing simply sentimental nor superficial about Christian prayer – it is deeply meaningful, very real and imminently practical.

Before we descend into the jungle and begin our journey or better yet, *our mission*, let's look out over the next four weeks and the terrain we will be covering. And first, so you know, this is not just "Steve Smith on prayer." This retreat is built from the approach that the Church has taken for centuries and even millennia. We are going to be following the road maps of many great theologians. First, for example, the great works of spiritual theology by Fr. Jordan Aumann, Fr. Garrigou-Lagrange and Fr. Adolphe Tanqueray. All of these theologians are building off of the tradition of the Saints. And so we'll be learning from St. Teresa of Avila (whom we've already quoted), St. John of the Cross, St. Bernard of Clairvaux, St. Ignatius of Loyola, St. Catherine of Sienna, St. Terese of Lisieux, St. Louis de Montfort, St. Alphonsus Liquori, Mother Teresa and on and on. All of whom have traveled these spiritual paths time and again. And most importantly, all of whom are going to THE source of spirituality and mental prayer – Jesus Christ, particularly as we encounter Him in the Gospels (but also in the totality of scripture and salvation history). So, we are in good hands and we are not deviating one iota from this tradition, including the tradition of how meditation and mental prayer is taught and how it unfolds in our lives.

Some of what we will encounter on this retreat may be familiar to you. Some of it new. Some of it may be challenging for you. I encourage you to stick with it, all of it. In fact, some parts of this retreat, if isolated from the whole could do more harm than good. This is how we make sure we are well grounded and have a solid foundation from which to confidently build our prayer life so that we can grow in peace, joy, happiness, inner harmony - in all ways. For my part I pledge to give my absolute best to distill and share years and years of following God along this path and also the guidance and training I've received from so many good and holy people.

Here is the terrain we will travel:

1. Week 1 – The Giant World of Mysticism. We will examine what mental prayer is and is not, and how it was revealed by God and developed by the Church. The roles that we play, and God plays. And, we will explore the three stages people pass through along the mystical path of relationship with God.

2. Week 2- Principles of Meditation. Christian Meditation is the starting point for people as they grow in mental prayer and personal holiness. We will learn what meditation is and the overarching principles necessary to progress in meditation. Most importantly we will learn why meditation is bigger than any single "method."

3. Week 3 – An Approach to Meditation. This retreat is careful to reinforce that mental prayer is about relationship with God, not about a single method or even worse, "a skill set." But it is helpful to have a starting point and we will learn some tried and true approaches to meditation and tackle the biggest hurdles, such as dealing with distractions.

4. Week 4 - Going Deeper into Christian Spirituality and Mysticism. We look at related topics such as contemplation, the movements of consolation and desolation, the tricks and tactics of the enemy, discernment of spirits, spiritual direction and the role of Mary and the Sacraments.

And this retreat has a plan for your growth in silent prayer and meditation - a plan for you to progressively increase to 15 minutes of daily meditation as follows:

1. Week 1 – Spend five minutes in silent prayer. You can pray with a specific theme from that day's retreat subject or you can

pray with scripture or talk with God about what's happening in your life. When in doubt, spend your time in silent prayer reflecting on our opening or closing prayer. The key is to spend this time in silence – or at most with gentle background music (the video version of this retreat and the *Interior Life* mobile app offer options for this).

2. Week 2 – Increase your time of silent prayer to 7 minutes. You should approach your time of prayer in the same was as for Week 1, with one exception. Make sure that at least the last 2 minutes of prayer are in true silence.

3. Week 3 – You will now start practicing authentic Christian meditation (not simply silent prayer) as you increase your prayer time to 10 minutes. You can start your prayer time with gentle background music but at least half of the time should be in complete silence. The Week 3 daily sessions will walk you through an initial approach to meditation.

4. Week 4 – Increase your meditation time to 15 minutes, with at least 10 minutes in complete silence.

Do your very best to follow that plan for increasing your time in prayer, but don't allow discouragement to enter in. If you are having difficulty increasing your time in prayer (e.g. increasing to 15 minutes), then focus on maintaining the duration that has been successful (e.g. 10 minutes). The goal of this retreat is 15 minutes of daily meditation, but it may take you longer than 30 days to reach arrive at that point. What matters most is to sustain steady progress and avoid back-sliding.

Some final thoughts: Prayer is a matter of spending time with the Creator of the Universe. Imagine you had an appointment with the president of your company, or some celebrity or whomever you hold in high regard – that appointment would become a top priority and you would prepare yourself and conduct yourself in a very particular way. Set about your time with God with that same mindset and everything else will fall into place.

I also want to reinforce that for the next 30 days you are on retreat. I know you have all your worldly responsibilities and activities and concerns, but amidst all of that you have decided to set apart this daily time for God, which is a wonderful thing. This retreat is about you and God, and He is so pleased to have this time with you – this is the delight that St. Teresa and Proverbs talk about. God, as is often said, is never out done in generosity. Have no doubt that through this gift of time that you are giving to God, He will pour tremendous grace into your life.

And now, let's return to gazing out to that mountain in the distance and the lush jungle that lies below, and through which runs your personal journey to Heaven. Spend the five minutes at the end of this session to talk with the Lord. Tell Him what is on your heart at this moment. Ask Him what he desires for you.

"On this mountain the Lord of hosts will provide for all peoples a feast of rich food and choice wines, juicy, rich food and pure, choice wines. On this mountain he will destroy the veil that veils all peoples, the web that is woven over all nations. He will destroy death forever." (Isaiah 25:6)

Let's close in prayer:

Lord Jesus Christ, help me to become ever more aware of your nearness and love for me. Amen.

Day 1 Postscript: A Few Thoughts About Setting

It is best to start the retreat on a Saturday. That way the first week of the retreat (which begins with Day 2) will fall on a Sunday, as will each week thereafter. And the retreat will end on a Sunday as well.

Find a peaceful place in your home for participating in this retreat and spending time in mental prayer. Wherever you do it, you should plan to continue spending your daily meditations there after completion of the retreat.

Some specifics – the setting should be a quiet place without loud noises, distractions nor disruptions. It may help to have a few holy objects, perhaps a lit candle, for recollection. "But when you pray, go to your inner room, close the door, and pray to your Father in secret." (Mt 6:6) Jesus is speaking about entering your very soul, but on a practical level we can't commune with God in the inner room of our soul if the physical room we are in is busy and distracting. People often create a small *oratory* (place of prayer) in their home – all it requires is a peaceful area with a comfortable chair (or kneeler if you prefer), a crucifix and any other devotionals or religious items that help you raise your mind and heart to God. In the video session of this retreat I show a picture of the oratory we created in a quiet corner of our bedroom.

You should participate in these sessions at the same time each day. We are creatures of habit and order. We have schedules for when we eat, sleep, work and recreate. Our prayer should be just as well ordered. It should also be at a time when we are able to be fully present with God. Can you do this on your lunch break? If there is no other option, then yes. But it's usually best to start your day with God in the morning, or to be with Him at the close of your day.

You may find it practical to separate the daily reflections from your time of silent prayer (weeks 1 and 2) and meditation (weeks 3 and 4). That is perfectly fine.

Pay particular attention to weekends. Most of us run into trouble maintaining our schedule on the weekends. The rigor and routine of our weekday schedules helps us lock in a prayer routine – but this often gets disrupted on the weekend. Make every effort to use the same prayer time and prayer place for weekdays and weekends. If that is not possible, then just make sure you have a consistent weekend routine.

Pearls from Day 1: Retreat Opening

We all desire fulfillment. God gave us that desire and wants to satisfy it with happiness in this life and Heaven in the next.

Thus, our ultimate goal is Heaven. We achieve that goal by following God's plan for our life. Following that plan will lead to living a holy life and that brings happiness, because for the Christian, holiness is the same as happiness.

Our primary way of communicating with God and following His plan for our life is *mental prayer* (silent, meditative prayer).

You can see how this flows – daily mental prayer with God will lead to holiness in this life, which is the same as happiness in this life. And holiness in this life will lead us to Heaven in the next.

In this retreat, we will be using the imagery of journeying through a jungle to a far-off mountain. That far off mountain is Heaven. Traveling through a jungle, unaided, is treacherous. But with the right Guides it can be beautiful and exciting. Prayer is how we communicate with God so that the Holy Trinity becomes our guide through the spiritual jungle.

It is important to establish a prayer routine. Mental prayer should be scheduled for the same time each day and done in a quiet, reverent setting. Pay particular attention to establishing a good weekend routine (to avoid the schedule disruptions that often occur on weekends).

Keep in mind that you are on retreat for the next 30-days. This is a special time for you and the Holy Spirit, who has a specific purpose for you being on this retreat and specific graces for you.

Your Pearls from Day 1

A place for you to capture your thoughts and inspirations from today's session.

WEEK 1
THE GIANT WORLD OF CHRISTIAN MYSTICISM

(each session followed by 5 minutes of silent prayer)

DAY 2: MENTAL PRAYER – *WHAT* IS IT AND *WHY* IS IT INDISPENSABLE?

> *Mental prayer* is often an unfamiliar term to people, but God intends mental prayer to be as natural as breathing. This week we will be looking at the who, what, why and how of mental prayer. Beginning today with the *what* and *why*...

Let's begin with prayer:

Come Holy Spirit, make of me a fitting dwelling place for the Lord. Amen.

YOUR JUNGLE MISSION

You found yourself lost in the jungle. At first you were confused and disoriented – "Where am I and how did I get here?" Those questions were quickly replaced by one far more pressing – "How do I get to some place safe? Because wherever I am, it definitely does not feel safe." That was when you realized how helpless you were. Lost in a jungle with no experience, no equipment and no one to help you. And that was when helplessness metastasized to cold, hard panic. You were lost, helpless, surrounded by a thousand deadly creatures, and heaven only knows how far from any type of shelter and safety. If you didn't start moving you would go out of your mind – you had to move somewhere, *anywhere*, just so long as you were moving and clinging to the blind hope that you'd stumble on a way out of that dreadful place.

That was when you met *Him*.

And just like that, there was hope. One moment you were in a full state of panic and surrounded by deadly things. The next moment you were following this strange man. You had no idea who He was. You had no idea where He was leading you. But your instincts were telling you that this strange, quiet man was your way out and that you should follow Him wherever He went.

You have so many questions for Him. You have so many questions *about* him. So much you want to tell Him and ask Him.

Our Starting Point

At some point we come to the realization that there is something greater than this earthly life. That God is real and that there is a larger purpose to our existence. That there is a different way we are supposed to live. This realization often crashes in on us when we're at a point of crisis. However it comes about, this realization is when we take the first steps of our spiritual journey. Yes, there may have been preparation for our journey involving many other people and events leading up to that moment, but our true faith journey begins when we come to our own personal awareness and acceptance of the spiritual dimension of reality – that there is a loving God, He has a plan for our life, we need Him and His plan is better than ours.

Yesterday we set the stage with imagery of a far-off mountain (our destination) and a jungle that lies between it and us. Prayer is how we navigate that jungle. Before we descend into the jungle, we need to spend some time in preparation. During the first two weeks of this retreat, we will be preparing for our journey. No one in his right mind would run headfirst into a dangerous jungle unprepared. If it seems that the imagery of a "dangerous jungle" is melodramatic, just stay tuned. In the days and weeks ahead, we will see exactly why a jungle is perfectly appropriate and why many spiritual masters have used similar imagery.

For today, we'll start by gaining a better understanding of mental prayer – what it is and why it's indispensable.

What Is Mental Prayer?

The two broad classifications of prayer are *vocal prayer* and *mental prayer*. I am sure you have some idea of what distinguishes each form, but we will go over both for the sake of completeness.

Vocal prayer, as its name attests, is prayer expressed in spoken words, sometimes with gestures. Vocal prayer can be expressed alone as well as in community, as with praise and worship services and vocal prayers during the celebration of Mass. Vocal prayer includes the simple prayers we offer throughout the day, like grace before meals. And, vocal prayer can be expressions of adoration, praise and petition.

One of the most important characteristics of vocal prayer that distinguishes it from mental prayer is that it is primarily a one-way communication. We tell God what is on our mind or heart. In and of itself this is wonderful, and God desires and encourages us to speak to Him in this way. But while vocal prayer can lift our spirit with awareness of God, it does not provide opportunity to quietly listen to God's speaking to us nor does it provide an environment to meditate on God and grow deeper in our knowledge and understanding of Him.

This is where mental prayer comes in. Mental prayer is the path by which we come to know God better, and thus love God and grow in virtue.

> "Mental prayer is a silent interaction of the soul with God. 'I will pray with the spirit, I will pray also with the understanding' (1 Cor 14:15). Every interior act of the mind or of the heart that tends to unite us to God, such as recollection, consideration, reasoning, self-examination, the loving thought of God, contemplation, a longing of the heart for God – all these may be called by the name of mental prayer. All these acts, even our examination of conscience, the purpose of which is to make our soul less unworthy of Him Who dwells in it, raise us up to God. All of these deepen our convictions, exercise us in virtue, and constitute our training for that heavenly life that is nothing else but an eternal, loving contemplation of the Godhead." (A. Tanqueray, *The Spiritual Life*)

And here is a simpler and more personal definition of mental prayer from St. Teresa of Avila: "Mental prayer in my opinion is nothing else than an intimate sharing between friends; it means taking time frequently to be alone with Him who we know loves us. In order that love be true and the friendship endure, the will of the friends must be in accord."

Wide and deep is the spectrum of what happens during mental prayer. Tradition distinguishes two important classes of mental prayer – meditation and contemplation:

> Meditation: Our activity is primary. We engage all our faculties (intellect, memory, imagination) to draw closer to God.
>
> Contemplation: God's activity is primary. He loves himself into our soul as a pure gift.

Why do we make these distinctions? What does this look like in practice? How should we meditate? How do we know if we are engaged in meditation or contemplation? Where do we start?

Let's take a step back and compare our relationship with God to our relationships with other people. An important part of developing into a mature person is to learn the art of getting to know someone. This starts with our earliest childhood friendships based on shared playtime and then we grow into the deeper friendships of adolescence and early adulthood. In time we come to the deepest human relationships of lifelong friendships and marital and parental love.

Along the way we learn how to relate to other people and share in their lives. We are aided in this by examples and instruction. Our parents model sacrificial love. Mentors and people we look up to guide us in our relationships. Great literature, the lives of saints and especially the life of Christ in the Gospels give us examples of how to live in relationship with others.

A large part of living in relationship with others is communication. Over time we learn that what someone is communicating to us is more than simply the words they say. There is context, intonation, non-verbal communication and so on. And, we learn that everyone communicates with us in different ways. Some friends are lighthearted and very verbal. Others are reflective and slow to speak. Still others are terse and to the point.

Our relationship with God is no less dynamic and unique. We grow and learn how to be in relationship with God. We learn that God speaks to each person differently, and we come to understand how He speaks to us. At the same time, we learn there are universal principles in how God speaks with everyone.

The purpose of the Catholic spiritual tradition is to guide people along the path of growing in relationship with God. Through this tradition questions about mental prayer, as listed above, become answered. Through this tradition we come to know God and how to open our mind and heart and hear His voice. Most importantly, we grow in love for God and neighbor and come to personally experience God's love for us. These are not simply sentimental words – this is the reality that unfolds through a life of prayer.

Day 2 (Week 1, Day 1)

Why Is Mental Prayer Indispensable?

As we will hear again and again, mental prayer is the life blood of our spiritual life. And our spiritual life is the life blood of our earthly life. See how that flows? If we are not spending time in mental prayer, our faith life (our relationship with God) will not grow and develop. It will remain sterile and two-dimensional, just as our relationships with other people would be lifeless if we never spent time with them. And, if our faith life (our relationship with God) is lifeless, all our other endeavors and relationships will suffer. There are countless examples of this from spiritual masters; we will sample a few.

From Fr. Philippe (*Time for God*): "Without a life of prayer even the Sacraments will have only a limited effect. Yes, they will give us grace, but that grace will remain unfruitful in part because the 'good soil' it needs is missing."

To paraphrase St. John of the Cross (*Spiritual Canticle*, Stanza 29): "It will not be difficult for you to understand that you would be much more useful to the Church and more pleasing to the Lord, not mention the good example you would give to those around you, if you devoted more time to prayer and to the exercises of the interior life." The prayer St. John is speaking of is mental prayer.

From Fr. Jordan Aumann (*Spiritual Theology*): "Experience shows that there is absolutely nothing that can supply for the life of prayer, not even the daily reception of the Eucharist. There are many persons who receive Communion every day, yet their spiritual life is mediocre and lukewarm. The reason is none other than the lack of mental prayer... We repeat that without prayer it is impossible to attain Christian perfection, no matter what our state of life or the occupation to which we dedicate ourselves."

From St. Alphonsus Ligouri: "Moreover, without meditation there is not strength to resist the temptations of our enemies, and to practice the virtues of the Gospel.... But man becomes docile and tender to the influence of grace which is communicated in mental prayer."

The most compelling reason why we should all be practicing mental prayer is that it is the example and teaching of Christ.

In scripture we have the example of Martha and Mary (Lk 10:38-42). Mary chooses the *better part*, mental prayer, in the form of contemplating Jesus. Our Lord Himself, tells us to go to our "inner room" (which is to say, our soul) and "...without me you can do nothing." (Jn 15:5) And, we have His personal example as Jesus routinely went away, in solitude, to spend time in prayer with the Father.

If we want to become fully ourselves, fully in love with God, fully available to God and to fully love and serve those around us, we must have an interior life built on mental prayer. The Saints are of one mind on this because it is the mind of the Church, because it is the teaching and example of Christ.

Let's return to our opening questions - What is mental prayer? Why is it indispensable?

The *what* - St. Teresa tells us mental prayer is an "intimate sharing between friends," having a heart-to-heart conversation with God.

The *why* - Mental prayer is indispensable because it's a key element of our relationship with God, spending one-on-one time with Him. Jesus, by his words and example, shows us that mental prayer is indispensable, and all the Saints affirm this.

This is where we will leave things for today. Yes, there are many questions yet unanswered but be at peace with the knowledge that you are entering a school of prayer and most if not all your questions will be addressed in the course of this retreat. This is a school through which many great saints and mystics have passed and illuminated the way.

Please spend 5 minutes in silent prayer (or with gentle background music); talking with God about today's session.

Let's close in prayer:

Lord Jesus Christ, help me to become ever more aware of Your nearness and Your great love for me.

Day 2 (Week 1, Day 1)

Pearls from Day 2: *What* is Mental Prayer and *Why* is it Indispensable?

God desires happiness (holiness) for us in this life and Heaven in the next.

Prayer is God's primary way for guiding us through this life.

Prayer can be distinguished as *vocal prayer* and *mental prayer*. Vocal prayer is just that – spoken prayer – and ranges from simple vocal prayers like grace before meals to the communal vocal prayers that are part praise and worship services and the Sacrifice of the Mass.

WHAT IS MENTAL PRAYER?

Mental prayer is both prayer of the mind and in the silence of our hearts. Mental prayer has the benefit of being ordered to meditating on God and talking with God. It is how we come to know Him and listen to Him.

St. Teresa of Avila describes it thus: "Mental prayer in my opinion is nothing else than an intimate sharing between friends; it means taking time frequently to be alone with Him who we know loves us."

WHY IS MENTAL PRAYER INDISPENSABLE?

Our faith, our spiritual life, is about relationship with God.

Loving relationships require that we spend time with the other person. We know this from our human relationships.

Mental prayer is the primary way that we spend "quality time" with God because mental prayer facilitates pondering Him and talking with Him – especially, listening to Him.

No other spiritual practices can provide for this growth in relationship in place of mental prayer.

Jesus communicates this indispensability by His teaching (such as pointing out that Mary *chose the better part* over Martha) and example (by regularly going off to spend time alone in prayer with the Father).

Day 2 (Week 1, Day 1)

Your Pearls from Day 2

DAY 3: *HOW* WE LEARN ABOUT MENTAL PRAYER - CATHOLIC SPIRITUAL TRADITION

> Today we are going to answer the question of why we are turning specifically to the Catholic tradition on mental prayer, and how it provides all that is needed for spiritual growth. You may not be Catholic; you may not be Christian. Or maybe you once were. There is so much brokenness in the Church today. Why for the love of God (literally), should we be turning to Catholic Christian tradition? Fair question. This is exactly the time to affirm your resolve and trust that there is a reason you signed on to this retreat and to hear the answer (spoiler alert – we don't completely answer the question today – the answer continues to show itself over the next four weeks).

Let's open in prayer.

Come Holy Spirit, make of me a fitting dwelling place for the Lord.

Your Jungle Mission

You quickly learned there were many others. Countless others, in fact, out there in the jungle, who had been found by the Savior. You'd taken to calling Him that, by the way. It came naturally and seemed the only fitting name since He came out of nowhere and saved you in your moment of helplessness and grave danger.

One of the many curious things is that everyone else naturally called Him "the Savior" as well. It seems they all had similar stories of being lost, desperate and saved from certain death by Him.

The other travelers were all ages and came from endlessly different backgrounds. About the only thing they had in common was that they didn't belong in the jungle any more than you did. That was why they called themselves nomads. Some of them had also only recently been saved. Others had been traveling with the Savior for a very long time and were quite knowledgeable about survival in the jungle.

You came to learn from some of these experienced ones that many, many nomads had traveled through the jungle before you. The Savior had brought them safely to a far-off mountain. And that was your destination as well – so long as you stayed close to the Savior and followed the Way.

You noticed how easily the experienced ones traveled through the jungle and asked them to show you how they did it. They explained that they were only imitating the Savior. Where He walked, they walked. What He avoided, they avoided.

You were eager to learn everything you could from these experienced ones and they were happy to show you the wisdom that was passed on from nomad to nomad.

How We Learn About Our Spirituality

Yesterday we considered what mental prayer is and why it is indispensable. From St. Teresa of Avila, "mental prayer is nothing but a friendly conversation with the One we know loves us." Isn't that beautiful?

The indispensability of prayer is based on God desiring *relationship* with us. God *is* relationship – that is the essence of the Trinity. All of salvation history, God the Son becoming man so that he could suffer and die to redeem us – all of it is for the sake of establishing relationship with us. You can't have a relationship with someone you don't know. You can't have a relationship with someone you don't spend time with. The primary way we come to know God and spend time with Him is through mental prayer. All the Saints attest to this because it is the teaching and example of Christ. After prayer, we come to know God through His teachings and by serving our neighbor so that we come to "love them as we love ourselves".

Now that we have established the basics of *what* mental prayer is and *why* it's indispensable, we turn to *how* we grow in mental prayer. Our "instructions" for mental prayer have been developed and handed down through Catholic tradition. We know that prayer is our personal GPS to stay on the right path while navigating through the jungle of life. But a GPS is of little benefit if we don't know how to operate it. This is where Catholic spiritual tradition comes in.

We can turn to healthcare for perspective on approaching our spiritual life. If we need to undergo a serious medical operation, we want to find a doctor who has performed the operation many times before. By many, we mean not just 5 or 10 or 20 times, but hundreds of times. We want the confidence that our doctor has encountered all the different types of circumstances that can arise – surprises are bad things when you are on an operating table.

Or consider our jungle mission. If we are about to set out in an unknown and treacherous jungle, we want an experienced guide at our side. We do not want a "city slicker" leading us through the jungle, we want someone who lives there and knows the jungle like the back of his hand. And we do not just want someone who lives there, we want someone who has made the journey to that far off mountain. And we do not just want someone who has made that journey, we want someone who has made it many, many times and encountered and overcome all of the hazards and can point out all of the beauty as well. And we do not just want someone who has made the journey many times, we want someone who has *led* countless others safely to that destination.

This reminds us of an important aspect of this mission - while the mountain top (Heaven) is the goal, we also desire success all along the way (our worldly and spiritual journey in this life). We do not want to just make it to the mountain top, bruised and battered and barely alive. True, it's better to arrive barely alive than not at all. But how much better it is to arrive strong, triumphant, and joyful, and reflecting on all the beauty and experiences of the journey we've taken. And as always – that doesn't mean that we won't face adversity in this life, we most certainly will, Christ tells us so. But even amid *external* adversity we can have *interior* joy by finding and serving God in all things.

Christ tells us that He came to give us life and life in the full. Certainly, He is talking about Heaven, but He's also talking about our life on Earth. We were created for holiness in this life and Heaven in the next. Jesus tells us that the Kingdom of God is *here*. In the Our Father we are taught to pray "Thy kingdom come", which includes coming right now, into our hearts. So, we seek not only the mountain top, but success, grace, and blessing along our journey.

Just so, we need a tried and true guide for our spiritual life. We look to Catholic Spiritual Tradition as that guide, and from here out we will turn our attention to why that is. On a side note, throughout this retreat we will generally use Catholic and Christian interchangeably since Catholic is Christian, particularly in the *spiritual* tradition (as opposed to the more *dogmatic* distinctions that principally separate Catholics and other Christian denominations). The Catholic tradition commonly self-references as Christian, for example Catholic daily prayer is called Christian Prayer. The Catechism of the Catholic Church (the official compilation of Church teaching) uses the term Christian repeatedly (as in Part 4: Christian Prayer). So, as with our Church, we use neither Catholic nor Christian exclusively when referring to the spiritual tradition.

Now, we live in a time and place where the culture puts a great deal of emphasis on individuality, personal expression, and a certain concept of freedom. Do any of the following sound familiar?

- what's good for me doesn't have to be good for you
- it's all good ... don't judge ....
- nothing is objectively true

The appeal of this world view, and the failure to share the truth and beauty of Christianity, has led to the rise of the "nones" (individuals with no religious affiliation) and, similarly, those who identify as "spiritual but not religious." If you happen to be inclined to this mindset, then thank you for being open to this retreat – and please, stay with us! The purpose of today's session is to give you confidence in why we are following a tradition that has been handed down over millennia.

In every other sphere of life our culture seems to recognize the value of having structures, institutions and individuals to provide formation (even self-proclaimed anarchists have a certain structure to the anarchy they profess). Parents move to a new home just to be in a better school district and then send their children to all manner of lessons for sports and artistic development. We talk about "lifelong learning" and "constant improvement." People love self-help courses and podcasts, and seek out experts and mentors who can help them quickly advance. All of that can be very good if ordered to God.

But when it comes to religion, the prevailing spirit is one of "anything goes." This contradiction doesn't stand up to scrutiny. The Christian God is a God of order, not chaos. All of scripture, in a sense, boils down to God teaching us how to love Him and one another and He is crystal clear that there is a right way and wrong way - and His way is the only right way.

By the fact that you are participating in this retreat you are aware of this need for order. The question is - why should it specifically be Catholic spiritual formation? There are many, many reasons why Catholic spiritual tradition is the true path to holiness. Four reasons that we will touch on in this session are: Catholic spiritual tradition comes from God (it is Divine); Catholic spiritual tradition is ancient; Catholic spiritual tradition is complete; and, Catholic spiritual tradition is for everyone.

Catholic Spiritual Tradition is Divine.

This goes without saying, but it bears stating – the single most important fact about Christian spiritual tradition is that it is Divinely inspired. This is reflected in scripture, all of which is inspired (St. Peter tells us that nothing in scripture is a personal interpretation). God also created the Church. Jesus Christ said to Peter, "You are Peter, and upon this this rock I will build my Church...." (Mt 16:18) And this *Church* is not merely buildings of worship, it is not just a community of believers, and it is not simply an institution; the Church that Christ founded is literally His body. The Church *is* Christ, which is why he said to Saul (before he became Paul), "Saul, Saul, why are you persecuting *me*?" (Acts 9:4) And the purpose of the Church (and the tradition that goes with it including the tradition of mental prayer) is to bring everyone to Christ and salvation.

Catholic Spiritual Tradition is Ancient.

In and of itself this is not a foundational reason for the validity of Catholic spiritual tradition, but it does demonstrate the authenticity and credibility of this tradition. The Catholic faith while ancient has also remained ever-vital and relevant. The roots of Catholic spiritual tradition are as old as it gets. Its beginnings are reflected in the historical, prophetic and wisdom literature of the Old Testament; many spiritual truths are contained in the stories of the Old Testament.

Take, for example, the model of the great patriarchs like Abraham and Moses and how, over time, they grew in relationship with God and learned to trust in Him completely. Look at the example of Elijah, who came to hear God not in the roar of thunder or hurricanes (as Moses heard God), but in the still, small voice (1 Kings 19:11-13). Through these events we see God deepening His relationship with His people. Or, take the book of Psalms, which speaks to the entire range human conditions and emotions. All of this predates far Eastern mysticism (e.g. Taoism and Buddhism) by centuries.

This ancient spiritual tradition was then advanced and perfected by Christ. Jesus says he no longer calls us slaves but friends and brothers. Through Jesus we become adopted sons and daughters of God the Father. And Jesus sends his Spirit to dwell within us. Through Jesus we are restored to God, we are brought into relationship, into the life of the Trinity. Following Jesus' example and teaching, the Apostles and the Church ever since have safeguarded this treasure and it has been expounded, exemplified, and taught by the Church and her great Saints and mystics over the last two millennia.

Let's take a further look at the ensuing two millennia and the major branches of mysticism.

People are sometimes surprised to learn that there is an Eastern tradition of Christian mysticism – Eastern as in Greek (as opposed to the Latin West). The Eastern Christian tradition does share certain characteristics with far-East spiritual traditions - but it departs from all other Eastern traditions in many important ways, for example in identifying the purpose of emptying of self is *to be filled* by the Triune God.

There are two main branches of the Eastern tradition. One branch traces back to the Desert Fathers, who fled the worldliness and depravity of the cities to seek Christian perfection in the solitude and isolation of the desert, particularly in Egypt starting around 300 AD. Most notable among them was St. Anthony of the Desert (as taught by St. Athanasius). This tradition takes on a character of ascetism (mortification and self-denial) in the service of purification and spiritual combat. The desert fathers had a deep understanding that the real battle is for our own heart, which is constantly being pulled from God to lower, worldly desires and temptations (more on that topic in Week 4).

The other branch of the eastern Christian tradition is characterized by the writings of Pseudo Dionysius in the late 5th century (but traces back to the earliest Church Fathers). First among his small collection of writings is his *Mystical Theology*. The author claims to be St. Paul's Athenian convert, Dionysius, but was in fact probably a Greek philosopher writing in the 5th century. His real name is unknown, but since he certainly was not the actual Dionysius of St. Paul's New Testament letters, he is known as pseudo-Dionysius. This tradition continued and, in a sense, culminated in the *Cloud of Unknowing* and other works by an anonymous author in the late 14th century. In this approach to mysticism God is encountered through negation (it is referred to as "negative theology"). God is thoroughly beyond our concepts of existing and being. In fact, God does not "exist" in the sense of our understanding of existence. So, we must empty ourselves of all our artificial constructs of God. Note the different character of this self-abnegation from that of the desert fathers, who approach self-denial as a form of spiritual combat.

Perhaps most familiar is the Christo-centric Latin tradition of the West. St. Ignatius of Antioch followed right after the Apostles with a mysticism focused on the Lord's passion. Not that the Eastern traditions aren't Christ-focused, but the Western tradition distinctly enters into the mystery of the Passion, recognizing it, in a loose metaphor, as the Big Bang of salvation history. All of world history and Old Testament Judaism prepare for, and collapse to, that single moment on Calvary. And then Christianity and grace and salvation explode forth. The Western tradition continued to flow through great Saints like Ambrose, Benedict, and Bernard and all the Benedictines, Dominicans and Franciscans of the Middle Ages.

These Eastern and Western traditions are then harmonized and synthesized during the counter reformation by great mystic saints like St Teresa of Avila, St. John of the Cross and St. Ignatius of Loyola. In fact, Carmelite (St. Teresa and St. John) and Ignatian spirituality are instrumental in this retreat. Fr. Adolphe Tanquerey offers the following synopsis of each school, "The Carmelite School insists that God is everything and man is nothing. It urges complete detachment in order to come, God willing, to a state of contemplation and inculcates the practice of the apostolate by prayer, example and sacrifice.", and, "The School of St. Ignatius makes a specialty of active, energetic and practical spiritual life aiming at forming the will for the personal sanctification and apostolic work" (A. Tanquerey, *The Spiritual Life*).

As a starting point we will focus on the deceptively simple and powerful Carmelite insights into the growth of our interior life through mental prayer and the Ignatian genius for integrating our interior and active lives. It is impossible to distill the breadth and depth of these two schools of spirituality into a few sentences – we'll be regularly learning from each and over time you'll develop your own sense for their distinct character.

And in our present day this heritage and blending of the entire dramatic range of mystical spirituality of which we humans are capable has been taught by modern theologians such as Fr. Thomas Dubay, Fr. Garrigou-LaGrange and Fr. Jacques Philippe. So, we have inherited this continuous chain of development from ancient roots, perfected by Christ and continuously developed and taught by the Church.

Catholic Spiritual Tradition is Complete.

The stunningly deep and beautiful tradition just described contains all that is *necessary* to ascend to the greatest heights of contemplation and holiness (which is to say, happiness). This tradition is also *complete*; there is no need to look elsewhere. Any other spiritual tradition has only small rays of truth at best, and much that can be harmful to our spiritual life and salvation. More will be said on Eastern mysticism as we go on, but as one example, Buddhist meditation while on the surface seeking a number of noble goals (peace, compassion, etc.) – completely rejects the understanding of the human person and of the Triune God as revealed to us in Christianity. Thus, Buddhist meditation cannot realize God's plan for us - perfectly becoming ourselves by becoming one with the Trinity.

Catholic Spiritual Tradition is for Everyone.

The word Catholic means *universal*. And this certainly applies to the Church's spiritual tradition and teaching. It speaks to every human heart and mind, in all times, all places and all circumstances. It is so simple that anyone can start right in and grow in holiness and relationship with God. It is so profound that no one will ever exhaust it.

These four considerations are closely tied to what are known as the *four marks* of the Church - the Catholic Church is One, Holy, Catholic and Apostolic. *One* is similar to complete. The Catholic Church is the One Church – yes, there are other Christian Churches, but they all have their roots in the Catholic Church which contains the fulness of Christian tradition. It is *Holy* – it is Divine, it is of God. It is *Catholic* – as noted above, this is synonymous with universal. And it is *Apostolic* – this is related to ancient roots consistently handed down through the ages. The Catholic Church can trace an unbroken line of succession of leadership directly to Christ and His apostles – each apostle laying hands on the next pope and generation of bishops and so on and so on to the present day.

Catholic Spiritual Tradition in Practice

Let's look at a simple example of the above concepts, particularly that Catholic spiritual tradition is Divinely inspired, is complete and is for everyone. Let's start with a simple question such as, "what is good?"

If we look to the wisdom of the world, in this case as memorialized by Merriam-Webster, we get the following definition (which is only a partial reproduction of the complete definition):

> "of a favorable character or tendency; bountiful, fertile; handsome, attractive; suitable, fit; free from injury or disease; not depreciated; commercially sound; that can be relied on; profitable, advantageous; agreeable, pleasant; salutary, wholesome; amusing, clever; of a noticeably large size or quantity; considerable; full; used as a word that gives force or emphasis to a statement; a good many of us; well-founded, cogent; true; deserving of respect; honorable; legally valid or effectual; adequate, satisfactory; conforming to a standard; liking only things that are of good quality...."

If we look to the wisdom of Catholicism, we get this: "Something is good if it is of God." The basis of this working definition is scripture, which tells us all good things come from God.

Which definition is easier to work with? The world's or God's?

A person could reasonably respond, "That's all nice and tidy, but how does that work in practice? How do I know what is *of God*?"

Day 3 (Week 1, Day 2)

Catholic spiritual tradition will take you as far as you want to go with this question.

First, we measure everything against our end-goal: Heaven. We are most concerned with what is good (and what is bad, or evil) to the extent that it helps us get to Heaven. So, if something is good it is of God and will advance us to Heaven and we should accept it. If something is evil, it is not of God and we should reject it.

The most basic source of good (in the form of behaviors) is the Ten Commandments as founded in scripture and articulated by tradition (you will not find a distinct list of ten commandments in scripture alone). You could probably stop with strict adherence to the ten commandments and a sacramental life and make it to Heaven just fine.

But if we go deeper (and God is always calling us deeper), Jesus advances the moral law of the Ten Commandments with the two great commandments (love God and love your neighbor) and also the beatitudes and teaching from His majestic Sermon on the Mount.

If we look even deeper, Catholic spiritual tradition expands on the scriptural teaching of the virtues (particularly faith, hope, love, prudence, justice, fortitude, and temperance, which between them lead us to sanctity and banish all vice).

And we can go still deeper. As Christians we are called to the *highest* good. How do I know how to choose between two competing goods? Let's say I'm asked to participate in a service ministry, but it will take me away from my family one evening a week (but it will also give service opportunities that I can do with my family). My primary responsibility is my vocation as a husband and father. Is it a greater good to say yes or no to the service opportunity? Catholic spiritual tradition gives magnificent teachings on this type of "discernment" all based on the example and teaching of Jesus.

In Catholic spiritual tradition we have an imminently complete and practical approach to life.

And mental prayer is an essential part of this tradition, so that we can be in relationship with God and live out His plan for our life.

Please spend 5 minutes in silent prayer; talking with God about today's session.

Lord Jesus Christ, help me to become ever more aware of Your nearness and Your great love for me. Amen.

Day 3 Postscript: A Few Thoughts for Retreatants who are Not Catholic

There is only one tradition of meditation in Western culture, and that is Christian mental prayer as it has been developed and handed down by the Catholic Church. That is why this book teaches from the Catholic spiritual and mystical tradition; there is simply no other school of Western meditation.

For our Protestant brothers and sisters, Catholic spiritual tradition on mental prayer really is your tradition as well. The foundation of prayer in the Old and New Testaments and especially the teaching and example of Christ are the same for all Christians. And the great contemplatives and mystics through the 14th century (prior to the Reformation) are at the heart of all tradition on mental prayer. Many great contemporary protestant theologians (such as C. S. Lewis and John Wesley) were influenced by these same Saints and mystics. We hope and expect you will feel right at home with this retreat.

There are, of course, areas of meaningful departure. The Sacraments are an important example. In the Catholic faith the Sacraments are instrumental in sharing in divine life and remaining in a state of grace and are thus integral with our spiritual life. Here, again, the Saints and spiritual masters who have passed on the tradition of mental prayer all had great devotion to the Sacraments, and so that is reflected in this book. The various Protestant traditions recognize sacraments to one degree or another and certainly recognize the spiritual concepts underlying the sacraments (such as the need for forgiveness and reconciliation) so, thank you for keeping an open mind and please prayerfully consider your approach to these elements of spirituality as they come up.

And now a few thoughts for non-Christian retreatants, or Christians who are drawn to look beyond our Christian spiritual borders. This particularly holds for individuals looking to alternative forms of spirituality and specifically to Eastern mysticism, mindfulness, and the like, which is ever more prevalent these days. At the root of it, alternate forms of spirituality are not pointing to the truth and reality of God, or at best are capturing only the smallest sliver of the light of God's truth. Note this also applies to most forms of what is commonly presented as "centering prayer" as well (this topic will be addressed elsewhere by *Interior Life*).

Imagine desiring a close relationship with a friend, but they rarely talk to you. They spend their time with other people, talking instead to them about things you would very much like to be sharing with them.

Imagine your friend trying to explain those other relationships: "I know you and I have this great friendship, but I feel more comfortable talking to this other person about what I should do with these important issues in my life." Or, "I really want to spend time with this other person because they make me feel peaceful and relaxed." It is much like this when we move away from Christianity to alternate attempts at spirituality. In these various alternatives there is a universalist inclination to think "God is all one," "All paths lead to God," "God loves me and accepts me on whatever path I take."

With all humility, let's attempt to place ourselves in God's position.

Scripture, history, and tradition reveal a Triune God (Father, Son and Spirit) who loves us so much that He sacrificed His only Son for us. *This* is where God desires to connect with us. God, Himself entered the world, became man, suffered and died a horrific death out of love for us. He desires to connect with us in *that* relationship that

He worked so hard and sacrificed so much to start building. To the statement "the Christian path is just one path among many", Jesus responds, "I am the way, the truth and the life; No one comes to the Father except through me." (Jn 14:6)

Christian spirituality is the path we must follow for happiness in this life and heaven in the next; we'd be doing you a disservice to say it any differently, and we're so grateful that you are here, trusting yourself to this path.

Day 3 (Week 1, Day 2)

Pearls from Day 3: *How* We Learn About Mental Prayer – Catholic Spiritual Tradition

Our goal is not just Heaven but holiness (and thus happiness) in this life. Everything else in life is secondary to this goal because this goal encompasses our entire life.

Mental prayer is an indispensable element of achieving this goal because it is key to our relationship with God (and neighbor).

Therefore, we need the best guidance available for our journey through mental prayer, and all of life. This is why we turn to Catholic Spiritual Tradition (CST). Note, that we will typically use "Catholic" and "Christian" interchangeably because much of the development of this tradition dates to the days when there was no distinction between Catholic and Christian.

Four, out of many, reasons we turn to CST are that it is Divine, Ancient, Complete and Universal.

Divine: God created the Church (Christ says to Peter, "On this rock I will build my Church"). And, Christ *is* the Church (Christ says to Paul, "Why are you persecuting *Me*"). The Church has continuously developed and shepherded this tradition since Christ's ascension to Heaven.

Ancient: CST's roots go back to Creation itself. God's initiative to grow His relationship with man traced through Old Testament covenants, patriarchs, and prophets. Spiritual truths in the OT predate other major world religions by centuries. Jesus perfects this tradition and the Church has expanded and proclaimed it for the next two millennia.

Complete: CST has the fullness of God's revelation, there is no need to look elsewhere. Any other spiritual tradition has at best only small rays of truth and much that can be harmful.

Universal: Catholic means "universal." CST is for all peoples, in all places and all times. Christ sent His disciples to all the nations. The Saints come from all corners of the globe and all facets of life. And we will find CST applies perfectly to our life whatever our circumstances and wherever we are in our relationship with God.

These four considerations are similar and related to the 4 marks of the Catholic Church – One, Holy, Apostolic and Catholic.

The fulness of the Christian faith is in the Catholic Church. Not only that – but the fulness of supernatural life as well. It is through the Sacraments of the Church that we can sustain the indwelling presence of the Holy Spirit.

Day 3 (Week 1, Day 2)

——————— Your Pearls from Day 3 ———————

DAY 4: THE *WHO* OF MENTAL PRAYER PART 1 - OUR ROLE AND WHAT IT MEANS TO BE HUMAN

> Think of any team activity you have done. A sport. School project. Service work. Whatever it may be. It's important to establish everyone's role and responsibilities – correct? Otherwise, it's a chaotic free-for-all. The same principle applies to prayer. Our prayer team is us and God. We need to know our role in prayer, and that entails understanding who we are as human beings. This may not be as obvious as it sounds...

Let's open with prayer:

Come Holy Spirit, make of me a fitting dwelling place for the Lord.

YOUR JUNGLE MISSION

You have been trekking through the jungle for a few days. The initial relief and euphoria from being saved are giving way to fatigue and a growing concern that this journey is going to be difficult; perhaps too difficult. You are being tested in ways that you never experienced before. The Savior keeps a disciplined schedule; up early, everyone has duties, there seems to be little idle time.

When you watch the other nomads you see that some of them, many of them, are having a much easier time of it than you. They seem to enjoy the challenges and the work and the discipline of it all. You start to think that maybe they're the lucky ones that are "cut out for this" and you're just not made for this type of journey.

Some of the experienced nomads sense your apprehension and start to share their experiences. They explain that the journey through the jungle is challenging for everyone at first. They reassure you that everyone is capable of making the journey, everyone has the skills and abilities needed to arrive at the far-off mountain. They also explain that everyone also has weaknesses and flaws, and that it is these weaknesses and flaws that make the journey difficult. The work of those new to following the Way to the mountain is to understand their weaknesses and flaws and master them. That's when the journey becomes easier; it becomes an adventure rather than a hardship.

UNDERSTANDING OURSELVES

Recall that over the last two days we covered the *What, Why* and *How* of mental prayer. *What* it is, is a conversation with God, who we know loves us. *Why* we need mental prayer is because Jesus shows and tells us that it's an indispensable part of getting to know the Triune God and having a real relationship with Him. *How* we learn about mental prayer is through Catholic spiritual tradition, which is divinely inspired, ancient, complete, and universal, among other things.

Today we will talk about our role in mental prayer – and to

understand that we need to know what it means to be a human being. Tomorrow we will look closer at God's role in mental prayer, and in doing that we will look closer at God's nature. We're going to cover quite a bit of ground today; it will pay dividends if you stick with it – much of why we do what we do (in all aspects of our life) is explained through the material we cover today and we'll be returning to these concepts throughout the retreat.

Let's return to our jungle mission. If you have ever gone deep into the woods for an extended period, you know one of the great challenges and benefits is that it reveals you to yourself. This isn't just psychobabble. There are aspects of our personality that we only discover when we allow ourselves to be pushed outside of our comfort zone. Can I endure physical discomfort? How will I handle a major mistake? Can I hold it together when my life is on the line? Long periods of silence, physical, mental and emotional exertion strip away superficiality and false notions and get us closer to the core of who we are. This is the reality behind outdoor learning and leadership programs such as *Outward Bound*.

And so, as we enter our spiritual jungle it's important that we understand ourselves in the full sense of what it means to be human. It's impossible to have a deep relationship with someone else if you don't know yourself first. This is partly why adolescents don't get married – they're still developing emotionally. Just as we need to understand ourselves emotionally and psychologically to have healthy human relationships, we need to also understand our spiritual nature to have a healthy relationship with God.

CHRISTIAN ANTHROPOLOGY – WHAT IT MEANS TO BE HUMAN

This is where Christian anthropology enters in and sheds light on our spiritual life. Christian anthropology is the study of the complete human person – body and soul - and it is indispensable for knowing who we are and how we relate to God (and one another for that matter). This may be familiar territory for you. But, for most people, including those of us who grew up in the Christian faith, these basic truths of life were long forgotten in the haze of the cultural revolution. Wherever you are on that spectrum, Christian anthropology is so particularly important to our prayer life that we will present a thumbnail sketch of the fundamentals so that we're all refreshed and starting from the same place.

We start with Creation and the book of Genesis. There is an order to the universe. God first created the inanimate *stuff* of the universe including the earth with its land, sea and sky. Then God turned to creating life. There is something unique and startling about life - everyone intuitively understands this. That something should live and grow and die has always captivated man. Life, even the simplest plant life, is a stunning concept. It is why we look for "signs of life" on other planets. Seriously - why do we care about that? It's more than idle curiosity or humdrum scientific inquiry.

Back to Creation, God first creates plants. It is at first a surprising concept that plants possess a soul. But with a little reflection it makes good sense. The soul is the "life principle" of the plant. A plant's soul is what distinguishes it from inanimate things like rocks and dirt. We tend to think that having a soul equates to having consciousness as we understand it. This is not the case. Plants have a *vegetative soul* that gives powers appropriate to a plant; powers to take in nutrition, grow and reproduce.

Moving up the chain of creation, God next creates animals. Animals also have a soul, a *sensitive soul*. An animal's soul has the powers of a vegetative soul (nutrition, growth and reproduction) but also has powers that are fed by the *senses* (thus it is a sensitive soul). These powers are movement, the five external senses, four internal senses and emotions. The power of movement (locomotion) and the five external sense are familiar concepts. Internal senses are memory, perception (the ability to receive information from the external senses), imagination (the power to form that sensory information into images and ideas), and estimation/cognition. That last power, estimation/

cognition, is the power to turn basic images and ideas into actionable thoughts. In animals this is very primitive – "that looks tasty, I will eat it;" in humans this power can be very sophisticated – "I think, therefore I am" as Descartes famously proclaimed.

Moving to the highest tier of creation, God created man. Man has a *rational* soul. Man's rational soul has all of the powers of vegetative and sensitive souls, and also has powers of intellect and will that give us capabilities of abstract thought and self-determination that animals do not have (this is why estimation/cognition is much more sophisticated for man than animals). Note that something extraordinary happens at this point in Creation – God breathes His Spirit into man. Man's soul is a *spiritual soul*. The human soul is also eternal, whereas plant and animal souls die when the plant or animal dies (for the animal lovers – St. Aquinas gives the comfort that if we need to have Fluffy with us in Heaven to experience perfect joy then God will raise Fluffy to Heaven).

Our spiritual faculties (intellect and will) are higher than our bodily faculties because it is in our spiritual nature that we are made in the image and likeness of God. God is pure spirit (only in Jesus Christ did God become man so that He could redeem us and lead us home). It was God, pure spirit, Who said "Let us make man in our image, according to Our likeness...." (Gen 1:26)

In the spiritual powers of our soul we are like the angels, who are pure spirit. In the sensitive powers of our soul (and in having a body) we are like animals. A common formulation is that our soul intermediates between our spirit and our body.

BEING	SOUL	POWERS (FACULTIES)
Human	Rational (Eternal Spirit)	Intellect Will

Animal	Sensitive	Movement
		External Senses
		   (sight, hearing, taste, touch, smell)
		Internal Senses
		   (perception, imagination, memory, estimation/cognition)
		Emotions

Plant	Vegetative	Nutrition Grown Reproduction

Turning to the rational powers of intellect and will, Pope St. John Paul II highlighted this as the source of man's unique capacity for relationship with God:

> Intellect gives the ability to know and understand. The action of the intellect is to know what is true (and God is the source of all truth). The intellect, in turn, engages lower mental functions such as memory and imagination to better grasp God's truth.
>
> Will is the governing faculty by which we freely choose and act. The action of the will is to love goodness (and God is the greatest good). The will is thus the source of love because love is primarily a decision (as opposed to popular thinking by which love is primarily an emotion).

God gave us our intellect so that we could know and love Him. Our intellect gives us the ability to ponder the deep truths and mysteries of our faith (as opposed to animals, whose material-only brains are limited to basic instinctual thought). Our intellect is also the seat of our conscience (which is the heart of the Natural Law). Thomas Aquinas points out that our conscience (and Natural Law) is demonstrated by Cain when he hides himself from God after killing Abel – he knew his action was evil because he had the light of reason.

GOD'S DESIGN	
INTELLECT	Ability to know and understand Action - know what is True **God** *is* Truth
WILL	Governing Faculty – freely choose and act Action - to love goodness **God** *is* Goodness (God is the greatest good)
EMOTIONS	Attract us to something perceived as good or desirable Move away from something perceived as bad or undesirable Automatic responses Support Intellect and Will

Our intellect, enlivened by the Holy Spirit, can engage our lower mental faculties (such as imagination and memory) to ponder, say, the mystery of the Trinity – three persons with one divine nature. Not only that, but our intellect, when properly guided and informed by faith and prayer can discern God's will for our life:

Do not conform yourselves to this age but be transformed by the renewal of your mind, that you may discern what is the will of God, what is good and pleasing and perfect. (Rom 12:2)

Note that intellect as a spiritual faculty is different than the worldly understanding of intellect. The world's understanding of intellect is limited to concepts such as accumulated knowledge, IQ and the ability to apply reason and objective thinking to complex matters. Such things are mostly limited to the functioning of our material brain (the gray matter in our skull). Our intellect, as a spiritual power, is much broader. Our physical brains (and thus knowledge and IQ) are a part of us and thus available to our spiritual power of intellect. But our intellect elevates our mental processes and incorporates purely spiritual abilities such as the Gifts of the Holy Spirit (e.g. wisdom and counsel – more on that in Week 4).

Thus, a person of very modest IQ can, in other ways, have a towering intellect. St. Joseph of Cupertino and St. Andre Bessette are outstanding examples of men of modest intelligence but deep wisdom.

Moving now to the will, our free will gives us the ability to choose God's will over our own passions and desires (again, as opposed to animals, which simply act on instinct). Once we have determined a course of action based on our intellect (and informed by faith), we engage our will to see our actions through. This is how it is with love. If the law of love tells us that we should act a certain way, for example by sacrificing for someone, it is by our will, conformed to our Father's will, that we see that action through even when it's difficult.

Not everyone who says to me, "Lord, Lord," shall enter the kingdom of heaven, but he who does the will of my Father who is in heaven. (Mt 7:21)

The spiritual faculties, as we have noted, are higher than the bodily faculties. And among the spiritual faculties the will is the higher than the intellect.

Even though the intellect usually comes first in terms of day-to-day activities (we *think* through something and then we *act* on it), our will is our higher spiritual power in terms of spiritual perfection. This is because our intellect will always be limited; we will never be able to know God perfectly since God is infinite and we are finite. He is Creator, we are creature. But we can love God perfectly because we can grow to perfectly submit our will to His.

Humans also have emotions (as do animals), which are the automatic response to what we perceive through our senses. Our emotions either attract us to something that we perceive as good or desirable, or they move as away from something that we perceive as bad or undesirable. Again, this is automatic. Whether or not we act on our emotions depends on our intellect and will (animals, on the other hand, operate only on emotion and instinct).

The proper ordering and integration of intellect, will and emotions (also termed passions and feelings) is the purpose of Christian formation. Our (properly formed) intellect should inform our will so that we choose Holy things. And the intellect and will should master our emotions. If we do this perfectly, we will be perfectly happy which, for the Christian, is synonymous with Holy.

We have painted a lovely picture of peace and harmony of the interior life of a human person. Our intellect discerns the right thing to do, by our free will we act on it, and our emotions and passions naturally incline us to want to do it.

Does your interior life resemble that?

Mine neither.

I can tell you mine looks much more like a Rorschach test than it does that lovely picture. And we know why - the *fall*. The fall of man had two particularly damaging effects on this design for interior harmony.

THE EFFECTS OF THE FALL

First, because of the fall, our intellect is darkened (we don't readily understand God's truth), our will is weakened (we don't readily choose the good or see our good choices through) and our passions are disordered (we desire things that aren't good for us). In other words, our fallen nature (also call "the flesh") is inclined to seek lowly things. This is *concupiscence* – our inclination to sin. St. Paul tells us quite plainly how this plays out:

> *Live in accord with the spirit and you will not yield to the cravings of the flesh. The flesh lusts against the spirit and the*

spirit against the flesh; the two are directly opposed. That is why you do not do what your will intends. (Gal 5:16-17)

Elsewhere St. Paul tells us that this is why we do what we know we shouldn't, and we don't do what we know we should. But please don't worry. It gets worse.

EFFECTS OF THE FALL – Part 1	
INTELLECT is DARKENED	Difficult to know truth
WILL is WEAKENED	We don't readily choose the good We don't see our good choices through
EMOTIONS are DISORDERED	Attract to things that are bad Move away from things that are good

The second destructive aspect of the fall is that not only are our emotions disordered (attracted to the wrong things), but our entire nature is disordered. Instead of our intellect running the show, our unruly emotions are clutching the steering wheel. To achieve their disordered end, our emotions thwart the proper functioning our intellect and will. Thus "...the spirit is willing, but the flesh is weak." (Mt 26:41)

Recall that our intellect should inform our will and the two, working together, drive our human activity. Our emotions (which exist at our animal level) should be subordinate and act to support our good thoughts and choices. Instead, our disordered emotions are now steering the ship. They are in charge and our darkened intellect and weakened will are slaves being dragged along for the ride (and are also at war with each other).

It doesn't stop there - *all* our sensitive faculties are disordered. Our memory and imagination need to be purified and disciplined.

But emotions lead the charge to overwhelm intellect and will. Our memory and imagination are dutiful soldiers, ready and eager to assist. Our beautiful picture of interior harmony and happiness has become a rather ugly and muddled mess.

How do emotions engage memory and imagination? Consider anxiety. Emotions stir up worries about the future. How? They pull up bad events from the past (*memory*) to *imagine* bad events in the future.

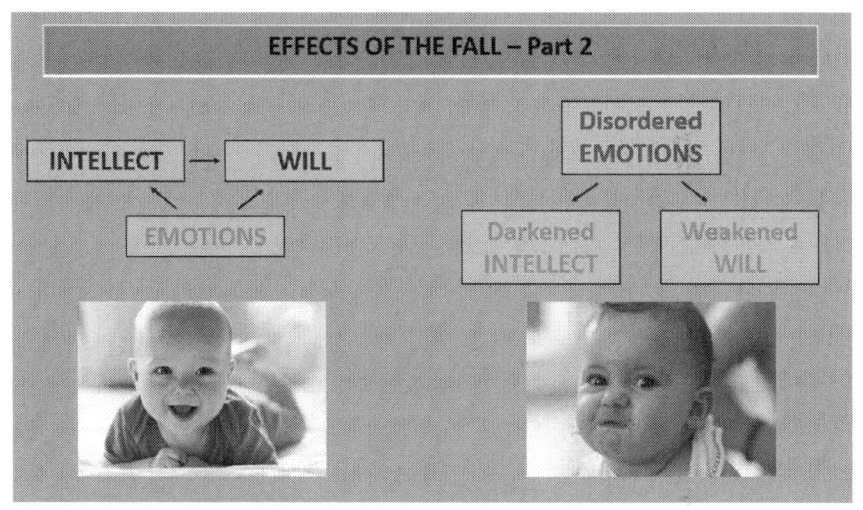

EFFECTS OF THE FALL – Part 2

INTELLECT → WILL
EMOTIONS

Disordered EMOTIONS
Darkened INTELLECT
Weakened WILL

(High-quality color versions of charts are available in the ebook and mobile app for this retreat)

Emotions can be very deceptive (another word for the devil is the deceiver…). Just so, our emotions deceive us with "imagined goods" – these are *false* goods (things that seem good but really aren't) or lesser goods (things that may be good in and of themselves but divert us from the greater goods that God desires for us).

For example, even when we are not seeking obviously sinful objects, we are inclined to ease and comfort. "Ease and comfort" can be deceptive. For some of us, it may be comfortable to bury ourselves in work. But work is a good thing – right? It depends on the situation and it requires a well-formed and well-ordered interior life to discern

Day 4 (Week 1, Day 3)

when it is time to separate from work and "waste" time with God, in recreation and with family and friends. Pope Benedict reminds us that "we are made for greatness, not comfort." St. Francis was so keenly aware of the weakness of the body (and emotions) that he referred to his body as "Brother Ass," equating it with a stubborn donkey that needs to be strictly disciplined.

What's worse, our emotions are so skilled in the art of deception that when we most need to engage our intellect and will is exactly when our emotions most powerfully kick in and before we know it, we "act without thinking". For this reason, we need to deeply understand how wounded we are from the fall and constantly remind ourselves of the proper functioning of our intellect and will and see them as distinct and superior to our emotions, memory and imagination. Most importantly – we need to constantly be calling on the help of the Holy Spirit.

Let's continue with another example - love and sacrifice. Because we have a spiritual soul, we are able to receive promptings from the Holy Spirit (through the proper function of our conscience, that "small voice"). Let's say we receive a prompting that we should sacrifice a weekend of our time to help a friend, knowing it will be difficult because we had much to do that weekend which will instead have to be accomplished at less convenient times. This prompting passes through our intellect to check that the prompting is reasonable and has the earmarks of coming from the Holy Spirit. We then engage our will so that we are determined to see this decision through and see it through as lovingly as possible.

The problem arises if the response of our emotions is "I don't want to do this." Our emotions will then assail our intellect with all manner of reasons (excuses) why it would be better not to help our friend ("they have plenty of other people to help them", or "it's really more important that I get my other activities completed," and so on). If we prevail in fighting off our emotions at the intellectual level and hold to the decision to help our friend, our emotions then get to work on our will. Laziness and fatigue creep in. Frustration as well, so that we are no longer a cheerful helper.

We need our intellect and our will to be stronger than our misguided emotions.

How do we do that?

We don't.

God's Grace – The Solution to the Fall

Everything is God's initiative. Whether we recognize it or not – it is only by God working in us that we can overcome the effects of the fall.

Yes, we must do our part and it takes a concerted effort to muster our intellect and will to choose well and see our good decision through to its proper end. More importantly it takes grace, so we should always be praying for God's grace to strengthen our intellect and will. In particular we should always be praying and working to improve in the four cardinal virtues of prudence (making right decisions and seeing them through), justice (knowing what we owe to God and neighbor), fortitude (the ability to withstand and overcome trials) and temperance (the virtue that militates against all sin and vice).

In the fourth week of the retreat we'll talk more about virtues. As we habituate the virtues, we can re-train our emotions and passions. Our emotions and passions were designed to be good and reinforce our intellect and will – growth in virtue (by God's grace) is how we reorder our passions to serve that original purpose.

This discussion of human anthropology brings us back to a recurring theme in this retreat – none of this is purely theoretical or informational or sentimental. All of this is meant to serve one purpose – that we grow in a loving relationship with God by better knowing Him and ourselves. All of this is meant to penetrate our intellect and move to our heart. A common roadblock at the early stages of mental prayer and developing our interior life is that we don't "feel" any different. But feelings are irrelevant. We don't have nerve endings in our soul. We must keep telling ourselves that our emotions lag reality. God *is* reality. Our intellect and will become more real as they draw closer to God. First, we get to know God; we get to thinking of Him all the time and seeing Him all around us –"Lord, help me find my car keys," "Lord, thank you for this sunrise," "Lord, please help my friend" - this is our intellect in action. Then we start responding to His promptings and changing our life to conform to His will – this is our will in action. With this comes loving thoughts of God, "Lord, I love you," "Lord, you are so wonderful," and loving thoughts of our neighbor. This may unfold slowly over time and we may not "feel" different along the way, just as a teenager doesn't feel any different from day to day while steadily growing from child to adult. Regardless of our *feelings*, the day comes when we *know* we have fallen in love with God because we realize that our lives could never again be complete without Him.

But there is always more; always mysteries to ponder in the Christian life. The definitions and concepts above are all abstractions – they don't get to the very root of it, because all these things are mysteries that we can never fully understand. We must always be pondering and probing the extraordinary gift that it is to be human – the incredible intermingling of body and spiritual soul. For example, St. Teresa of Avila challenges that we know what our homes look like, but we don't know what our own soul looks like. She muses at the distinction of the Soul and Spirit:

> "As I was saying, it is possible to make observations concerning interior matters and in this way we know that there is some kind of difference, and a very definite one, between the soul and the spirit, although they are both one.... It seems to me, too, that the soul is a different thing from the faculties and that they are not all one and the same. There are so many

and such subtle things in the interior life that it should be presumptuous for me to begin to expound them."

So, what does your spiritual soul look like? How does God see you? What exactly does it mean that He resides in you? As we'll continue to learn, these are among the many mysteries we have to ponder and bring to God in mental prayer.

Please spend 5 minutes in silent prayer; talking with God about today's session.

Let's close in prayer:

Lord Jesus Christ, help me to become ever more aware of your nearness and your love for me.

DAY 4 POSTSCRIPT: HUMAN CONSCIOUSNESS, MYSTICAL EXPERIENCES AND MODERN SCIENCE

There is a still-mysterious boundary between the basic thinking and functions of our brain (the squishy gray stuff in our skull) and the sophisticated thoughts and willful actions that come from our *mind* and *heart* (i.e. our spiritual powers of intellect and will). Science continues to confirm this. Many scientists are now taking the position that science must completely rethink the nature of consciousness, because the approaches to date, such as mapping electro-chemical activity of the brain, are wholly insufficient to explain human consciousness. Whether they know it or not, scientists are getting the slightest glimpse of the mystery of human being's spiritual soul.

It's important to emphasize that man is not just a really smart monkey or a highly evolved chimpanzee. Man is a completely different order of being from any other animal, however intelligent the animal may seem, and science will never be able to explain the deepest mysteries of our consciousness. The big bang provides a useful analogy. The start of the universe, as first theorized by Catholic priest Fr. Georges Lemaitre, was orchestrated in such a way that science is not capable of seeing before it. Science acknowledges this. The start of the universe is a *singularity* – all information is destroyed in a singularity so that science cannot "see" one nanosecond before it. It is like cracking and scrambling an egg – you can't undo it and put the egg back to what it was like before the cracking and scrambling. If you had never seen an egg before, and someone gave you a scrambled version of it, you would be hopeless to try to figure out what it looked like before the scrambling. Cracking and scrambling are akin to the singularity of the Big Bang – science will never be able to figure out what everything looked like before it occurred.

Atheist scientists may shrug their shoulders and say, "we don't need God - we can explain the *stuff* of the universe without him," but they must acknowledge that they can't say *how* the universe came to be or *what* purpose it has. In fact, science will never even be able to fully explain the stuff of the universe. For example, based on our current knowledge, to examine the most fundamental building blocks of matter would require a particle accelerator the size of the milky way galaxy. And, you and I know, even if science were able to come up with a device of that scale, it would only reveal some unexpected and even deeper mystery about the "stuff" of the universe that would require an even more colossal gadget. Because the most basic cause and sustaining force of the universe is God. And God is infinite so it would require an infinitely colossal gadget to observe Him. In short, only God and His revelation can answer the most basic questions about His creation.

The same is true of human consciousness. Scientists are at work on the "hard problem of consciousness" – trying to understand what makes humans different from all other primates and mammals. And that is a wonderful and noble endeavor, so long as it is ordered to God and Truth. A similar pattern will emerge with this endeavor as emerged with the study of creation of the universe and the smallest building blocks of matter, there will be some kernel at the heart of the phenomena of human consciousness that science will be unable to probe and answer. Science will ultimately have to concede its inability to characterize the very heart of what it means to be human. In fact, science is already beginning to reveal an astounding and insurmountable gap between human consciousness and animal consciousness. Atheist scientists will shrug their shoulders and brush aside these traces of God's fingerprints on human consciousness. This is because they are thinking of humans as having only a material brain; a lump of gray matter that just happens to weigh a little more than a chimpanzee's. In fact, we know that we have a mind that is greater than just our material brain. Our mind, and our consciousness is based in our soul; our eternal, spiritual soul.

A final thought on our minds and mystical experiences. It is well established that psychedelic drugs (psilocybin in particular) can induce what seem to be mystical experiences with life-long effects. To a lesser extent different environmental factors and activities (e.g. transcendental meditation) can also induce seemingly mystical experiences. What this shows is that God gave us brains that are "hard wired" for transcendent mystical experience. The catch is that wiring is not for us to abuse and manipulate to our own ends (just like we should not abuse and manipulate our body's ability to reproduce). That wiring was created by God for His purposes. As part of our loving relationship with God we need to let Him determine when and how He uses that wiring to grace us with authentic mystical experiences (which He often does as we'll discuss in Week 4).

Day 4 (Week 1, Day 3)

Pearls from Day 4: The *Who* of Mental Prayer part 1 - Our Role and What It Means to be Human

To enter fully into relationship with God, we need to know what it means to be human.

Christian Anthropology explains who and what the human person is - based on both reason (knowledge we can obtain with our own mental abilities) and revelation (knowledge that we can only receive from God). Humans are at the top of Creation and it's important to understand how we relate to other living things.

BEING	SOUL	POWERS (FACULTIES)
Human	Rational (Eternal Spirit)	Intellect Will — IMAGE AND LIKENESS OF GOD

Animal	Sensitive	Movement
		External Senses
		   (sight, hearing...)
		Internal Senses
		   (perception, imagination, memory,
		   estimation/cognition)
		Emotions

Plant	Vegetative	Nutrition Grown Reproduction

Humans, plants and animals all have a soul and powers (or faculties) appropriate to their state of being.

Our spiritual faculties (intellect and will) are higher than our sensitive faculties (which we share with animals). This is because we are made in the image and likeness of God, and God is pure spirit.

GOD'S DESIGN	
INTELLECT	Ability to know and understand Action - know what is True God *is* Truth
WILL	Governing Faculty – freely choose and act Action - to love goodness God *is* Goodness (God is the greatest good)
EMOTIONS	Attract us to something perceived as good or desirable Move away from something perceived as bad or undesirable Automatic responses Support Intellect and Will

In a well-formed person, the intellect should inform the will so that the will makes good choices. The emotions (as well as memory, imagination and cognition) merely support the intellect and will; they are subordinate.

EFFECTS OF THE FALL – Part 1	
INTELLECT is DARKENED	Difficult to know truth
WILL is WEAKENED	We don't readily choose the good We don't see our good choices through
EMOTIONS are DISORDERED	Attract to things that are bad Move away from things that are good

The will is higher than the intellect because while we can never know God perfectly (He is infinite and we are finite, we can never fully know Him), we can always love perfectly (we can always choose God's will).

There are two ways the fall has damaged the human person. First, our intellect is darkened, our will is weakened, and our emotions are disordered (we desire unholy things).

Day 4 (Week 1, Day 3)

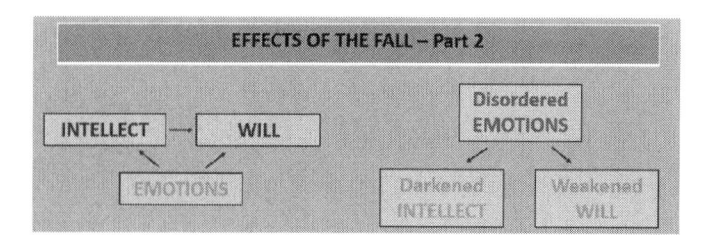

EFFECTS OF THE FALL – Part 2

INTELLECT → WILL

EMOTIONS

Disordered EMOTIONS

Darkened INTELLECT

Weakened WILL

Second, our faculties themselves are disordered. Instead of our intellect and will being the highest faculties, our disordered emotions tend to dictate how we behave.

One of the great missions we have in this life is to properly integrate our spiritual and sensitive powers and order them to God.

Your Pearls from Day 4

DAY 5: THE *WHO* OF MENTAL PRAYER PART 2 – GOD'S ROLE AND THE LIFE OF THE TRINITY

> Prayer is all about the relationship between us and God. Yesterday we learned about what it means to be us - human. We are a composite of body and soul. Today we turn our attention to God, who is infinitely beyond us, but desires to be known by us all the same.

Let's open with prayer:

Come Holy Spirit, make of me a fitting dwelling place for the Lord.

Your Jungle Mission

You are starting to understand yourself a little better. You're discovering strengths and gifts and reserves that you never knew were within in you. You're also recognizing some of your areas of weakness that hold you back and make parts of the journey very difficult. For example, sometimes you think you know best which way to go and are frustrated when it seems like the Savior is taking a more difficult route. Other times you find yourself envious of other nomads who seem to be having an easier time than you. Still other times, fatigue takes hold and you want to hang back and relax even though you know it's better that your press onward. Your fellow nomads remind you that recognizing these stumbling blocks is half the battle.

You are also taking the advice of the other nomads that you need to carefully copy whatever the Savior does. The challenge you've encountered with that advice is that He isn't always within eyesight. Sometimes He's off scouting ahead, at other times He is searching for someone who wandered off and got lost. You found yourself floundering when He was away. But some of the experienced nomads explained to you that the Savior doesn't leave you on your own, that He is present with you in His *Spirit*. What's more, they explain that the Savior has a Father who is always watching over all of the nomads and working with His Son and His Spirit to ensure that no harm comes to them.

They explain to you that an important part of the journey is to get to know the Father and the Spirit – especially since the goal is to be united with them someday at the Mountain Top.

From Yesterday

As a recap of yesterday, we are body and soul, with physical and spiritual powers associated with each, and which have been disordered by the fall. It is our task during our time here on Earth to learn to cultivate our spiritual faculties, intellect and will, by which we are made in God's image and likeness. It is also our task to properly subdue and direct our lower, sensitive faculties, which we share with animals; our emotions (also known as our passions, feelings and desires), imagination, memory and cognition. This is so that we can best love and serve God and the people He places in our lives and be led to our Heavenly destination.

Day 5 (Week 1, Day 4)

That explains us and our mission here on Earth. What then of God? Who is He and what is His role in our spiritual life? The place to start is with the mystery of the Trinity.

Catholic Understanding of Mystery

One of the many beautiful and unique aspects of Catholicism is the understanding of "mystery." First, Catholicism sheds great light on what the word "mystery" means to a Christian, which is not what the world thinks of the word. Catholic tradition also clarifies how mystery relates to faith, and it provides the most complete understanding of the many specific mysteries of the Christian faith.

The focus of Christian meditation is to penetrate the great mysteries of our faith. Christians understand mystery not as a murky and impenetrable unknown but as something so glorious and limitless we can never fully comprehend it (like the expanse of the universe). Spiritual mysteries are revealed to us by God and, while not fully knowable in this life, can be explored and partially understood through prayer and our spiritual power of intellect.

Turning to the great mystery of the Trinity, scripture and Catholic tradition teach us that God is Three Persons sharing one divine nature. We can't fully understand this. But God desires us always to enter deeper into this mystery and come to know Him as best as we can.

We know that God the Father created us and all the universe. We know this first and foremost because we are told this by God (revelation) and we can also approach this from reason (as the ancient philosophers did). But before that act of creation, God simply *was* (this is another mystery, the mystery of God's eternal being and nature). What was God doing before creation? God's two great actions are to know and to love. That should sound familiar from yesterday. This, again, is why our highest faculties are our spiritual powers of intellect and will. This characterization of God is also a great mystery. We naturally relate with the phrase "God is love" because it is a familiar concept and because "love" seems the most fitting characteristic to associate with God. Placing "knowing" on a par with love is less obvious, so let's start with that.

GOD THE FATHER'S ACT OF KNOWING AND GOD THE SON

We can back into the concept of God's act of knowing (really, His *self*-knowing) by considering life on earth. As we move from plant to animal to human the most significant distinction between each class of being is the degree of sentience (or consciousness or self-awareness). Plants have no sentience. Animals have only a vague or shadowy sentience in that they possess powers of perception, rudimentary emotions, and instinctual responses. Humans possess a high degree of sentience. In this hierarchy God is telling us something, through his Creation, about the importance of sentience since the creature possessing it in the fullest measure was made in the image and likeness of God. Secular philosophy innately grasps the significance of sentience as demonstrated in maxims such as "know thyself" and "I think, therefore I am."

What then of God? How does His sentience manifest itself? Does God think? Does He reflect on Himself? Certainly, God can't have questions about Himself, since He is all-knowing. Does God even need to think at all? Or is thinking beneath God since it implies things that need to be "thought out"? Or, does God simply *know*? If God simply knows, what does His knowing look like (so to speak)?

Great philosophers and theologians, St. Aquinas and St. Augustine first among them, have made some headway with these sorts of questions, but ultimately only God Himself can provide the answers - and He does in scripture. The Old Testament provides some hints, such as "I came out of the mouth of the Most High" (Eccl. 24:5). But it is the opening of John's Gospel where the second person of the trinity is given His full self-revelation:

Day 5 (Week 1, Day 4)

In the beginning was the Word, and the Word was with God, and the Word was God.
He was in the beginning with God. (Jn 1:1-2)

Word in this scripture passage is translated from "logos," which implies both Word and Reason, but theologians focus on word. Before we utter a word, we have an image of the word in our mind. But our image of something is only the faintest representation of what it is. As you form the word "desk" in your mind you have some concept of what the desk *is*. But hardly a complete image. Do you know what type of wood it is made from? Do you know which exact tree, from which exact forest, provided the wood? How old was the tree? What animals made their homes in that tree? How many atoms are contained in the desk? If we knew those things, we would be taking just the first step to knowing the desk the way God knows everything.

Putting this together – it is of our nature to be self-aware, but our self-awareness is stunningly limited; we know so little about ourselves. By loose comparison, it is in God's nature to be self-aware, but He is completely and perfectly self-aware. Thus, God's self-knowledge begets Himself – to do anything less would imply incomplete self-knowledge. Thus, God the Son, begotten by the Father's self-knowledge, is fully God. God's self-knowledge is so powerful and complete that it is a living Word; it is God Himself.

As another very loose analogy you might think of a writer who creates particularly vivid characters, say, Anne Shirley or Bilbo Baggins. By the end of the novel you feel as if you are saying goodbye to a close friend. If the thoughts of a human writer can make a mere character in a book seem to live and breathe, we can start to see how the thoughts of our omnipotent and eternal God beget an actual person - His Son.

And God the Son, Jesus Christ, became man and redeemed us. Here another mystery enters, Jesus Christ true God and true man. Jesus is no less God, "I and the Father are one," (Jn 10:30) but also fully human. Jesus takes on our humanity so that we might take on his divinity.

THE FATHER AND SON'S ACT LOVE AND THE HOLY SPIRIT

Let's turn our attention from God's act of knowing to his act of loving. This is also a great mystery. God the Father and God the Son exist in a continuous cycle of self-giving to one another. Here we see again why, for humans, our power to love is higher than our power to know. We can never know something perfectly – just look at the simple example of a desk. But we can love perfectly. By God's grace we can fully give ourselves to God (this is the example of the Saints). The mutual love and self-giving of God the Father and God the Son is ever-present in scripture. God the Father is always pointing to his Son:

> *Behold, my servant whom I have chosen; my beloved in whom my soul is well-pleased; I will put my Spirit upon Him, and he shall proclaim justice to the gentiles. (Mt 12:18)*
>
> *While he was still speaking, a bright cloud overshadowed them, and behold, a voice out of the cloud said, "This is My beloved Son, with whom I am well-pleased; listen to Him!" (Mt 17:5)*
>
> *and a voice came out of the heavens: "You are My beloved Son, in You I am well-pleased." (Mk 1:11)*
>
> *Then a cloud formed, overshadowing them, and a voice came out of the cloud, "This is My beloved Son, listen to Him!" (Mk 9:7)*
>
> *Then a voice came out of the cloud, saying, "This is My Son, My Chosen One; listen to Him!" (Lk 9:35)*
>
> *For He rescued us from the domain of darkness and transferred us to the kingdom of His beloved Son. (Col 1:13)*
>
> *So also Christ did not glorify Himself so as to become a high priest, but He who said to Him, "You are my son, today I have begotten you." (Heb 5:5)*

For when He received honor and glory from God the Father, such an utterance as this was made to Him by the Majestic Glory, "This is My beloved Son with whom I am well-pleased." (2 Peter 1:17)

And God the Son is always giving Himself back to the Father:

And He went a little beyond them, and fell on His face and prayed, saying, "My Father, if it is possible, let this cup pass from Me; yet not as I will, but as You will." (Mt 26:39)

And He was saying, "Abba! Father! All things are possible for You; remove this cup from Me; yet not what I will, but what You will." (Mk 14:36)

Father, if You are willing, remove this cup from Me; yet not My will, but Yours be done. (Lk 22:42)

Jesus said to them, "My food is to do the will of Him who sent Me and to accomplish His work." (Jn 4:34)

I can do nothing on My own initiative. As I hear, I judge; and My judgment is just, because I do not seek My own will, but the will of Him who sent Me. (Jn 5:30)

For I have come down from heaven, not to do My own will, but the will of Him who sent Me. (Jn 6:38)

This eternal act of love between Father and Son brings us to God the Holy Spirit. Just as God's self-knowledge is so complete and powerful that it is a person (Christ), so too the communion of love between the Father and Son is so great it is a person, the Holy Spirit (in creation this is mirrored by husband and wife – whose love is so fruitful and real that it becomes a person – a child).

God the Spirit flows from the Father and the Son and is with us as Counselor and Consoler - "But the Paraclete, the Holy Spirit, whom the Father will send in my name, he will teach you all things." (Jn 14:26) Now, a Spirit exists where it acts. For human beings, our spirits are inextricably bound to our bodies; we are enfleshed spirits. The

Holy Spirit is pure spirit and is present in all places. The Holy Spirit is also present within us (so long as we are in a state of grace – that is, not corrupted by mortal sin) "Do you not know that you are a temple of God and that the Spirit of God dwells in you." (1 Cor, 3:16) But if the Spirit is in us, so too is the Father and Son. So while the indwelling of God is most properly associated with the Holy Spirit, the indwelling makes present the Trinity.

Whoever loves me will keep my word, and my Father will love him, and we will come to him and make our dwelling with him. (Jn 14:23)

Here we see the indwelling of the Holy Spirit tied with "whoever loves me will keep my word." This is an example of the reality that we must be "in a state of grace" for the Holy Spirit to remain in us. If we are living in unrepented mortal sin the Holy Spirit will not dwell within us – because we are making the decision for our soul to not be a fitting home for Him. Human beings naturally recognize the importance of forgiveness (psychiatry recognizes one of the best things for mental health is to forgive and seek forgiveness). Christianity in all its forms recognizes the importance of repenting our sins. The Catholic Church provides the completeness of forgiveness of sin through the Sacrament of Reconciliation. This is discussed further in Day 28. Suffice to say, if you are a Catholic and have not recently celebrated the Sacrament of Reconciliation, you should (and continue to go monthly), especially if you are aware of serious sin in your life. You'll be so glad that you did. If you are not Catholic you should still make a genuine act of repentance (again, see day 28) – this is a beautiful offering to God - and please prayerfully consider coming home to the Catholic faith.

When we lift our spirit to God in prayer it is perfectly acceptable to have any one of the three persons of the Trinity as our focus, or all three.

Day 5 (Week 1, Day 4)

OUR INCARNATIONAL FAITH

Faith and prayer, and all of life for that matter, are particularly *incarnational*. It is the God-Man, Jesus Christ, who redeemed us, mediates for us and came to earth and shared in our humanity so that we might share in his divinity. These also aren't just romantic phrases. This is *very real*. We truly share in Christ's divinity by being transformed into His likeness, by having our fallen nature literally transformed by God's grace. St. Paul repeatedly instructs us about putting on the "new man" – which is to rid ourselves of our fallen nature and, through Christ, reclaim who God created us to be (this is akin to what some refer to as ridding the *false self* and becoming our *true self*). A primary way we open ourselves to the grace of being transformed into Christ is through mental prayer. We will find it is meditation on the mysteries of Christ's life that most powerfully cultivate our interior life, reveal us to ourselves, and heal, purify and harmonize our wounded humanity. And as we grow closer to the Son, we necessarily grow closer to the Father and the Spirit. And we will also grow closer to all the other members of the Body of Christ in our human relationships.

The saints give us a wonderful analogy of a wagon wheel. Jesus is the hub of the wheel. Each one of us is holding onto one of the spokes of the wheel. The closer we move toward the hub, the closer we are in relationship with Jesus. If we move away from the hub, toward the rim, we are isolating ourselves from Jesus. Obviously, we want to be right at the hub, clinging to Christ. But notice what else happens - as we get closer to the hub, we also get closer to all of the other spokes. In other words, as we grow closer to Jesus we grow closer to everyone else who is moving toward him.

Returning to our faith being incarnational, Jesus is the key that unlocks the Trinity.

We all long to be reunited with our heavenly Father. Even if we don't consciously know it – at the deepest part of all of us, our spirit longs for this. Jesus Christ restores that relationship: "….no one comes to the Father except through me." (Jn 14:6) Jesus tells us that through Him we become adopted children of the Father. We can look to the story of the Prodigal Son. We can imagine our Heavenly Father watching for us, running to us with open arms – and it is Jesus who leads us back to the Father.

And Jesus gives us the gift of His Spirit to assist in our spiritual journey here on Earth. We speak of the "promptings of the Spirit." These are movements of our heart that draw us to God's will for us at specific moments in time. We see this in action in the call of Samuel ("Speak, Lord, your servant is listening." 1 Sam 3:9) We also see this reflected in God calling to Elijah, in a whispering voice on the mountain top. God speaks softly. Many great orators use this same technique. By speaking softly, you draw people's attention to you. But, for our part, we need to be listening carefully. This again is where mental prayer enters. We need to cultivate a facility for silence, so that we can hear God's promptings in the silence of our heart, and we can respond as Samuel, "Speak, Lord, for your servant is listening."

The purpose of mental prayer is to share in the life of the Trinity. We go to the Father through the Son with the help of the Holy Spirit. The Father and Son eternally existing in a perfect exchange of love, from which proceeds the Holy Spirit. Grace, blessedness, holiness – all boils down to sharing in the life of the Trinity, being a part of their loving embrace.

That addresses our understanding of who the Trinity are. This brings us to the other subject of this session – the role of the Trinity in mental prayer. This is quite simple; God has the primary role in our mental prayer. It is only by God's grace that we can enter into the life of the Trinity. First by the *sanctifying grace* of baptism that restores our relationship. God then continues to offer us *actual grace* (grace that *acts* in our life) - a supernatural gift that spiritually strengthens us to carry out our earthly vocation and raise our intellect and will to God. As always, these aren't vague, sentimental words. When we overcome a great hurdle in life and say "it was by God's grace" – that is a truism – much of what we do in this life is only through the supernatural gifts that God gives us when we open ourselves to sharing in the life of the Trinity.

Please spend 5 minutes in silent prayer; talking with God about today's session.

Let's close in prayer:

Holy Trinity, may You make Your home in us and draw us ever deeper into Your life of love. Amen.

Pearls from Day 5: The *Who* of Mental Prayer part 2 – God's Role and the Life of the Trinity

God is Three Persons with one divine nature. This is a great mystery.

For Christians, mystery does not mean something completely hidden and unknowable. Spiritual mysteries are truths that are so grand we can never fully comprehend them (like the mystery of the Trinity). We are called to accept God's revealed mysteries by faith, but to also explore them with our power of reason.

God the Father's two great actions are *to know* and *to love*. Therefore, humanity's highest powers are the spiritual powers of intellect and will.

God's self-knowing is so complete and powerful that it begets a person, the Second Person of the Trinity, His Son. "In the beginning was the Word, and the Word was with God, and the Word was God." (Jn 1:1)

In God's act of loving, God the Father continually pours out His love to His Son. God the Son is continually giving Himself back to the Father. This mutual act of self-giving love is so complete and fruitful that it is a person - the Holy Spirit.

The three persons of the Trinity always act together. But specific operations are most properly associated with each: creation to God the Father, redemption to God the Son and sanctification to God the Spirit.

We must be "in a state of grace" for the Holy Spirit to remain in us. If we are living in unrepented mortal sin the Spirit will not dwell within us. The Catholic Church provides the completeness of forgiveness of sin through the Sacrament of reconciliation. This is discussed further in Day 28.

Day 5 (Week 1, Day 4)

We can pray with any one of the three persons of the Trinity, but our faith is particularly *incarnational*. This is because God redeemed us and leads us to Heaven by becoming a man – Jesus.

Jesus is the key that unlocks the Trinity. Jesus reunites us with our Father: …. "No one comes to the Father except through me." (John 14:6) And Jesus gave us the gift of His Spirit to dwell within us.

Humans are meant to share in the divine life of the Trinity. Grace is another word for sharing in that divine life, and mental prayer is an important part of how we receive that grace.

God's role in mental prayer is primary. It is only by God's grace that we can enter into the life of the Trinity. First, by the *sanctifying grace* of baptism that restores our relationship. Then, God continues to offer us *actual grace* (grace that *acts* in our life) - a supernatural gift that spiritually strengthens us to carry out our earthly vocation and raise our intellect and will to God.

———— **Your Pearls from Day 5** ————

Day 6 (Week 1, Day 5)

DAY 6: THE INTERIOR LIFE IS NECESSARY TO SUSTAIN THE ACTIVE LIFE

> "You can't judge a book by its cover." "It's what's on the inside that counts." "How many licks does it take to get to the center of a tootsie pop?" We are fascinated with what's on the inside. And with good reason. Our interior life really is *what it's all about*. If we get our interior life in order, everything else falls into place. So today we will consider carefully what is meant by "interior life" and how it relates to our entire life.

Let's open with prayer:

Come Holy Spirit, make of me a fitting dwelling place for the Lord.

YOUR JUNGLE MISSION

You've come to realize that the jungle is teaming with life and activity. Much of it quite beautiful. Some of it, very dangerous. Some things are deadly in and of themselves – snakes, big cats, poisonous plants. A great many other things are deceptively dangerous because they appear attractive – waterfalls, lush valleys, exotic creatures - but they distract and allure you from the path that would lead you to the mountain top.

All of it is so very demanding – physically, intellectually and emotionally. Each morning you need to prepare for the day ahead – prepping physically and mentally, and organizing your gear for the type of terrain you'll encounter. And then you're on your way, trekking through the jungle. As evening comes you scout out a resting place for the night and search for food and water. You attend to the needs of your fellow nomads. Before you know it, it is time for bed. There's so much to do and you just want to keep pressing ahead as quickly as you can.

The strange thing is that the Savior doesn't seem to share your sense of urgency. He appears perfectly content to take His time (although He certainly accomplishes everything that needs doing). Most of all, He wants to set aside specific times of the day to talk with you. It's often right when you want to move ahead at breakneck speed with the tasks at hand. Stranger still is that when you take the time away from all your pressing tasks to sit quietly with the Savior the rest of the day goes smoothly.

But those days when you are in too much of a hurry and pass up your time with Him, everything falls apart.

Your Interior Life

And so it is with the world around us. As sure as God made little green apples, this world is a busy, distracting, and alluring, place. 24/7. Nonstop. You may have noticed that the world has a way of crowding in whenever you make plans to separate from it. You know what happens when you try to set aside some quiet time or go on vacation. It's even worse when we set aside time for God. When we decide to make time for prayer, or make plans to go on a retreat, all manner of distractions, everything from small brush fires to major conflagrations suddenly brew up.

Day 6 (Week 1, Day 5)

Trust in this – the world is actively opposed to you spending quiet time with the Lord. If it seems difficult to set aside a few minutes of quiet with God, it is because it is.

But the outside world isn't the only jungle we face. Our interior world can be every bit as challenging. We find out how true this is whenever we first attempt to sit in silence for a few minutes. Or just 20 seconds. It is mystifying the flights of fancy that occur in less time than it takes to tie a shoelace. And it's not only challenging, it's treacherous – the exterior world can only tempt us, our agreement with sin happens in our interior.

So, we need to get our interior life figured out. Because our interior life is the key to both our eternal life *and*, as it turns out, our exterior life in the here and now. And when we join our interior life to God amazing things happen.

For the past two days we discussed you and God – the lead roles in this loving relationship. We learned how all of us are damaged by the fall. Our intellect is darkened. Our will is weakened. Our passions are disordered. And yet we are called to go out in the world and make it holy. How can we possibly do that when our faculties seem hopelessly broken? The answer is *grace*. God's grace heals our faculties, especially our *interior* faculties. As your interior faculties heal and become sanctified your exterior activities become holy. That is the power of grace. And you receive God's grace by being in *relationship* with Him.

With that, we'll look at these aspects of your interior life:

1. Your interior life and the necessity of grace
2. Your interior life should ultimately permeate and transform your entire life
3. Your interior life is superior to your active life

Your Interior Life and the Necessity of Grace

What, exactly, is your Interior Life? In its most primitive form, the interior life is simply what takes place in our mind – thoughts, instincts, aspirations.

But that really isn't *life,* that's just interior. Life is relationship ("it is not good for man to be alone"). And simply living in our own heads isn't relationship, it's just ego - us talking to ourselves (or worse, the enemy smuggling lies and deception into our consciousness).

Fr. Garrigou-LaGrange (from *The Three Ages of the Interior Life*) offers keen insight into the interior life:

> "As soon as a man seriously seeks truth and goodness, this intimate conversation with himself tends to become conversation with God. Little by little, instead of seeking himself in everything, instead of tending more or less consciously to make himself a center, man tends to seek God in everything, and to substitute for egoism love of God and of souls in Him. This constitutes the interior life. No sincere man will have any difficulty in recognizing it. The one thing necessary which Jesus spoke of to Martha and Mary consists in hearing the word of God and living by it....
>
> ...The interior life is precisely an elevation and a transformation of the intimate conversation that everyone has with himself as soon as it tends to become a conversation with God."

There's a lot contained in that brief passage from Fr. Garrigou-LaGrange, and we'll return to it in a moment.

But first - the interior life presupposes grace. We can't truly know God without the sanctifying grace that is given at baptism and which restores our relationship with God. On a side note, a person may ask, "what about adults who have not been baptized, but have an awareness of God, and are even drawn to God?" Good question. That innate pull toward God is a form of grace called *prevenient grace*.

This is grace that precedes human decision. Sort of like your stomach rumbling is prevenient to you ordering a pizza. This is the grace by which God begins to draw a person to Himself before that person is even aware of it. That person still has the power of free will to turn aside from God, but the initial attraction is the work of God – prevenient grace.

In any event, we receive sanctifying grace at baptism, and with that our relationship with God is restored. From that point on we must continue to cooperate with God and receive His "actual grace" – which is to say grace that is *active*. This is God's on-going gift of grace that helps us to conform our will to His and, along with sacramental grace, remain in a *state of grace*.

We are going to delve much deeper into these forms of grace in Week 4. What matters here is that we can't truly know God without sanctifying grace. This doesn't mean we can't encounter God in our life or reason quite a bit about God without grace. Let's consider our prior discussion of mystery. The Greeks went exceptionally far in their understanding of God operating purely from philosophy; most of yesterday's discussion of the soul originated with Greek philosophical thought – there's a tremendous body of philosophy behind all of that, such as Plato's analogy of the cave and the role that *forms* play in creating reality (Dr. Peter Kreeft has many good books on these topics for further reading).

But reason alone only gets us to understand God in the same limited way that I would understand you by reading your resume or biography. If I want to really *know* you, I need to have a relationship with you.

God, as He always does, initiates this deep, personal relationship with us. He comes and manifests Himself in our interior. This is the indwelling of the Holy Spirit. This is the grace we receive at baptism.

Now it is up to us to respond to God's grace. That's all it takes. When we receive and affirmatively respond to God's grace, that grace turns to glory; it actually accomplishes things in our life. Here is an example comparing a friend's invitation to dinner and God's prompting to grace:

Dinner with a Friend	Prompting from God
Amy calls and invites you to get pizza.	God prompts you to volunteer as a tutor.
Amy also says "I'm buying – dinner is on me. All you have to do is show up!"	God assures you that He will provide the grace (in the form of virtues and gifts) to carry it out.
It's up to you to simply say "yes" and show up at dinner and be fully present.	It's up to you to simply say "yes" and follow through by doing your best.
If you do, your relationship grows because you share dinner and conversation with your friend.	If you do, your relationship with God grows because you shared in God's work by helping your neighbor.
Grace (your friend's invitation and paying for the meal) has been turned into glory (deepening friendship).	Grace (God's invitation and the gifts He gives to accomplish it) has been turned into glory (deepening relationship with God and neighbor).

What happens if we say "no" to God? The grace remains, but is inoperative, like putting a fresh battery in a flashlight but never turning it on. More generally, when a person habitually rejects God's grace, it becomes a sort of self-condemnation; the person distancing themselves from God, by turning from God and toward self. There are countless ways this can occur: we have an inner prompting to start going to Church but decide not to. Or, we have an impulse to reach out to someone on the margins, but we let the busyness of life get in the way. Or, we recognize an unhealthy pattern in our life, but make no effort to break it. Fr. Garrigou-LaGrange describes it thus:

> "If a man is fundamentally egotistical, his intimate conversation with himself is inspired by sensuality or pride. He converses with himself about the object of his cupidity, of his envy; finding therein sadness and death, he tries to flee from himself, to live outside of himself, to divert himself in order to forget the emptiness and the nothingness of his life. In this intimate conversation of the egoist with himself there is a certain very inferior self-knowledge and a no less inferior self-love... The intimate conversation of the egoist with himself proceeds thus to death and is therefore not an interior life."

Chilling, isn't it? But there is merit in facing such cold realities head on – it is very clarifying for why we need to cultivate an interior life and help others do the same.

Stepping back into the light, we see that the interior life is meant to grow into a loving relationship with God. Here we think of St. Teresa's definition of mental prayer being a conversation with Him who loves us. But our interior life extends beyond mental prayer.

Your Interior Life and Your Entire Life

Recall Fr. Garrigou-LaGrange's definition of interior life noted that over time "man tends to seek God in everything." Elsewhere, Fr. G. continues:

> "In this interior conversation with God, which tends to become continual, the soul speaks by prayer, *oratio*, which is prayer in its finest form... Prayer takes the form now of petition, now of adoration and thanksgiving; it is always an elevation of the soul toward God.... The saints truly follow this way, and then between their souls and God is established that conversation which does not, so to speak, cease."

Our interior life becomes everything. We might think of soldiers going off to war – their wives and families are always on their minds and hearts; in everything they do there is the underlying thought of home. As our interior life grows, everything we do is taken up into it.

Mental prayer is not the totality of our interior life, but it is the all-important heart of our interior life. Mental prayer is the well where we return to refresh our self and stay close to God. The deeper our devotion to mental prayer, the more we can turn the rest of our life over to God in an unceasing conversation. And there is a symbiosis in that the more we bring all things to God, the richer our mental prayer becomes.

That then is the first key concept of the interior life – that it is meant to permeate and transform our entire life. Fr. Jean Baptiste Chautard puts it this way: "Active works must begin and end in the interior life, and in it, find their means." (*Soul of the Apostolate*). And St. Jose Maria Escriva says: "It is in the midst of the most material things of the earth that we must sanctify ourselves, serving God and all mankind." (*Conversations with Msgr. Josemaria Escriva*).

Your Interior Life is Superior to Your Exterior Life

The second key concept of our interior life is that it is superior to our active life as simply stated by Fr. Chautard: "In their turn, Popes, holy doctors of the Church, and theologians affirm that the interior life is, of itself, superior to the active life."

From Stefan Cardinal Wyszynski (*Sanctify Your Daily Life*): "Interior life is the basis of exterior life and of all physical, educational, social, and scientific work. The starting point for every kind of work ought to be the interior life, just as the branch comes forth from the life of the vine itself."

And, again, from Fr. Garrigou-Lagrange – "Hence, to have an interior life, an exceedingly active exterior apostolate does not suffice, nor does great theological knowledge. Nor is the latter necessary. A generous beginner, who already has a genuine spirit of abnegation and prayer, already possesses a true interior life which ought to continue developing."

This should be extremely encouraging! Like all things in the spiritual life, what really matters is our willingness. As St. Teresa says, "What matters is not to do much, but to love much."

How It All Works

While all of this may be encouraging and edifying, it is also a bit esoteric. Let's come back to ground level and see how this looks in action. First, let's clarify terminology.

Interior life is everything that happens in our mind. Recall that your mind is more than your physical brain – it is also your spiritual powers of intellect and will. And by definition, your interior life incorporates both your conscious and subconscious mind. This would include the understanding of human consciousness such as Freud's theory of ego, superego, and id or Jung's theory of the collective unconscious. *Everything* that makes *you* be *you*, is part of your interior life.

Our exterior life is all our exterior activity in the world.

Often there is overlap between our interior and exterior. Think of something that requires a great deal of concentration. Anything creative. Playing a sport. Doing your taxes. Your interior is closely aligned with your exterior activity.

Other times there is little overlap. Take driving a car. How often have you been driving down the highway and your mind wanders and you have no recollection of guiding the car for the past 30 miles?

The same distinctions are true for spiritual matters. If you *pray* a rosary for someone, is it an interior or an exterior activity? It's both. Your interior and exterior activities are aligned. The opposite also holds true. How often do we go to Mass and while our bodies are there our minds have travelled to dozens of destinations?

The goal of our life is for our interior life and our exterior life to be fully aligned and to be fully brought into our relationship with God. For this to happen we must grow our relationship with God by spending time with him and, as we have been discussing, that happens first and foremost through mental prayer.

The figures on the following page illustrate how this works. These figures are conceptual; they aren't a scientific mapping of the human person - they simply illustrate the relationship between interior, exterior and mental prayer.

In these figures, bear in mind that the interior life means all of our interior - conscious, subconscious, ego, id, superego, memories, instincts, imagination – every bit of our interior can be available to God, every bit (even our subconscious) can be brought into relationship with Him, healed, harmonized, *sanctified*.

You will see the last three figures are identified with the purgative, illuminative and unitive ages – we will discuss these terms tomorrow (after which you should take another look at these figures).

The great contemplatives are our models in this. They bring everything into their contemplative lives. *Everything* they do becomes prayer because they have lives of deep mental prayer.

With these figures in mind, recall our two key concepts of the interior life (with quotes from Fr. Chautard):

1. It is meant to encompass our entire life. "Active works must begin and end in the interior life, and in it, find their means."
2. It is superior to our active life. "In their turn, Popes, holy doctors of the Church, and theologians affirm that the interior life is, of itself, superior to the active life."

Day 6 (Week 1, Day 5)

Interior: Everything involving our mind and spiritual faculties of intellect and will. Note, this includes conscious and subconscious. All our mind is available to God and can be transformed and sanctified.

Exterior: Our physical activity in the world.

A person almost devoid of spiritual activity. A classic example is a person simply going to Church on Sunday. A small part of the exterior activity is turned to God (physically going to Church) and a small part of the interior is turned to God (praying in Church and perhaps a few prayers during the week). God is absent from the rest of their life.

A person starting to grow their interior life through authentic relationship with God (purgative age). The darkest blue is the time of mental prayer. From this well spring, more of the person's interior and exterior life is being brought into that relationship as they grow in relationship with God and in virtue.

A person far along in their relationship with God (illuminative age). Their mental prayer is deep and consistent; they have grown far in virtue so that most of their interior and exterior life has been brought into relationship with God.

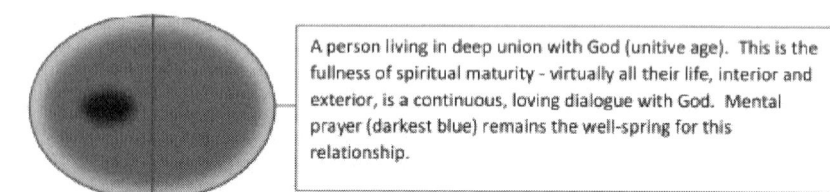

A person living in deep union with God (unitive age). This is the fullness of spiritual maturity - virtually all their life, interior and exterior, is a continuous, loving dialogue with God. Mental prayer (darkest blue) remains the well-spring for this relationship.

(High quality color graphics are available in the ebook and mobile app for this retreat)

Closing Thoughts

Our interior life and our time of mental prayer is also a school of virtue. St. Teresa of Avila, when asked to teach postulants about mental prayer, did so by teaching about virtue. The two go hand in hand. As we grow in relationship with God we will naturally grow in virtue. And as we grow in virtue we will naturally desire to grow in our relationship with God. Thus, unless we grow in relationship with God, we will not be able to act virtuously, we will only act. Our service won't be joyful. We won't be open to promptings of the Holy Spirit. We won't be able to persevere through trials.

And we won't know what to say yes to and when to say no. It is easy to be consumed with activity in the world, that doesn't mean the activity is fruitful. And by this we particularly mean fruitful in the fullest sense of the word – fruitful in filling our lives with meaning and building up the Kingdom of God.

With the topic of the busyness and activity of the world, we have now come full circle. Our interior life (anchored in mental prayer) is necessary for our active life in the world to be fruitful. Our interior life is meant to encompass all that we do – to make everything an unceasing conversation with God who loves us and desires to share in all that we do.

Please spend 5 minutes in silent prayer; talking with God about today's session.

Let's close in prayer:

Jesus, draw me to You in my interior life so that I can bring You to the world in my active life.

Day 6 (Week 1, Day 5)

Pearls from Day 6: The Interior Life is Necessary to Sustain the Active Life

We all possess self-awareness and have an interior world of dialogue with self – this is sometimes thought of as our *ego*. But this isn't "life" in the fulness of the word. Life is relationship, and conversation with self is not relationship.

But how are we to have a relationship inside of our own mind? The answer, of course, is found in God.

We develop an interior life (instead of simply an ego) when we become aware of God and "tend to seek God in everything, and to substitute for egoism love of God and of souls in Him." (Fr. Garrigou-LaGrange, *Three Ages of the Interior Life*).

Our interior life requires *grace*. We can't know God and grow in relationship with Him without his grace. First the sanctifying grace of baptism and then God's on-going actual grace and sacramental grace that sustain and strengthen us.

We must say "yes" to God's grace. God will prompt us to share in his work (serving people around us) and give us the grace to accomplish it. If we say "yes" the grace is turned into glory. If we say "no" the grace never transforms into glory, it is inoperative, like putting fresh batteries in a flashlight but never turning it on.

KEY CONCEPT #1: OUR INTERIOR LIFE IS MEANT TO ENCOMPASS OUR ENTIRE LIFE

Our interior life flows from our mental prayer and is intended to eventually permeate and transform our entire active life as well – so that everything we do becomes a loving dialogue with God.

KEY CONCEPT #2: OUR INTERIOR LIFE IS SUPERIOR TO OUR ACTIVE LIFE

Scripture and tradition have always given pride of place to the interior life (e.g. the story of Martha and Mary, and the example of Jesus' solitary prayer). Our interior life perfects our active life.

Your Pearls from Day 6

DAY 7: THE THREE AGES OF THE INTERIOR LIFE

> We now know that our interior life is the key to sharing in the life of the Trinity and healing our fallen and disordered nature. And we know that mental prayer is the "key to that key," it is the heart of our interior life. Is that all there is to it? In the rest of life there are ways that we progress and mature. It turns out that our spiritual life also follows a pattern of growth – the Three Ages of the Interior Life.

Let's begin with opening prayer:

Come Holy Spirit, make of me a fitting dwelling place for the Lord.

YOUR JUNGLE MISSION

It was the lichen. That was your undoing.

You were happily chatting with Oscar and Wendy. They only recently joined the nomads - making them the newest of the band of sojourners. They had also been pulled from harm's way by the Savior. They were telling you all about their struggles and how the challenges they were facing had started to take a toll on their marriage; they were at one another's throats with frustration, indecision and disagreement about which way to go to get out of the jungle. They were about to separate, and each go their own way and probably would have each fallen into perilous circumstances. That was when He showed up. And now here they were and suddenly everything was different. As they told their story you could sense their relief and the peace and light that was returning to their relationship. It was like watching a wilted plant return to life after being watered. You were taking pleasure in the moment.

You were also enjoying being "the experienced one" for a change. Oscar and Wendy had question after question about the jungle, the nomads and, especially, about Him. Many of them were the same questions you first had. They also thought up a few that had not occurred to you. You did your best to answer them and were surprised at how much you knew. You were able to tell them about the nomads and the Way you were all traveling. You shared what you knew about the far-off mountain. They were particularly curious about the Savior's Father and His Spirit. They had all kinds of questions about those Three and were asking rapid fire. You were doing all you could to strain your memory and answer as best as possible; there was something about the bond of love between the Father and the Savior ... how again did that go?

And that was when you heard "watch out for the lichen!"

And down you went like a sack of potatoes. Bill, who had tried to warn you and one of the truly experienced nomads, was right by your side helping you assess the damage. Twisted ankle and scraped knee. As you hobbled to your feet Bill observed, "Rookie mistake. The rock around here is covered with lichen. Gets real slippery. But you'll never forget that lesson."

Make that twisted ankle, scraped knee and wounded pride.

You may no longer be the newest of the nomads, but you still had plenty to learn. Which prompted you to reflect that there was quite a spectrum of experience among the nomads. Some were fairly new, like yourself; shedding bad habits and learning new disciplines. There were others who seemed to have all the basics down, but still struggled from time to time. And then there were those that seemed almost like Him – they were completely at ease. It also seemed that they spent most of their day with Him – how did they find the time?

THE THREE AGES

Christian tradition has always taught three stages of spiritual development through which we all may pass: the purgative way, illuminative way and unitive way. These are the three ages of the interior life.

The material for today's session is primarily culled from Fr. Tanqueray (*The Spiritual Life*) and Fr. Garrigou-Lagrange (*The Three Ages of the Interior Life*). But these ages (or ways) are founded in scripture, expounded by Tradition, and affirmed by reason.

As an example of how they are reflected in Sacred Scripture, consider our Lord's words: "If any man will come after me, let him deny himself, and take up his cross daily, and follow me." In self-denial and self-renouncement - *let him deny himself* – we see the purgative way. The carrying of one's cross already presupposes the positive practice of virtue, or the illuminative way. *Follow me* is intimate union with Jesus, union with God, and hence, the unitive way.

The apostles themselves passed through these three ages. Their purgative way extended from Christ calling them (and their conversion) up to Christ's Passion (His suffering and death). Their illuminative way extended from Christ's Passion to Pentecost (receiving the Holy Spirit). And they continued along the unitive way from that time on.

The three ages are reflected in the Catholic sacrifice of the Mass. The purgative way is the penitential rite. We enter into Mass by expressing sorrow and repentance for our sins. The day's readings, the Liturgy of the Word, bring us to the illuminative way. And the high point of the mass, Communion, the Liturgy of the Eucharist, brings us to the unitive way.

St. Paul repeatedly infers the three ways. Early Church Fathers elaborated on the Three Ways. And as noted above, our faculty of reason affirms the truth of the Three Ways in our own human development. Now we will look at each stage in greater detail.

Purgative Way

The characteristic of the Purgative Way, the state of beginners, is the purifying of the soul for the purpose of drawing closer to God. God dwells in our soul. He sees all. Nothing is hidden. It takes extraordinarily little self-reflection to shudder at the thought of the foul things we have tucked away in there. We clean our house before guests arrive. How much more do we need to purify our interior house (our soul) to make it suitable for the Lord!

We also associate the purgative way with this: "The fear of the Lord is the beginning of wisdom; a good understanding have all those who practice it" (Ps 111:10 and Sir 1:14). *Fear of the Lord* is not the fear of undeserved abuse from a tyrannical master. *Fear of the Lord* is first and foremost fear that we might offend our loving Father who sacrificed His only Son for our salvation. To be sure it is also a fear that is rooted in the knowledge that we do grave harm to ourselves when we act in ways counter to God's will, but this is a less perfect, self-focused fear.

Simply the desire to travel the mystical path and enter the purgative way reveals a soul that is yearning for God. A person has already traveled far along the road of faith to come to commit themselves to the purgative path – desiring to unite themselves more fully to God.

The Liturgy of the Hours beautifully captures the scriptural expression of a purgative mindset by compressing the end of chapter 6 and the start of chapter 7 of 2nd Corinthians:

> *You are the temple of the living God, just as God has said:*
> *"I will dwell with them and walk among them. I will be their God and they shall be my people."*
> *Since we have these promises, beloved, let us purify ourselves from every defilement of flesh and spirit, and in the fear of God strive to fulfill our consecration perfectly.* (2Cor 6:16;7:1)

It is of significance that this scripture passage is taken from the celebration of the *Solemnity of All Saints* - because this is the mindset of a Saint – to purify ourselves so that we are a fitting dwelling place for the Lord.

When we begin to turn our lives over to God in earnest, our *fear of the Lord* reveals many bad habits and attachments that need be purged. This is accomplished through the sacrament of reconciliation, prayer, penance, mortification, warfare against capital sins and warfare against temptation. We will get deeper into these in the Week 4 topic of spiritual combat. Passage along the purgative way results in:

1. Purity of Heart – We come to avoid all mortal sin and abhor deliberate venial sin.

2. Mortified Passions – We gain the self-control over our disordered passions. This enables us to practice the positive side of virtue and thus gradually come nearer to the Divine Model.

3. Profound Convictions on all the great truths – our souls come to deeply comprehend and believe God's truth, particularly through discursive meditation.

There is a comic strip view of the purgative way as a way of sadness and self-loathing (you might envision Monte Python characters strolling around whipping themselves with thorn branches). It is, in fact, wonderful and liberating to enter along the mystical path and unite ourselves with God. As always, those aren't empty words - you will be amazed at the freedom that comes as you turn away from sinful patterns that bind all of us.

Much of the purgative way is consolation and refreshment. When a soul turns to God and enters into mental prayer God often fills the soul with many "sensible" consolations – that is, consolations that are perceived by the senses – feelings of peace and rich inspirations, images and insights during the course of meditation. This is what our senses and emotions were made for! There is an increasing awareness of the goodness of God all around us, and we sense God's providence constantly at work. Consolation and lifting of our spirit work hand-in-hand with our recognition for the need to purge ourselves of worldly attachments so that they don't impede our awareness and response to higher things. This is *detachment* and we'll also return to this in Week 4.

Purgative practices are very much in the spirit of Lent. It is curiously self-serving. In Lenten fasting we give up something good (like meat) for something better – God. This helps us heal from disordered attachments to those goods. St. Paul puts his finger on it, as usual, when noting how athletes deny themselves all manner of things. This is a productive self-denial so that we bring out greater aspects of ourselves. It's not a pointless annihilation of self – it is to bring forth our true self.

Athletes deny themselves transient and insignificant pleasures for something much greater – so that they can compete well, so that in the epic moments of life they can have the joy of doing great things and the satisfaction that comes from living up to their potential. In the thrill of competition, they bring forth the best of themselves. As St.

Day 7 (Week 1, Day 6)

Paul says, if they do that for a crown of leaves, how much more should we do so for everlasting life?

We can all get a taste of that in this life. When we give things up in a purgative way, it's not about pain and suffering and drudgery. Yes, it can be hard at times – self-denial and discipline can sting because of our fallen nature – but we realize quickly that the fruits of self-control are well worth it. And we start to recognize that we have reserves of virtue that were not there before. Things that used to be hard come naturally and are even welcomed. People see a difference in us. So, we "give things up," but we do so for God. And because God is not outdone in generosity, God reflects it back to us 10 or 30 or 100-fold. That's the spirit of the purgative way. We enter into a loving relationship and clear out everything that hampers that relationship.

Better yet – the purgative way leads us to a place where our sacrifices become meritorious and redemptive. We "offer them up" with Christ's sacrifice on the cross, and those sacrifices become a source of grace for the world.

This is how purgation leads to sanctification. We are told by St. James:

Blessed is he who perseveres in temptation, for when he has been proven he will receive the crown of life that He promised to those who love Him. (Jas 1:12)

And a few verses later St. James warns what happens when we are not able to rise above our fallen nature:

Rather, each person is tempted when lured and enticed by his desire. Then desire conceives and brings forth sin, and when sin reaches maturity it gives birth to death. (Jas 1:14-15)

So, let us persevere along the purgative way!

The primary prayer of the purgative way is discursive meditation.

Meditation simply means meditative prayer in which we bring all our faculties - memory, imagination, intellect – to bear, so that we come to deep understanding and conviction of the great mysteries of the faith. It is discursive meditation because we flow from topic to topic, not in a disorderly way, but unhindered. We are led by the Spirit. One day we might be led to meditate on Jesus' feeding of the multitude. Another day we might be drawn to Jesus' first public ministry at the wedding feast at Cana. What was the role of Mary? Why did Jesus use the words He used? What was the significance of changing water into wine? What was the impact on his followers? Discursive meditation is prayer of the intellect – through our meditation we come to better know and understand God.

Meditation is also a time of silence. Silence is what sets mental prayer apart from all other prayer. It is not an empty silence. It is a sacred silence. It is a silence of listening. It is a silence of letting God be God. It is a silence of allowing God to do His work in our soul.

ILLUMINATIVE WAY

The illuminative way is so named because the great aim of the soul is now the imitation, the following of Christ, by the positive exercises of the Christian virtues; Jesus is the Light of the World, and whosoever follows Him walks not in darkness. "He that follows me walks not in darkness but shall have the light of life." (Jn 8:12)

A soul that has purified itself and mortified the passions through the purgative way, progresses along the Illuminative Way by:

1. Affective Meditation and Contemplation – Affective meditation is a simplification of meditation that prepares a soul for contemplation. Affective meditation differs from discursive meditation in that there is less effort on our part. More of the "work" is done by the Holy Spirit. As we come to know God by meditating on His truths (discursive prayer) we grow in love for him. Our hearts are drawn more to

simply communicating our affection (love) to God. Thus, we transition from a primarily intellectual prayer (discursive prayer) to a prayer of the will (affective prayer). Just as the will is the higher of the two spiritual powers, so affective meditation is a higher form of prayer. But it can't be forced. We must be docile to the Holy Spirit, Who leads us from one form of prayer to the next when we are ready.

Affective prayer then gives way to infused contemplation. In the context of mental prayer, infused contemplation is often called just contemplation (it is understood that it is mystical prayer as opposed to ordinary contemplation, like contemplating a lovely sunset). In affective prayer our activity is simplified, but there is still an emphasis on our activity. Contemplation is wholly a work of God. We cannot initiate contemplation. All we can do is put ourselves in the presence of God. And even that is not necessary, per se. God will bestow contemplation when and where He will. St. Teresa of Avila would be drawn into contemplation and mystical visions at very unexpected moments.

2. Growth in Virtue – a sustained effort to practice the moral and then theological virtues and avoid even the most venial sins.

3. Warfare Against the New Offenses of the Enemy – while we labor in the acquisition of the virtues, our spiritual foes are not idle. They return stealthily to take the offensive, either by causing in us a re-awakening, in a more subtle form, of the seven capital sins (such as *spiritual* pride – "look at how holy I am!"), or by leading us to complacency ("the fires of purgation have passed, I no longer need to practice such intense self-denial...").

Unitive Way

Once we have purified our soul and adorned it by the practice of the virtues, we are ripe for habitual and intimate union with God, that is, for entrance into the unitive way. Persons belonging to the unitive way exhibit the following:

1. Great Purity of Heart – not merely the expiation and reparation of past faults, but detachment from whatever may lead to sin, horror for all deliberate venial sins and even for any willful resistance to grace. Purification is completed in the unitive way by passive trials.

2. Great Mastery Over Self – acquired by the mortification of the passions and the practice of the moral and theological virtues. The original order of the human nature is to some extent restored, and the soul is now in full control and can give itself entirely to God.

3. Constant Need of Thinking of God – real suffering is experienced at not being able to be constantly occupied with the thought of God, and strenuous efforts are made to keep His presence in mind when duties demand attention to earthly cares.

The unitive way is marked by total self-mastery – we are no longer driven by disordered emotions and unhealthy attachments; and by this we become truly our self. There will still be temptations from our fallen flesh, but we are completely immune to them. St. Paul is speaking of the unitive way with his stunning testimony: "I have been crucified with Christ; yet I live, no longer I, but Christ lives in me; insofar as I now live in the flesh, I live by faith in the Son of God who has loved me and given himself up for me." (Gal 2:19-20)

Those on the unitive way transition to times of contemplative prayer. This includes a progression from the simple unitive way to infused contemplation. In brief, the Simple Unitive Way is marked by the cultivation of the gifts of the Holy Spirit and simple contemplation (also called the prayer of simplicity or acquired contemplation). This type of contemplation is a further simplifying and deepening of affective meditation; our efforts are minimal and ever reduced to simply placing ourselves in the presence of God.

Infused Contemplation is purely supernatural; it cannot be acquired by any effort on our part. Much more will be said about meditation and contemplation in weeks 2 and 3.

The Three Ages in Practice

As we noted at the outset, there are many parallels of the Three Ways in everyday life. Take skilled trades. To this day most tradesmen start as apprentice/beginner, progress to journeyman/adept/proficient, and finally become master/expert. It is the same in the arts. We start as a beginner, then become an intermediate, and some progress to being true masters of the art.

But there is an important difference between how God works and how the world works. In the world there is increasing reward with each stage, be it money, power, prestige or social standing. In our spiritual life God loves us right where we are, and he loves us perfectly. With God, our compensation, if you will, is the same no matter what we do – we can't make Him love us any more, nor can we make Him love us any less. Simply look at the parable of the prodigal son, or the parable of the generous landowner and the workers in the vineyard.

That's how God approaches things. Now let's look at ourselves.

Our motives are not as pure as God's. Much of our desire to advance is based on pride (we want it for our own glory) instead of love (we wish to advance for God's glory). Here again, is the fruit of the purgative way. We shed our selfish motivations. In fact, we'll never progress from the purgative path until we shed that selfy-ness. If we are trying to achieve contemplation and mystical union as a prize to be won, we will never get there, because it is driven by self. We must be led to it by opening ourselves to God. God is guiding us on our path. If we give ourselves over to His will, He will place us exactly where we are supposed to be at that point in time, be it purgative, illuminative or unitive. Recall our jungle mission – God is guiding us and showing us the path which He desires for us.

This is one of many reasons why God gives a peace that the world cannot give. The world only compensates you to the extent that you *perform*. God loves everybody perfectly, regardless of our performance. He loves you perfectly right where you are. A stunning thing happens when we put God first - even our worldly endeavors become redeemed. Suddenly playing music, creating art, doing our professional jobs, raising our families, is not about worldly accolade or compensation. Our prideful interior drive, the one that is never satisfied, starts to simply bleed away because we're now doing things out of love of God and neighbor.

That's all there is to it.

It is no longer about competing or being the best for a bigger salary or higher position or to gain the esteem of others – how all that plays out is neither here nor there, it's not on the radar. We do what we do because it is the state in life that the Lord has called us to and we are doing it to serve Him and our neighbor. If we rise in the eyes of the world and have increased success – fine. If we don't – fine. Because it was only ever about serving God's call. This is where the peace comes from. Once we are serving Him, we are "rewarded" by Him, in this life and the next. God's reward is Himself, experiencing the fruits of the Holy Spirit, beatitude in this life and the consolation of spending eternity with Him in the next.

When this sinks into our heart everything else takes on a different character. It is like looking at a dark ominous jungle, but then suddenly sunlight breaks through, illuminates the jungle and it's transformed to something beautiful. There is a scene just like this from Tolkien's *Return of the King* in which Frodo and Sam are entering the dark, dank and depressing lands of Mordor. But suddenly the sun breaks through, just for a moment, and there is brightness and hope. Their circumstances haven't changed, but the sun transforms them. That is how our life is transformed through relationship with God and passage along the Three Ways.

One final thought on the framework of the three ages. To be certain, this mystical framework is extremely helpful and beneficial – because it is the way most of us progress. But we don't want to be overly rigid in our application of this tradition. God is bigger, and our relationship with Him is richer, than any single framework. The framework is only in the service of the relationship and is never the main thing or the goal. It neither defines nor takes precedence over the relationship. We should not jump to the conclusion that "I'm not matching up with the framework, so something is wrong."

Our spiritual journeys follow a jagged path, though by the grace of God we hope to be always moving steadily closer to that far-off mountain - to God and to Heaven. There is no specific "Eureka!" moment when we know we have moved from one age to the next and we will often shift between ages for a time. Most importantly, it is good to be aware of these three ages for an overall understanding of how spiritual maturity unfolds. Intense self-assessment is, itself, pointless and counterproductive. We'll return to the topic of spiritual growth in the fourth week when we discuss spiritual direction.

For all of us the focus is to do our best to draw ever closer to God and neighbor and trust that God will take it from there.

Please spend 5 minutes in silent prayer; talking with God about today's session.

Let's close in prayer:

Lord Jesus Christ, help me to be ever more aware of Your nearness and Your great love for me. Amen.

DAY 7 POSTSCRIPT: THE THREE AGES, TERESIAN MANSIONS AND NIGHTS OF THE SENSES AND SPIRIT

The Carmelite order provides the most comprehensive teaching on the ages of the interior life. First among the Carmelite mystics are St. Teresa of Avila with her analogy of the seven mansions of the soul (*Interior Castle*) and St. John of the Cross with his teachings on the dark night (*The Dark Night of the Soul*). The standard relationship of these to the *three ages* is tabulated below. Fr. Thomas Dubay's *Fire Within* provides an excellent summary of Carmelite mystical spirituality.

Age	Mansion	Type of Mental Prayer
Purgative	1st	Meditation Transitioning from discursive to affective
Purgative	2nd	Meditation Transitioning from discursive to affective
Purgative	3rd	Meditation Transitioning from discursive to affective
Dark Night of the Senses		
Illuminative	4th	Infused Contemplation Transitioning to conforming union
Illuminative	5th	Infused Contemplation Transitioning to conforming union
Illuminative	6th	Infused Contemplation Transitioning to conforming union
Dark Night of the Spirit		
Unitive	7th	Transforming union

Day 7 (Week 1, Day 6)

Pearls from Day 7: The Three Ages of the Interior Life

In many aspects of life, we can identify three stages of progress. For example, in human development: childhood, adolescence, adulthood. In skilled trades: novice, journeyman, master/expert. In the arts: beginner, intermediate, master.

In the spiritual life, if we enter the mystical way, we move through three ages: purgative, illuminative and unitive. These three ways are founded in scripture and expounded by tradition (the following is based on A. Tanquerey, *The Spiritual Life*).

The Purgative Way is the way of beginners (although a person has advanced far in relationship with God to simply desire to enter the purgative way). It is marked by:

1. Purity of heart – We come to avoid all mortal sin and abhor deliberate venial sin.
2. Mortified passions – We gain the self-control over our disordered passions. This enables us to practice the positive side of virtue and thus gradually come nearer to the Divine Model.
3. Profound convictions on all the great truths – Our souls come to deeply comprehend and believe God's truth, particularly through discursive meditation.
4. The prayer of the purgative way is meditation – In *discursive* meditation we move from topic to topic (discursive) and apply all our mental faculties to come to know and believe God's truth. Over time our meditation simplifies and becomes simple expressions of love and affection, thus this is known as *affective* meditation (or affective prayer).

The Illuminative Way is thus named because the great aim of the soul is now the imitation of Christ (we walk by His light). It is marked by:

1. Contemplation – prayer simplifies further from affective meditation to infused contemplation. Contemplation is wholly a work of God, we can do nothing to produce it, we only receive.
2. Growth in virtue – a sustained effort to practice the moral and then theological virtues.
3. Warfare against the new offenses of the enemy – while we labor in the acquisition of the virtues, our spiritual foes are not idle and we must increase our vigilance.

The Unitive Way is a life of habitual and intimate union with God. It is marked by:

1. Great purity of heart – not merely the expiation and reparation of past faults, but detachment from whatever may lead to sin, horror for all deliberate venial sins and even for any willful resistance to grace. Purification is completed in the Unitive Way by passive trials.
2. Great mastery over self – acquired by the mortification of the passions and the practice of the moral and theological virtues. The original order of things is to some extent restored, and the soul now in full control, and can give itself entirely to God.
3. Constant need of thinking of God – real suffering is experienced at not being able to be constantly occupied with the thought of God, and strenuous efforts are made to keep His presence in mind when duties demand attention to earthly cares.
4. Mystical union - the most advanced form of contemplation. The soul is fully transformed and in a state of deep communion with God.

Day 7 (Week 1, Day 6)

─────────── **Your Pearls from Day 7** ───────────

DAY 8: WEEK 1 – PUTTING IT ALL TOGETHER – WHAT IS YOUR *WHY*?

> This brings us to the end of Week 1. Today we return to our motivation – why are we doing this – and by "this" we mean *everything*.

Let's begin with opening prayer:

Come Holy Spirit, make of me a fitting dwelling place for the Lord.

Congratulations for completing Week 1 and thank you for your commitment to this retreat. Once again, your time on this retreat is a gift to God (and *from* God). Whatever else transpires, however good or challenging any given session is, you are offering your time, your mind and your heart to God through your dedication to this retreat and that's love. My first spiritual director would ask the rhetorical question - "What do people do when they are falling in love?" And then answer it – "they *waste* time together." So even if some days have felt wasted (hopefully not!), be assured that it is a productive waste of time.

Day 8 (Week 1, Day 7)

Your Jungle Mission

This was a good day. Of course, you learned from the Savior that every day is a gift and that His Father was watching over the nomads and turning all things to good, even what seemed to be a hardship at the time.

But this was a particularly good day because you overcame a challenging situation. You were able to do your part by using the knowledge and skills you'd been steadily accumulating along the Way. And now you were sitting with the Savior and reflecting on the events of the last 24 hours.

Last night the nomads made camp in a glade with a pond fed by a spring. It was a beautiful setting made even better by the gentle sound of the water flowing into the pond. Your sprained ankle was healing but still painful and the combination of the cool water and peaceful setting made for the first decent night's sleep you had in days.

The next morning a fragment of the nomads made known that they planned to stay behind. The Way through the jungle was looking ever more difficult and the place you were now had fresh water and fruit trees and seemed the perfect place to stay and rest. Just for a little while. Or maybe longer.

Between your sore ankle and fatigue from many sleepless nights, their plan was tempting. Very tempting. You wouldn't stay behind too long. Just a day or two to rest up in this lovely setting.

Unable to convince the small fragment otherwise, the rest of the nomads set out on the next day's journey.

Soon after they left, you took to thinking about some of the disciplines that the Savior had taught you. To constantly renew your mind and make your "yes mean yes". You thought back to what life was like before you were found by the Savior. You also reflected on the fact that the Way through the jungle wasn't really all that hard. Yes, you suffered some bumps and bruises, but the Savior quickly healed them, and they were more than made up for by the joy of progressing through the jungle in the company of the Savior and your fellow nomads. And then there was that far off mountain. It sounded so beautiful how the Savior described it. And you would finally meet His Father in person.

You shared all of this with the fragment, and helped them to remember their own stories and reasons for traveling to the mountain top. You helped them break free of the spell of the glade. And so you pulled your things together and set out after the nomads.

It was little surprise that you soon came upon Him – waiting and watching for you.

And now you were sitting with Him in the evening twilight and He's explaining how pleased He is that you decided for yourself to follow Him, and brought the others with you.

Your Why?

Today we are going to end with a question - why are you making this retreat? And why, particularly, do you want to grow in mental prayer? Yes, we received an answer to the *Why* of mental prayer in Day 2 – because it is the example and teaching of Jesus and it is how we grow in relationship with God. This is the true answer to "why is mental prayer indispensable?". But it is a general answer. Today we want to dig more deeply into *your personal why*.

Day 8 (Week 1, Day 7)

And while we are digging more deeply, what, in your heart, do you desire from this retreat?

We will work our way to these questions with some related questions and motivations...

WHY DOES IT SEEM HARD AND COMPLICATED?

Why is this journey portrayed as difficult and dangerous? Why is our spiritual journey equated with a jungle? Didn't Jesus make salvation easier than that?

It's true that in theory we could just get baptized, strictly live out the Ten Commandments, receive the sacraments and slide into Heaven.

But Jesus wants more for us. He invites us into the fullness of life, not life for non-concentrators. He wants us to rise above our fallen nature and live out beatitude, as envisioned for us in the Sermon on the Mount.

But why does it have to be hard? Don't we just have to accept Jesus as our savior, keep on the straight and narrow, and we're good to go? Yes. And no.

Jesus does say salvation is simple. He says His burden is easy and His yoke is light. Jesus' way is simple.

But He also says whoever would be His disciple must deny themselves and take up their cross. That instruction is also simple. But it isn't easy. It's actually very hard. At first.

It's hard because the fall substituted our love for God and our desire for greatness with a lusting for comfort and ease. And the world and satan continuously assault us with temptations that play to that lusting. Venerable Fulton Sheen, writing in the 1960's and 1970's, commented even then how hard it was to be a Christian. He noted that it used to be easy (i.e. in the 1930's and 40's), because all of society was Christian. But it had become hard because all of society was now pushing against Christianity. And that was Bishop Sheen speaking 50 years ago; we know which direction society has slid since.

Jesus doesn't want mediocrity for us. He calls us to live life to the fullest. That is the message of the Sermon on the Mount. We shouldn't be living the minimal life of the 10 C's (don't murder your neighbor), we should live beatitude (don't even speak ill of your neighbor, instead, love him as yourself).

So, our way to Heaven is simple - model ourselves after Jesus. Doing it can be extremely hard. It requires *grace*. And for grace to work, we must cooperate with it. As you know, God doesn't magically change us. If we pray for patience God doesn't simply whack us with a "patience stick." Instead, He sends us opportunities to grow in patience – if we accept those opportunities we are cooperating with God's grace, that grace becomes glory, and we will grow in patience.

And so it is with the mystic path and mental prayer. It is a coin with two sides, one side is simple and rewarding, the other side is not easy.

"Point yourself to the mountain top and start walking in that direction." Simple.

"Watch out for that python! Hey, is that quicksand?" Not easy.

You've decided to take up this challenge – and that is a very good thing indeed. Let's take some time to consider your motivations for this adventure, because motivation is a powerful God-given facility that we need to tap into.

MOTIVATION #1: THINK OF HEAVEN

Heaven is a fine motivator. We are doing this so that we will all be in Heaven someday. When it comes to Heaven, what we know best is that we know truly little. "Eye has not seen." Few theologians take a stab at Heaven, and when they do it is much more a poke than a stab, because Heaven is too wonderful. The moment we try to put it into human words and images we so diminish it that we can take no more of it. Here is C.S. Lewis on the matter (from *Collected Letters*):

> "No, I don't wish I knew Heaven was like the picture in my Great Divorce, because, if we knew that, we should know it was no better. The good things even of this world are far too good ever to be reached by imagination. Even the common orange, you know, no one could have imagined it before he tasted it. How much less Heaven."

Be that as it may, Venerable Fulton Sheen gives a glimpse of Heaven by contrasting it with our Earthly constraints of time and space. How many times have you experienced something wonderful and thought, "I wish so-and-so were here to share this?" Heaven is eternal. It exists outside of time and space. In Heaven all things simply *are*. In Heaven there will be no more wanting for that missing person; we will be able to celebrate Christmas and Easter at the same time with all our loved ones. Or something like that. Or nothing like that. Again, eye has not seen.

But here is another Heavenly motivator – our degree of blessedness in Heaven depends on what we do here on earth.

From theologian Frank Sheed (*Map of Life*):

> "Not all souls will be equal in heaven. The soul grows naturally by development of the intellect and will. Supernaturally – which is what matters here – it grows by the possession of the Supernatural Life. But this it must receive upon earth, for after death it cannot merit. Therefore, souls united with God have not all reach the same degree of development when they come to die. But, greater or smaller, all souls are functioning in heaven with intellect and will at their highest intensity upon

their highest object: therefore, every soul will know perfect happiness."

St. Therese of Lisieux (actually, her sister speaking to her) explains this with a thimble analogy. If we fill both a large tumbler and a small thimble with water, they are both completely full. Just so, whether our soul is the size of a tumbler or a thimble when we get to Heaven, our soul will be filled completely with God. But the tumbler-sized soul will be able to receive more of God – more of God's truth, beauty and goodness. Fortunately for us, all sin – particularly envy, in this case – is vanquished in Heaven. So even if we have but a thimble, we won't be jealous of the tumblers; we'll all be rejoicing in the glory of God and that our cup is full. But, why not aspire to a tumbler? Mental prayer and growth of our interior life, by which we sanctify our active life, is the path to a tumbler-sized soul.

Still, Heaven can seem far off – far off in time, far off in space, far off emotionally and at times far off spiritually. Let's look even closer to home...

Motivation #2: Our Pearls - Why We Believe in God in This Life

Our life of mental prayer isn't only for entry into Heaven, it is for happiness in this life. It is extremely helpful, therefore, to have spiritual pearls that remind us of why we are doing this in the here and now. Why do we believe in God at all? And why do we believe that God loves each of us, individually?

I am going to share some of my pearls (in no particular order). I go back to these routinely to renew in my soul the reality of God. Your pearls, of course, are probably much different. And if you have not had the opportunity to search for the pearls that you will carry in your pocket, then that is the purpose of today.

Steve's Pearl #1 - The Martyrdom of the Apostles. This is the classic argument for Jesus' divinity and for Pentecost. What else would drive

12 men to pour out every ounce of their life for a single cause – to spread the Gospel. All of them suffered and 11 of them gave their lives in brutal martyrdom. Here's Chuck Colson on this point –

> "I know the resurrection is a fact, and Watergate proved it to me. How? Because 12 men testified, they had seen Jesus raised from the dead, then they proclaimed that truth for 40 years, never once denying it. Each one of them were beaten, tortured, stoned and put in prison. They would not have endured that if it weren't true. Watergate embroiled 12 of the most powerful men in the world-and they couldn't keep a lie for three weeks. You're telling me 12 apostles could keep a lie for 40 years? Absolutely impossible."

Steve's Pearl #2 - Historical Coincidences. We noted the significance of mountains at the outset of this retreat. Abraham is called to sacrifice Isaac on Mount Moriah and it's generally understood that would be the same location where Christ was crucified approximately 2,000 years later. Think of all the history and chance happenings during that intervening period, and yet those two events, the one that prefigured the other, are tethered together in time and space. Salvation History is chock full of this.

Steve's Pearl #3 - Jesus' Brilliance. He always has the perfect response. Many fine authors create many fine characters who can outwit their opponents. But none can hold a candle to Christ. If Christ had not lived and the Gospels not been written down, no author would have ever invented anything remotely close.

Steve's Pearl #4 - Science. Time and again, science confirms the greatness of creation and the supernatural realm. No sooner do scientists think they are about to get to the "big answer" then they find there's a deeper underlying mystery. This happened with the creation of the universe. This happened with the discovery of dark matter. This is happening with the study of human consciousness.

Steve's Pearl #5 - My Beautiful Wife (and thus my beautiful daughters). My wife and I come from the same small town (population less than 4,000 souls when we lived there). But we didn't meet there. We had to move to a large city 1,000 miles away and move into the same high rise at the same time so that we were there just in time to stop by the building Christmas party. Where we met. Top that.

Steve's Pearl #6 - Personal Revelation. Here is a picture where our Heavenly Father made himself more real to me than I am to myself. Below that is a picture where I had a similar experience of Jesus and the Holy Spirit (pictures only in the Video version of the retreat).

Steve's Pearl #7 – The People in My Life. God has placed so many wonderful people in my life – all of them tied in one way or another to His plan for my salvation. Sometimes I get very direct glimpses of how God is working through the people in my life, which reminds me that God is working through them *all* the time.

Steve's Pearl #8 and Counting - Many Other Personal Miracles. Too many to list here, but many small miracles – divine appointments, events so statistically unlikely that they had to have been divinely orchestrated.

I return to these pearls of personal revelation and experiences of God's goodness time and again. When I am feeling dry and need to stir up my spirit and conviction, these are my aids. First and foremost, I call to Jesus, as well as our Blessed Mother and my Guardian Angel. And then I turn to these pearls.

What are your pearls?

Motivation #3: Growth in Happiness

There is nothing wrong with having your own happiness as a motivation for mental prayer and growing in relationship with God. But we must allow God to purge (there's that word again) our misguided ideas of happiness and embrace His much better plan for our happiness.

It is perfectly normal, healthy and *human* to desire:

- good health and security
- fulfillment in relationships
- to make the most of our abilities
- to overcome a great weakness
- to have an authentic experience of God and all that is sacred and holy

These and many more personal desires are exceptionally good motivations to devote yourself to mental prayer.

MOTIVATION #4: PURE LOVE OF GOD

Ultimately our highest motivation is to do everything for love of God. Everything else is an imperfect motivation, because it's based on seeking our own satisfaction – "I'll be so happy in Heaven." But, that is OK – we're still desiring the right things, even if for imperfect motives. Over time our love will be purified and what we will desire most is God for His sake, and in that all our other desires will be satisfied.

You've already had a taste of this type of love.

Think of a point in time in your life when you were with someone in a great trial – a child, a parent, or perhaps a complete stranger – but someone in true agony or distress. In that moment, your heart went out to them and you acted. You did all you could for them in that moment, even if simply to comfort them. In that moment there was no thought of self – "oh, I hope people are watching, seeing how kind and helpful I am!" – there was none of that. In that brief moment, all your will, all your energy was focused on that one person. That is what we are growing into with God. You may well be on your way to that point. In time, maybe not until we are in Heaven, we will all reach a point where we are consumed with the things of God - loving God and neighbor.

That type of love is your destiny.

That type of love is worth journeying through a jungle.

Please spend 5 minutes in silent prayer; talking with God about today's session, perhaps reflecting on your own pearls.

Let's close with prayer:

Lord Jesus Christ, help me to be ever more aware of Your nearness and Your great love for me. Amen.

DAY 8 POSTSCRIPT: A SIDE NOTE ABOUT FLOWERY TALK AND DOUBTS AND YOUR PEARLS

We often speak in absolutes during this retreat, statements like "We do this out of love for God." This is a stylistic necessity. If we qualify every statement, it will be clumsy in the extreme, "We do this out of love for God, even though it may be imperfect love and maybe we don't even *feel* love at all, but we don't trust our emotions, so just trust that your desire to love God is love because love is a decision...." That kind of legalistic qualifying hullaballoo makes your head spin.

Instead, we simply speak in absolutes. Certainly, you have doubts. Everyone does in their own way. "...Lord I believe, help me in my unbelief!" (Mk 9:24)

Maybe you are carrying a cross of *great* doubt, or great dryness. Maybe no "pearls" come to mind for you, or those that do are not overly convincing. Then please hear this – something moved you to go on this retreat. Even if it was pure curiosity – *something, or someone, moved your curiosity* to attend a retreat focused on God. Receive this as God's message that He loves you so very deeply and desires you to enter a lifelong relationship with Him. Receive this moment, right here and now, as one of your pearls.

Day 8 (Week 1, Day 7)

Pearls from Day 8: Week 1 – Putting It All Together

WHY DOES IT SEEM HARD AND COMPLICATED?

Jesus' plan for salvation is simple. Follow Him. But doing it is not easy. It can at times be very difficult to be a Christian and grow in holiness. We can only do so with God's grace – and with God's grace all things are possible! But we must cooperate with that grace for it to transform to glory and be active in our life.

It's important to take time to consider your motivations for this journey, because motivation is a powerful God-given facility that we need to tap into.

MOTIVATION #1: THINK OF HEAVEN

When it comes to Heaven, what we know best is that we know truly little. "Eye has not seen." Few theologians take a stab at Heaven, and when they do it is much more a poke than a stab. Because Heaven is too wonderful. The moment we try to put it into human words and images we so diminish it that we can take no more of it. Nonetheless, Heaven is an extremely worthy subject of our meditation.

Another aspect of Heaven that should motivate us is that our degree of blessedness in Heaven depends on what we do here on earth. St. Terese of Lisieux employs the comparison of two souls – one is a thimble the other a large tumbler. In Heaven both will be filled, but the tumbler will be able to receive more of God's truth, goodness and beauty. We should aspire to the tumbler. Our interior life is how we increase the capacity of our soul to love God and neighbor.

MOTIVATION #2: YOUR PEARLS - WHY YOU BELIEVE

What are your *pearls*? What are the great truths and experiences of God's goodness that you come back to, to stir up your faith? If you don't have any, now is the perfect time to reflect on them.

MOTIVATION #3: GROWTH IN HAPPINESS

There is nothing wrong with having your own happiness as a motivation for mental prayer and growing in relationship with God. But we must allow God to purge our misguided ideas of happiness and embrace His much better plan for our happiness.

MOTIVATION #4: PURE LOVE OF GOD

Ultimately our highest motivation is to do everything for love of God. Everything else is an imperfect motivation, because it is based on seeking our own satisfaction – "I'll be so happy in Heaven." But that's OK – we are still desiring the right things, even if is for imperfect motives. Over time our love will be purified and what we will desire most is God for His sake, and in that all other desires will be satisfied.

Day 8 (Week 1, Day 7)

——— Your Pearls from Day 8 ———

WEEK 2
MEDITATION DISPOSITIONS AND PRINCIPLES

(each session followed by 7 minutes of silent prayer)

Day 8 (Week 1, Day 7)

DAY 9: DISPOSITIONS AND PRINCIPLES VS TECHNIQUE AND METHOD

> Welcome to Week 2 of our retreat! Next week we descend into the jungle. This week we complete our preparation. When we think of preparation we think of methods and procedures – it's human nature. But God's ways are not our ways. Our preparation and entry into a life of mental prayer unfolds a bit differently....

Let's begin with opening prayer.

Come Holy Spirit, make of me a fitting dwelling place for the Lord.

Your Jungle Mission

You were often intrigued by "life hacks". You were impressed by people that seemed to have a trick or gadget or some shortcut to get around life's many challenges. Of course, part of you was always skeptical that "if something seemed too good to be true..." And, you thought, never was it known to be said, "anything worth doing is worth doing with a shortcut and a life hack."

But still there was so much to learn about trekking through the jungle. It seemed there should be an easier way to learn

Day 9 (Week 2, Day 1)

the ins and outs. You asked some of the experienced nomads why they didn't have lots of fancy gear. "Don't need it." You asked if there was a guidebook. "Weren't you given a Bible and Catechism?" Yes, but they are so long. You asked if anyone gave thought to ways to make the journey a little easier. "That's why we follow Him. What could be easier than that?"

Then it dawned on you that the nomads that had the easiest time were the ones that stayed closest to Him and spent the most time with Him.

You were catching on that success in the jungle wasn't so much about *how* as *who*.

METHODS AND TECHNIQUES

As we noted in the introduction, in human endeavors we usually seek techniques, methods, guides and best practices. A *method* is thought of as a system or recipe. And *technique* is a matter of style and skills.

These are not our starting point for mental prayer, and they will have truly little to do with mental prayer. The reason for this goes back to our definition of mental prayer. Mental prayer is about a loving relationship and conversation. When we have a conversation with someone we love, we are not thinking about the mechanics of the conversation:

- Should I be formal? "Well, hello and greetings upon thee on this fine day."
- No, no, no – that's too stiff. Should I be laid back? "Hey ... cool ... right on ...."
- That's too laid back. And creepy. Should I be bright and cheery? "Super awesome to see you!!!!!"

That was a cartoonish example, but you get the idea. There is a place in human relations for carefully guarding our speech, for example, in legal proceedings, in formal work meetings and so on. But those aren't loving conversations.

Call to mind your first formal interview. Whatever it may have been - for a job, to get into college, an internship. I remember my first high school job interview. It was with Richard, the assistant manager of a *Friendly's* restaurant. Looking back on it Richard was barely more than a kid himself, but to my mind I was all but meeting with the Governor. I was nervous, stiff and had no idea how I was supposed to act, so I went with formality and military rigidity. Of course, to him I was just a clueless high school kid and so he was completely at ease, while for me it was an awkward exchange. But ... I did get the job. I worked hard at my duties of dishwashing (I have great respect for restaurant workers) and I developed a comfortable working relationship with Richard. I could be myself, and I knew what to expect from him in return.

The formal rigidity of my initial interview was appropriate for the moment, but hardly a genuine conversation between friends. The latter relationship of being at ease with a person is moving in the direction of how we should approach God. Yes, there is the tension that we should be in awe, but at the same time our loving God desires our heart and for us to be completely open to Him.

> *When you pray, do not be like the hypocrites, who love to stand and pray in the synagogues and on street corners so that others may see them. Amen, I say to you, they have received their reward. But when you pray, go to your inner room, close the door, and pray to your Father in secret. And your Father who sees in secret will repay you. In praying, do not babble like the pagans, who think that they will be heard because of their many words. Do not be like them. Your Father knows what you need before you ask him.* (Mt 6:5-8)

Day 9 (Week 2, Day 1)

And so, we reinforce again and again, prayer is about relationship. It has nothing to do with method or technique.

There is a liberating aspect of the knowledge that prayer is not a technique. Technique is difficult. Technique is mandatory for worldly accomplishments. In my case, I am a pianist, and not a particularly accomplished one at that. Yet I had to practice long and hard for the modest skills that I have. To become a world-class pianist, I would have had to practice day and night, and even then, my technical limitations would have precluded playing Rachmaninoff. Technique is mandatory to become an accomplished pianist – just as it is to be a great baseball player, or a masterful painter, or a masterful computer scientist, or a masterful whatever. Furthermore, certain aspects of technique are born in us – either we have them or we don't. I will never be a starting quarterback no matter how hard I practice.

And since prayer is all about relationship, it almost goes without saying it is *not* about method. To attempt to distill relationships into a method is to attempt to coerce someone to respond to you on your terms.

GETTING TO KNOW GOD

The purpose of mental prayer is simply getting to know God, so that we fall deeper in love with Him.

Saint Ignatius of Loyola, in his *Spiritual Exercises,* insists we beg for this grace: "Intimate knowledge of Jesus, that we love Him more ardently and follow Him more closely." In other words, we are begging for *relationship*.

And St. Teresa of Avila, in the *Interior Castle*, tells us that even simple vocal prayer is about relationship: "Since vocal prayer is prayer it must be accompanied by reflection. A prayer in which a person is not aware of whom he is speaking to, what he is asking, who it is who is asking and of whom, I do not call prayer however much the lips move."

We are often our own greatest impediment to meditation. Many bible verses speak to us about praying from the heart. That may sound easy at first. I think, "Of course I'm going to pour out to God what's on my heart, I have no problem being honest with God." But there are different layers of honesty and self-knowledge. Scripture in fact tells us "... we do not know how to pray as we ought." (Rom 8:26) Things are not always as they seem at the surface level.

Here we recall the distinction between our lower nature with its sensitive powers of emotions and feelings. These don't often reflect *reality*. Reality, meaning, how things *really are*. Reality is different from how we think and feel that things are. We routinely think something is different than what it really is. Look at any legal dispute – both sides think and feel they are right. For the Catholic mind, reality is synonymous with Truth, and God is Truth. Thus, beneath the surface of our prayer there is the *reality* (or truth) at the deepest levels of our being, our soul.

Many times, our thoughts and feelings are distorted by layers of disorder and worldliness, or simple superficiality. We pray, "God, I desire such-and-such for this person in my life" and "God, I need this to happen" and so on. Below the surface of those petitions are deeper desires for meaningful relationships, purpose in life, and to give and receive love. And, of course, below those deeper layers, is the very heart of it – our soul yearning for God. Therefore, that same passage from Romans continues "the Spirit itself intercedes with inexpressible groanings."

None of this can be distilled into a method or technique.

This is yet another reason why entering relationship with God in prayer is a wonderful journey – it is not only discovery of God but discovery of self; recognizing who we really are, who God created us to be. In mental prayer, God reveals us to ourselves.

It all starts with endeavoring to be open and honest with God. We all have defense mechanisms, we all have emotional and spiritual wounds, parts of ourselves we want to keep hidden and personas that we put on to meet the expectations that others have of us. But how do we distinguish our deepest and most meaningful friendships? They are the ones where we can "just be ourselves" (or at least as near to that as we can get).

This is closely related to the other characteristic that distinguishes true friendships – you can't force them. You can't *make* someone be a "true friend."

These two related characteristics of true friendship - (1) they are real, we can't force them; and (2) in them we are completely ourselves - are at the heart of why prayer is not about technique or method.

Dispositions and Principles

To be a world class person of prayer requires only that (1) you be you, (2) you make an act of faith to pray with God each day, and (3) you make a genuine effort to grow in virtue (love of God and neighbor and denial of self).

But our entry into mental prayer is facilitated by awareness of certain dispositions and principles.

Dispositions relate to the character of our mind and heart (refer to retreat Day 4 – our role in mental prayer). *Principles* are guiding spiritual concepts of how we interact with the Trinity in prayer (refer to retreat Day 5 – God's role in mental prayer).

This distinction of principles and dispositions is based in large part on the teaching of Fr. Jacques Phillippe (particularly in *Time for God*) and is aligned with the teaching of all the great mystical Saints.

Dispositions

The importance of entering a relationship with proper dispositions is just as true in human relationships. If we are intensely self-absorbed, we are not going to be a particularly good friend. If we are not patient, we are not going to be a particularly good friend. If we are not generous, we are not going to be a particularly good friend.

To get a better feel for our spiritual dispositions let's return to our jungle mission. Certain dispositions are absolutely necessary to successfully navigate our way through an unknown and forbidding jungle. We must *believe* in our goal and the ability to achieve it. If we don't believe that the distant mountain is worth reaching, and that we can reach it, we'll never make it. Every good coach, mentor and trainer knows this. The student's success depends in large part on the desire and ability to envision success. We will also need *persistence*. The way will be difficult; every great undertaking is. And we will need *humility* – "pride cometh before the fall." If we don't make an honest evaluation of ourselves, take our journey seriously, and seek help where we are lacking, we will soon find ourselves in trouble.

These are the dispositions we will develop for our spiritual journey: faith, purity of intention, humility, and fortitude. These dispositions focus on our role in mental prayer and how we open ourself up to God's grace.

Principles

What about principles? Well, as we have noted before, we need a guide. Even though a trail has been blazed for us, that doesn't make it effortless; we still must make the journey. And there are yet many dangers along the way such as distractions, fatigue and even dangerous and poisonous creatures. We need an expert guide.

There is something unique about our guide, our guide is three Guides; the Trinity. Our Guides have gone before us and blazed the trail. Our Guides travel with us and accompany us along the trail that they made, doing the hard work, wielding the machete to clear away overgrowth, and scaring off wild animals. Our Guides are watching over us, from that far-off mountain top. And our Guides don't only travel before and beside us, they also literally travel within us, encouraging us to move forward. Our fundamental principles for our jungle mission are nothing more or less than to cultivate complete trust and reliance in our entirely capable Guides.

This idea of principles is also reflected in our human relationships. The way we relate to a parent is different than the way we relate to an old friend which is different than the way we relate to a spouse. Just so, we will have unique ways of relating to our Guides.

These are our principles: primacy of God's action and Love, Jesus Christ and our incarnational faith, and the indwelling of the Spirit. These principles focus on God's role in mental prayer and how we relate to Him.

Tomorrow we will move to our first disposition, faith and trust in God. As with all aspects of our interior life this is simple, but not easy. We humans have a powerful desire to control our circumstances.

Approach vs Method

A closing comment about dispositions and principles. All that has gone before is completely true and in keeping with the teachings of Christ, and the Saints and spiritual masters on this topic. But there is the practical reality that we all must start somewhere with meditative prayer. This is also based on the teaching and example of Christ. When His disciples asked Him to teach them to pray, He gave them (and us) the gift of the Our Father.

So too, the Saints have developed introductory approaches to meditation. We need to sit with the Lord for 15 minutes and do *something*. Even if that *something* is learning to do *nothing*. In the third week of this retreat we will learn and practice a practical approach to Christian meditation (the entry point for mental prayer).

We call this an "approach" and not a "method." This isn't just fancy wordsmithing. Well, in a way it is, but for a very good reason. We want to stay as far away as possible from the concept that prayer can be boiled down to method and technique. The approach we will practice is just one of many ways you can enter into your relationship with God. It is practical and time-tested. It's a place to start, so that God can lead you from there.

But first come the dispositions and principles.

Today we will extend our silent prayer to 7 minutes. You might use this time with God to return to your pearls from yesterday. These are the precious gifts that God has given only to you, your very personal connections to God. These pearls are His personal expression of His love for you.

Let's close in prayer:

Lord Jesus Christ, help me to become ever more aware of Your nearness and Your great love for me. Amen.

Day 9 (Week 2, Day 1)

Pearls from Day 9: Dispositions and Principles vs Technique and

METHOD

Most human endeavors involve method and technique. A *method* is thought of as a system or recipe. And *technique* is a matter of style and skills. Method and technique are absolutely necessary to become great at human endeavors – playing an instrument, playing a sport, professional accomplishment.

Prayer, however, is about loving relationship and conversation. We know from our human relationships that they are not about technique or method.

The good news is that to be a world class person of prayer requires only that (1) you be you, (2) you make an act of faith to pray with God each day, and (3) you make a genuine effort to grow in virtue (love of God and neighbor and denial of self).

Many bible verses speak to us about praying from the heart. That may sound easy at first "of course I'm going to pour out to God what's on my heart. I have no problem being honest with God." But there are different layers of honesty and self-knowledge. Therefore, scripture tells us "...for we do not know how to pray as we ought." (Rom 8:26)

This is also why there are certain dispositions and principles that are very helpful to enter into prayer and into relationship with God.

Dispositions and principles are entirely different from method and technique. By dispositions we mean behaviors and characteristics of our heart and mind (our higher spiritual powers). Thus, dispositions are related to Day 4 of the retreat (our role in mental prayer).

By principles we mean guiding spiritual concepts – particularly who the Trinity is and how we interact with them in prayer. Thus, principles are related to Day 5 of the retreat (God's role in mental prayer).

The four dispositions we will develop for our spiritual journey are: faith, purity of intention, humility, and fortitude.

And the three guiding principles: primacy of God's action and law of Love, Jesus Christ and our incarnational faith, and the indwelling of the Holy Spirit.

Day 9 (Week 2, Day 1)

Your Pearls from Day 9

DAY 10: DISPOSITIONS PART 1 – FAITH AND TRUST AS THE BASIS FOR MENTAL PRAYER

> Today we look at faith and trust as the basis of mental prayer. Yet again, we discover something that is simple (trusting in God) while at the same time, something that is not easy (trusting in God). Why? Because we humans have a tremendous drive to control our circumstances...

Let us begin with prayer.

Come Holy Spirit, make of me a fitting dwelling place for the Lord. Amen.

YOUR JUNGLE MISSION

You are always encouraged by your time with the Savior. When He looks at you and tells you that you can do something, you believe Him. In fact, you don't just believe Him – that is, believe the words He's saying - you believe *in* Him. It seems there is something special about Him that makes the words He says true.

As you go about your day, if you hold to His words and example and trust in them, things go smoothly. And should a challenge arise you are at peace and confident that you'll get through it successfully.

At least, that's how it is most of the time.

But there are those times when you falter. This often happens when you're far away from Him. And a challenge arises. You immediately spring into action without giving thought to the teaching you received from the Savior. And even if His teaching does occur to you, it is accompanied by doubt that it will really help in your present circumstances. What's more, you forget to call on His Spirit (a habit you've been slowly developing). Once that seed of doubt gets ahold of you it quickly grows into self-doubt and then outright fear.

Fortunately, He has a knack for showing up before things become a complete disaster. Little more than a reassuring look from Him is all it takes to restore your confidence. Then you are back on your feet and realize with Him by your side you are fully capable of overcoming what a moment ago seemed insurmountable.

From Yesterday

Yesterday we discussed certain dispositions that are necessary to successfully make our journey to the distant mountain. By dispositions we mean frames of mind, behaviors, habits and, most importantly, virtues. Dispositions relate to our role in mental prayer, and our primary role in mental prayer is to receive God's grace.

But receiving God's grace is meant to be active, not passive. We must cooperate with God's grace so that it *transforms to glory*. If we don't cooperate with grace it just sits there – dormant, sterile, fruitless.

Let's see how we receive and grow in faith.

The Disposition of Faith

Belief is a powerful force.

If we do not believe in what we're doing, and our ability to do it, we are doomed from the start. Venerable Fulton Sheen tells the story of men who were hypnotized and told that their strength had become greater than before. They proceeded to lift weights 40% heavier than they had ever lifted. Then they were told they were not as strong, and the weight they lifted was 40% less. Medical science demonstrates this with the familiar positive effects of placebo pills (and the negative "nocebo" effect). And of course, athletes are well familiar with this concept. If you envision yourself succeeding, such as making a winning shot, you are much more likely to do so. What we believe, effects how we perceive ourselves, the world, and thus, how we act. Recognize, though, that these "beliefs" are not tricks. The athlete must still be an athlete; his belief, or vision of success, simply helps him perform at a higher level.

This brings us to faith, and its necessity for us to advance in the spiritual realm. Faith is a gift from God. We can't create faith in our soul. It is an *infused* virtue (more on that term later). Faith is the virtue by which we believe the revealed truth of God. As with our example about belief, faith is not some type of trickery; it is a gift from God, but it also requires us to participate in it.

For example, faith works in conjunction with our reason. We have very good reasons to believe in God. We have very good reasons to believe in the necessity and power of mental prayer. But there is still a mystery to it all. This should be familiar from last week's discussion of the Christian meaning of mystery. Some things in the spiritual life we must accept by faith, but we can penetrate the mystery to some degree with our reason (which then helps us to receive the grace of faith).

Let's look to Fr. Garrigou-LaGrange (*Three Ages of the Interior Life*):

Day 10 (Week 2, Day 2)

"Infused faith makes us believe all that God has revealed because He is Truth itself, (infused faith) is like a higher spiritual sense which allows us to hear a divine harmony that is inaccessible to every other means of knowing. This explains why there is an immense difference between the purely historical study of the Gospel and of the miracles which confirm it and the supernatural act of faith by which we believe in the Gospel as in the word of God."

This is like our athlete – he already has physical abilities, but his belief allows him to perform at a higher level. It is much more so with faith and our higher faculties of intellect and will – they can't perform at a higher, a spiritual level, without the virtue of Faith. Our faith allows us to experience reality at a higher level than our reason and senses alone permit.

Faith is integral to mental prayer and our relationship with God. We can't see God in the ordinary sense. And we can't have a conversation with God in the same way that we have conversations with friends. But by faith we believe that God can and does enter into a relationship with us. Fr. Philippe (*Time for God*) identifies three critical aspects of faith as it relates to mental prayer:

    a. Faith in God's presence (that He is always there with you).

    b. Faith that we are all called to meet God in mental prayer.

    c. Faith in the fruitfulness of a life of prayer (even if we don't "feel" anything happening at certain times).

Let's pause for a brief refresher on virtue. There are three supernatural virtues, also called the theological virtues – faith, hope and love. They are *super*natural because they are completely beyond our nature. We can't acquire them on our own, no matter how hard we might try. Therefore Fr. Garrigou-Lagrange uses the word "infused". Faith, hope and love (charity) must be infused into us by God.

The natural virtues are different (chief among them are the cardinal virtues of prudence, justice, fortitude and temperance).

They are also referred to as *acquired* virtues, because we can acquire them, to an extent, through our own efforts – they are part of our nature. To illustrate this in the absolute extreme, you can readily call to mind very *un*Godly people who all-the-same possess a twisted type of virtue. They can be cunning, which is related to prudence. They can be driven, which is related to fortitude. They can be disciplined, which is related to temperance. And so, we can acquire the natural virtues on our own, even without God (although we can never *perfect* them without God's grace).

Thus, Christ gave His disciples the mission to baptize, so all the world could receive the sanctifying grace of Baptism. With that sanctifying grace we receive not only the indwelling of the Spirit but also the gift of the theological virtues (faith, hope and love) and the ability to grow in the perfection of the other virtues.

Regarding faith, we can't know God without Him being present in our soul. Let us look at this with a rough analogy. Say you have a friend who is determined to convince you to turn over all your money, every last dime, to his financial advisor, Bill. But you have never met Bill. Are you going to give Bill all your money? No. It doesn't matter how many nice things your friend says about Bill, you're not going to give him one dime until you meet him, talk with him, get to *know* him. So it is with faith in this very loose analogy. People can say all manner of nice things to us about Jesus, but until we are able to meet Him and get to *know* Him, in our soul, we won't have an active supernatural faith in Him. This type of knowing is especially important in Christianity.

From the Baltimore Catechism, "We were made to *know* Him, love Him and serve Him." This does not mean to know God like we know a TV character. It is to know Him intimately in our soul. Ancient Hebrew has a word for this type of knowing – *yada*. In the book of Exodus, the line of Pharaohs had always respected the Israelites out of reverence for their famous patriarch, Joseph (like our George Washington). But then a new Pharaoh comes into power and he begins persecuting the Israelites "because he did not *know* Joseph." Obviously, he knew who Joseph was in a historical sense, but he had no admiration for Joseph, he did not honor Joseph's memory nor hold him in esteem. He did not *know* Joseph.

Faith is the basis of how we come to *know* God.

Enemies of faith are presumption and fear. Presumption is an unwarranted feeling of righteousness and the attitude that God is going to do exactly what we desire. The Pharisee praying in the Temple and holding himself above the tax collector was presumptuous (Lk 8:9-14). Fear is doubt in God's loving providence. The Israelites doubting God at the Red Sea and wishing they were back in captivity is this type of fear (Ex 14:10-14).

Presumption and fear are both facets of selfish pride. All sin and vice are. Likewise, all virtues are facets of selfless love. With presumption we think we don't really need God because we're perfect just as we are, we have it all figured out and God will serve our will. With fear we think we need to act, we need to take control, because we can't count on God, because He isn't doing what we hope for Him to do.

Thus, presumption and fear are also the same in that both attempt to make God small and make ourselves large. Faith is exactly opposed to this. Faith makes God big. "I must decrease that He might increase," said John the Baptist.

This is key when we talk about growing in holiness, expanding our interior life, and joining all our activity with our interior life so that we sanctify it and the world around us. These are, indeed, noble and worthy goals. In fact, they are so noble and worthy that they are not for us to do. We do not do any of it. God does. If we let Him. If we are small, then He will guide us in all things. Our only role is to let God be God. Whatever weaknesses we have, He will fix them. If there are broken relationships in our life, He will heal them. If we are facing a situation that seems impossible, remember nothing is impossible for God. But we must let God be God. We must trust Him.

Trust

Trust is a marvelous facet of the theological virtue of faith. Trust is very illuminating. Taking myself as an example, it can be easy for me to think that I have strong faith – I believe in our Trinitarian God, I believe Jesus was born of the Virgin Mary and suffered and died for my sins, and on and on. I accept and believe the precepts of our faith. But how well do I trust in God?

Trust and beliefs are related but distinct facets of faith. Trust, in fact, puts our beliefs to the test – do we really believe what we say we believe? Trust is a very personal aspect of faith. How much do I trust in God? The opposite of trust in God is how much I trust in myself. The two are mutually exclusive. The closer I get to placing all trust in God and none in me, the better I am.

The Catechism (CCC 2547) sheds further light on the topic of trust: "Abandonment to the providence of the Father in heaven frees us from anxiety about tomorrow." Tomorrow, by the way, is the land of outcomes, and outside of my control. The Catechism also tells us that trust is uniquely tied to the beatitude of poverty – the more I trust in God the more I realize that I am completely poor (what do I have that isn't a gift from God?) Blessed are the poor, for *theirs is the Kingdom of Heaven.* And Heaven happens to be our desired destination.

It is exceedingly difficult to let go of the illusion of control: "If I just do this certain thing, this certain way, everything will turn out the way I want." This calls to mind the issue of method and technique, and why we avoid them at all cost in our prayer life. And this idea of control in our spiritual life is not anything new. This is actually an ancient heresy known as Pelagianism – the idea that we can earn our desired outcomes. We need to abandon that illusion of control.

Day 10 (Week 2, Day 2)

Everyone entering deeper into relationship with God has this fear: if I let go, God is going to ask something of me that I am not able or prepared to give. We may not think that is our fear at first, because we haven't yet delved that deeply into our own heart, but that fear is in all of us. God, however, does not work that way. Faith and growing our interior life are not some divine trap that God will spring on us. God never asks anything of us that we cannot give. Might it sting and might there be challenges as we grow in faith? Sure. But when they come, they are not from God. Our challenges, hurdles and crosses are laid for us by our three enemies (the world, satan and our fallen nature). The stinging when it comes, is God's healing touch, like medicine poured out on a wound.

This brings us to another unique aspect of trust – it is one of the virtues (like fortitude) that grows through tribulation (see Rom 5:3-5 and CCC 2734). Our trust grows when we prevail over adversity by the grace of God. Think again, of the Israelites at the Red Sea with the Egyptian army bearing down upon them. Think of Abraham climbing Mount Moriah with the expectation of sacrificing his son. Think of the Apostles huddled in the upper room. Think of anyone who suffered adversity in the name of the Lord – all of them ultimately prevailed!

Faith, then, is an infused virtue. It is pure gift. We can't attain one iota of it on our own. But we can receive more and more of it by opening ourselves up to it. The more we trust in God, the more we let go of the illusion of control, the more faith will pour into us.

And, as we discussed last week, we need to trust that God is there even if it doesn't "feel" like it. God is operating in the spiritual realm, the realm of our soul, whether we feel it or not. Mother Teresa, once again, is a powerful testimony to this. Her soul was in communion with God even if for many years she could not feel His presence.

We must pray for more faith "Lord, increase our faith!" and then put it into action- "Jesus, I trust in you." In our mental prayer, this is trusting that God is with us and doing His good work in our soul, so long as we just keep faithfully showing up and placing ourselves in his loving care

Please spend 7 minutes in silent prayer; talking with God about today's session.

Let's close in prayer:

Lord Jesus Christ, help me to become ever more aware of Your nearness and Your great love for me. Amen.

Day 10 (Week 2, Day 2)

Pearls from Day 10: Dispositions Part 1 – Faith and Trust as the Basis for Mental Prayer

In worldly endeavors we recognize the importance of belief and envisioning success. If we don't believe in a cause, we won't fight for it. If we can't envision success, we won't achieve it.

In the spiritual realm this equates to the theological virtue of Faith. We have faith that God exists. We have faith that Christ died for us and won our salvation. This faith motivates us to grow in holiness in this life.

The theological virtues (faith, hope and love) are infused virtues. They are pure gifts from God. This contrasts with the natural (or acquired) virtues. Particularly the Cardinal Virtues - prudence, justice, fortitude and temperance. It is within our *nature* to be able to *acquire* these virtues by our own actions. Faith, hope and love are *super*natural, beyond our nature, and must be given to us by God.

The enemies of faith are presumption and fear. Presumption is an unwarranted feeling of righteousness and an attitude that God is going to do exactly what we desire. The Pharisee praying in Temple and holding himself above the tax collector was presumptuous (Lk 19:9-14). Fear is doubt in God's loving providence. The Israelites doubting God at the Red Sea and wishing they were back in captivity is this type of fear (Ex 14:10-14).

For us to receive the gift of faith we must become small and let go of our efforts to control our circumstances. As John the Baptist declares, "I must decrease that He might increase." (Jn 3:30)

Trust is a marvelous facet of the virtue of faith. Trust and beliefs are related but distinct. Trust, in fact, puts our beliefs to the test – do we really believe what we say we believe?

Trust it one of the virtues (like fortitude) that grows through tribulation (see Rom 5:3-5 and CCC 2734). Our trust and faith grow when we prevail over adversity by the grace of God.

We must pray for more faith, "Lord, increase our faith!" and then put it into action, "Jesus, I trust in you." In our mental prayer this is done by trusting that God is with us and doing His good work in our soul, so long as we just keep faithfully showing up and placing ourselves in his loving care.

Day 10 (Week 2, Day 2)

Your Pearls from Day 10

DAY 11: DISPOSITIONS PART II – PURITY OF INTENTION AND HUMILITY

> "Then the Lord God formed the man out of the dust of the ground." (Gen 2:7)
>
> "All we are is dust in the wind." (Kansas)
>
> "'For you are dust, and to dust you shall return' …. That's why I do not dust, it could be someone I know." (Gen 3:19 and anonymous homemaker)

It's good to know where we came from, it keeps us grounded. In fact, our first parents came from the dust of the ground. Humbling, isn't it?

And humility, it turns out, goes hand-in-hand with purity of intention.

First, let's open in prayer.

Come Holy Spirit, make of me a fitting dwelling place for the Lord.

Day 11 (Week 2, Day 3)

Your Jungle Mission

Everything was always better when you were with the Savior. He always found the best pathways through the jungle – the surest footing, the best view, the least nuisances and dangers.

The Savior had a knack for cooking the tastiest dinners, healing wounds and repairing damaged equipment. He seemed to know everything about the jungle, all the plants, animals and insects. He could anticipate how weather patterns would develop. And He was a magnificent teacher. He could make anything understandable and always had intriguing stories to breathe life into the lessons.

He was always very alert and in the present moment. He was completely focused on the people and conversations around Him. And yet He also seemed to be anticipating the needs of the future, from small to large. One afternoon while you were talking with Him you noticed he would snip a few leaves from passing branches. Sure enough, that evening those same leaves simmered in the stew, giving it a wonderful flavor. One of the nomads was suffering a sore knee and the next day there was going to be a particularly long hike. The Savior had gotten up early to search out a sturdy branch and masterfully fashion it into a well-fitted crutch.

Of course not everything He did was completely to your liking. It was difficult, at first, to accustom yourself to His rhythm of life. Some days He wanted to press further along the day's hike than you did. Other days, when you were eager to push ahead, He chose to linger and rest and talk and appreciate the jungle. And then there was the food. Everything He cooked was so delectable you found yourself wanting third and fourth helpings. But that wasn't the way of it. No one ever left hungry, but no one ever over-indulged (which was probably a good thing, but not easy when it was all so tasty).

Over time you came to realize there was something more attractive about Him than what He did for you, as good as all those things were. There was something more fundamental, satisfying and enriching about Him. There was a simple goodness about Him. Not just that He was good; He radiated a goodness that elevated everything around Him. At times you found your heart burning when you were with Him, out of love for Him and everyone else with you because you found yourself seeing everyone else in a new light when you were with Him.

A time came when you sought Him out each day not because of His knack at orienteering through the jungle or making fine dinners or healing wounds. You sought Him out each day simply because you couldn't imagine not being by His side and because you knew that was where He desired you to be.

Focus and Purity of Intention

Yesterday we discussed the importance of Faith. In our spiritual life this is our belief in God and trust in His plan for us in this life and His desire for us to spend eternity with Him in Heaven.

As we shift our focus to purity of intention, we pause a moment to focus on ... *focus*. Now, every human endeavor requires focus. The ability to focus is one of the greatest factors for success in achieving a goal. A popular story in the business world involves two of the world's wealthiest men – Bill Gates and Warren Buffet. As the story goes, Bill Gates and Warren Buffett were once at dinner at the home of Bill Gate's parents. During the evening Bill's parents asked each of them to each write on a piece of paper the single most important trait

Day 11 (Week 2, Day 3)

for success. One wonders what prompted Bill's parents to play this particular "get to know you" game. But as the story continues, when they showed their answers, each had written "focus."

This is true for our analogy of trekking through a jungle to reach that far-off peak. If we lose our focus and start taking side trips to explore some interesting sight, we not only delay our journey, but we risk something happening that will prevent us from continuing and achieving our goal.

Focus in the spiritual realm is associated with purity of mind and purity of intention. Our time in prayer can't be a self-centered activity; our focus needs to be turned from self to God. Here we can think of Peter and the disciples on the stormy sea (Mt 14:22-23). Peter gets out of the boat to walk over the water to Jesus. So long as Peter looked at the Lord he walked on the water. When he turned his gaze from Jesus to the surging sea his thoughts turned to fear, and he sank.

This is the subtle distinction between focus and faith. Faith comes first, and therefore it is our first disposition. We start with believing in God. Peter believed in Jesus. Once we establish our faith, we must keep that faith at the forefront of our intellect and will. *That* is spiritual focus and that is purity of intention. When Peter lost his focus on the Lord he began to focus on the *stormy* sea, and then came the fear (the great enemy of faith).

So, our focus must turn again and again to God. To have this focus, to be single-minded in our love for God and doing His will in all things, is to act with purity of intention. If we love God purely, we will not be troubled nor discouraged if it doesn't "feel" like mental prayer is working.

And there is this - "Blessed are the pure of heart, for they shall see the face God." (Mt 5:8) When nothing distracts us from God, we start to see His face in everything.

We also must guard against praying to God as a technique to get good things from Him - "I have to pray today so that God will bless me." Putting it in the context of human relationships, it would indeed be an unhealthy marriage or friendship if we only spend time with that person so that we will get something from them.

I know anyone reading this book understands that God isn't a celestial ATM (prayer goes in, blessing comes out...). But this aspect of purity of intention can be trickier than it seems. The enemy is very crafty at rebranding the idea that "if I pray, good things will happen" as something altogether different and noble. For example, we pray for healing for a friend. It is indeed good to desire physical health for our friends and loved ones, but even prayers of physical healing must be accompanied by "thy will be done". It could be unknown to us is that it is very necessary for the *spiritual* health of our friend that they suffer an ailment so that they learn to cling to God. It is a simple fact of human nature that at times hidden deep down in our prayer is the idea that *if I do this, God will come around to my way of thinking*.

The transformation we need is not for God to come around to our way of thinking, but for our thinking to become God's thinking (and our loving to become God's loving) – even in those instances when we're not able to foresee how God is working events for the good. That sort of transformation depends a great deal on the openness of our hearts to be transformed, and that depends on the purity of our intention (that we come to prayer out of love for God and with no other agenda). As the saying goes – we need to cultivate a love for the gift-giver, not the gifts.

Purity then is an act of both intellect and will. Here the adage of "fake it until you make it" comes to mind. We are not really "faking it" – but we do have to take command of our emotions. We are naturally self-absorbed and come to prayer wanting God to attend to our needs. We must force ourselves to put that aside and pray for the grace to desire God for His own sake, and then gratefully accept the gifts God desires to give us. Likewise, we have to force ourselves to gratefully accept if He doesn't seem to be giving us the gift we thought we needed. Call to mind that you are praying to God who created you, who knows you better than you know yourself and who showers you with all good things. Make it an act of will, an act of gratitude, an act of self-sacrifice, an act of generosity, to bring yourself back to this intention again and again and again.

Humility

Purity of intention goes hand-in-hand with the virtue of Humility (in fact, all virtues work in harmony). Humility comes from the Latin word "humus" – or earth. Humble people are grounded, close to their roots, close to *reality*. Humility is also related to meekness. A meek person is perfectly who they are, no more and no less. A meek person does not know false modesty. Jesus casting the money changers out of the temple was meekness in action every bit as much as Jesus washing His apostles' feet; because it was Jesus being perfectly himself and perfectly aligned with the will of the Father in each situation. Even in righteous anger, Jesus was *grounded* in doing the will of His Father. This is humility.

It is easy to see how humility and purity of intention are related. Purity of intention not only helps us to focus on God, but also helps us to see ourselves for who we are and thus grounds us, helping us to remain humble. Humble people recognize their lowliness and so they trust not in themselves but in God, which leads to purity of intention.

St. Teresa of Avila tells us "The whole edifice of prayer is founded upon humility." And from 1 Peter 5:5 "God opposes the proud but gives Grace to the humble."

Christ warns us, "Amen, I say to you, unless you turn and become like children, you will not enter the Kingdom of heaven. Whoever becomes humble like this child is the greatest in the Kingdom of heaven." (Mt 18:4,5)

With that, St. Peter brings us to the flip side of humility - "pride." Just as all the virtues are wrapped up in love, so too all sins have their root in pride. In pride we place ourselves above God and from that lofty position we give ourselves permission to act on whatever sinful impulses come our way. Oh, to be sure we find ways to justify them, we employ situational ethics and every other trick in the book – merely to distract ourselves from the prickling of our conscience that tells us we are defying God.

Humility is the virtue that counteracts pride, which is why humility is the *queen of virtues* (it is no surprise that Mary, Queen of Heaven, is most known for her humility!) We must pray for and practice humility. Fr. Garrigou-LaGrange gives us two methods for practicing humility:

1. "The remedy for pride is to tell ourselves that of ourselves we are not... And if grace is in us it is because Jesus Christ redeemed us by His blood." It is only by the gift of God that we exist at all, let alone that we experience any form of goodness in this life.

2. "The remedy for pride is also to tell ourselves that there is in us something inferior to nothingness itself: the disorder of sin and its effects." Without the redemption purchased for us by Christ, we are *worse than nothing*, we deserve and are destined for pain and suffering.

That is strong medicine, but pride is a deadly disease and we can't trifle with half measures. How else to practice humility? The *Imitation of Christ* (by Thomas a Kempis) gives some concrete examples:

1. A lowly and simple man who serves God is better than a learned and accomplished man who does not.

2. Love to be unknown and esteemed as nothing. Do away with all ambition. To the extent that worldly success or admiration comes to you, count it all as to God's glory.

3. If you see someone else do something wrong and sinful do not consider yourself any better. We are all frail and never know

Day 11 (Week 2, Day 3)

when we might slip into sin ourselves. See no one as less frail than yourself.

4. Be not ashamed to wait on others for the love of Jesus Christ, and to be looked upon as poor in this world.
5. Trust not in your own knowledge, but in the grace of God.
6. Continual peace dwells with the humble, but in the heart of the proud is frequent envy and indignation.

The first four are self-explanatory, but will profit us if we reflect on them in prayer. Number five reminds us to always check our own thinking and motives. Obviously, we are called to utilize our knowledge to move through each day, but the warning hinges on the word "trust." While we engage our intellect and think for ourselves, we should always be invoking the Holy Spirit and our Guardian Angel to guard our thoughts. And, we should always be wary of our own failings and thus seek to stay close to God in all that we do.

Number six gets to the heart of discernment. We can judge how we are doing by the fruits that grow in our soul - the fruits of the Holy Spirit. This is the guidepost *par excellence* because here there can be no forgery. Only God can give true interior peace. Pride yields only interior conflict such as envy ("why is so-and-so getting the promotion?") and indignation ("why do I have to do *this*, it's a waste of my abilities!"). True interior peace, even amidst trials, comes from God alone.

We see that our dispositions build on one another. This is because these dispositions are, in fact, virtues and virtues always rise and fall together. None of us are perfectly pure nor perfectly humble. And we may, in fact, have a long way to go. Be not discouraged! Truly humble people are never discouraged because they trust in God, not themselves. We must pray to God for these graces and exercise our faith and trust in God and that He will grant us continued increase in purity and humility and any other virtues we require to progress in prayer and holiness.

God is always listening, always waiting to shower us with grace. We need only to spend a little quiet time with Him and ask!

Please spend 7 minutes in silent prayer; talking with God about today's session.

Let's close in prayer:

Lord Jesus Christ, help me to become ever more aware of Your nearness and Your love for me. Amen.

Day 11 (Week 2, Day 3)

Pearls from Day 11: Dispositions Part II – Purity of Intention and Humility

Purity of Intention

Focus is an important mindset for any human endeavor.

Focus in the spiritual realm is associated with purity of intention. Once we establish our faith, we must keep that faith at the forefront of our intellect and will. That is spiritual focus and that is purity of intention.

If we love God purely, we will not be troubled or discouraged if it doesn't "feel" like mental prayer is working. "Blessed are the pure of heart, for they shall see the face of God." (Mt 5:8)

We pray not to find self-fulfillment or self-satisfaction, but to please God. We must cultivate a love for the gift-giver, not the gifts.

Purity is an act of will. Even though we can't love God purely we should aspire to – we should aim for it and practice it as well as we can and with the trust that God will purify us.

Humility

Purity of intention goes hand-in-hand with the virtue of humility because humble people are always aware of their smallness and God's greatness, and thus their complete reliance on Him.

Humility comes from the Latin word "humus" – or earth. Humble people are grounded, close to their roots, close to *reality*.

From St. Teresa of Avila – "The whole edifice of prayer is founded upon humility." And from St. Peter - "God opposes the proud but gives Grace to the humble." (1 Pt 5:5)

Humility is the virtue that counteracts pride, which is why

humility is the *queen of virtues* (it is no surprise that Mary, Queen of Heaven, is most known for her humility!)

Humble people do not carry on about their wretchedness – they consider it good fortune, since it gives God a chance to show how merciful he is.

It is exceedingly difficult for us to accept that we are so poor (spiritually); that is why people naturally tend to avoid silence.

Humble people are never discouraged because they trust not in themselves but only in God.

Your Pearls from Day 11

DAY 12: DISPOSITIONS PART III – FORTITUDE

> If you are feeling some fatigue, maybe even wondering why you started this retreat and are considering calling it quits, rest assured that's perfectly natural! Fortunately for us, we can tap into the *supernatural* power of fortitude. Hold on tight.

Let's open with prayer:

Come Holy Spirit, make of me a fitting dwelling place for the Lord.

Your Jungle Mission

You've entered into a particularly difficult stretch through the jungle. The difficulty isn't physical. In fact, this stretch is among the easiest you've encountered. The difficulty is the monotony.

Mile after mile, day after day, week after week, all the same thing.

At first the sights and sounds were exotic and beautiful to behold. But even those captivating sights eventually became routine. "Oh look, another giant kapok tree ... oh look, another

Day 12 (Week 2, Day 4)

pristine waterfall ... oh look, another colorful toucan." And then fatigue set in. You started thinking that maybe it would have been better to have stayed behind, back at that glade with its lagoon and fruit trees.

Fatigue and boredom. Boredom and fatigue. A deadly combination.

In fact, it really was almost deadly. You had become so numb to your surroundings that one afternoon you nearly walked straight into a pride of momma lions watching over their cubs. Fortunately, He was at your side and gently steered you away from disaster.

With each mile seeming no different than the mile before, each day blending into the next, and no end in sight - it was getting harder and harder to stay alert and motivated.

You fell in with some of the experienced nomads and asked how they were holding up. They affirmed that these stretches of the journey were more difficult than those that were physically demanding. The stamina that was required was stamina of the intellect – to stay alert and remember your training. And stamina of the will – to keep going. They also assured you that this stretch of the jungle was forcing you to grow by leaps and bounds in fortitude – and that would make the rest of the journey much easier.

Fortitude

Any great human endeavor requiring sustained effort to achieve a high goal reaches a point of malaise. There is always that middle part of the journey, where the newness has worn off, the prize looks impossibly far off, and the drudgery of the effort seems too much to bear and no longer worth it.

And so it often is with prayer. When we first strike out to deepen our prayer life we are engaged and energized. At some point, we hit the wall. This is when we engage the great battle to simply be faithful to our time of mental prayer, come what may, according to the definite plan we have established.

Part of this battle is with our *feelings*. Those troublesome feelings – where the weakness of our flesh thwarts the good intentions our intellect and will.

We come to a point where prayer doesn't "feel" like it's doing anything. Many people experience strong consolation at the very start of mental prayer (such as feelings of peace, positivity, and inspiration). This is God drawing them into prayer. But at some point, God desires us to start to stand on our own two feet, and the consolations dissipate. Then begins the battle between our will and our feelings.

Fr. Philippe advises that what is important is that mental prayer of "poor quality" but regular and faithful, is worth more than prayer that is "sublime" but only now and then. There is no true love without fidelity.

Another obstacle that feelings will quickly put in our path is the feeling that "I really don't have time for this – I have more important things to be doing." This is partly an issue of fear, which you will recall is an enemy of faith. Fear that we won't get everything else done – as if God isn't bigger than our to-do list.

But there is a broader underlying issue with the perception of not having enough time for prayer – priorities. "There is no one who has left house or brothers ... who will not receive 100 fold in this lifetime."(Mk 10:29) You may be familiar with this anecdote about Mother Teresa in one form or another: She was being chauffeured by a priest who was recently given major new responsibilities (he may have been installed as an Auxiliary Bishop) and in making nervous

Day 12 (Week 2, Day 4)

small-talk to the future Saint mentioned the promotion left him with little time to pray. Mother Teresa immediately called him to a session of school and instructed him that with greater responsibilities he should be spending *more* time in prayer, not less. That's just how it is. Fr. Jean-Baptiste Chautard (*The Soul of the Apostolate*) puts it quite plainly – "the busier you are, the more you need the interior life."

Remember from the other day – the contemplative life is necessary for the active life. Time given to God is not stolen from other people or activities – it perfects the time spent with others.

Faithfulness to mental prayer is also a school of freedom – discipline in mental prayer, instead of just praying "when we feel like it," sets us free in the other areas of our life. We are exercising our first disposition - trust in God. When we honor our divine appointment with mental prayer, we are trusting that God will order the other commitments in our life so that all is accomplished to His satisfaction.

Recall this from Fr. Philippe – "Without a life of prayer there is no holiness – without a life of prayer even the Sacraments will have limited effect and deep conversion experiences won't be lasting." That explains a lot – doesn't it? Don't we often wonder why it seems like we are not getting anywhere in our spiritual life?

If we are not seeing authentic fruit from our spiritual life, it is probably because we're not making the commitment to mental prayer necessary for it to flourish.

Receive this not as condemnation but motivation. God knows that the enemies of our nature are working against us and, particularly, our prayer life. God knows that we are assaulted with every obstacle and seemingly good reason why we should not commit to mental prayer. Because of this, God is always working to draw you to Him, including through the somewhat strong medicine such as the advice from Fr. Philippe (and all the Saints).

Remember this – there is an ordering to Christian prayer:

- First comes consistency (aka persistence)
- Consistency leads to Quality
- Quality leads to Quantity

Let's look further at these three – Consistency, Quality and Quantity.

1. Consistency and the Virtue and Gift of Fortitude

Ok, so if prayer is so important, and if we know for a fact that the enemy (our flesh, the world and satan) will conspire to try to stop us in our good intentions to pray 15 minutes each day – what do we do about it?

The same things we always do. We turn to God and his arsenal. Among the big guns in His arsenal are the virtues. We need a bazooka. A howitzer. And that is *fortitude*.

Fortitude – The Virtue

Fortitude is one of four Cardinal virtues (along with prudence, justice and temperance). From CCC 1808: "Fortitude is the moral virtue that ensures firmness in difficulties and constancy in the pursuit of the good. It strengthens the resolve to resist temptations and to overcome obstacles in the moral life."

For beginners in the spiritual life, fortitude helps dispel fear of effort and fear of risks. Fear of effort? Yes, in a curious way. Fortitude dispels the flawed thinking that there is something better or more pleasurable that I should be doing ("Fear of Missing Out"). Fear of risk? Yes. Are friends or family members going to think you are becoming a "holy roller"? Or, now that God has you cornered, is He going to start asking things of you that you are not prepared to give? Fear is a sneaky thing (because it comes from the enemy) and can take many forms. Fortitude dispels it.

As we progress in prayer, fortitude takes a different character and propels us in generosity (and another great virtue – magnanimity, spiritual generosity) – to greater imitate Christ and more heroically give of ourselves in prayer and striving in virtue.

This discussion of fortitude reminds us of the big picture. The big picture of the purpose of fortitude in our jungle mission is to bring us to the mountain. The big picture of the purpose of fortitude in our prayer life is to bring us to God – in this life and in the next.

Fortitude - The Gift

Fortitude is also a gift of the Holy Spirit (discussed more in Week 4). We receive a supernatural dose of fortitude with Sacraments of baptism and confirmation. As with all gifts we must pray to receive the grace ever more and exercise our will to better partake of the gift of fortitude. We must pray for it and recognize that while we can do nothing without God's grace, we "...can do all things in Him who strengthens us." (Phil 4:13)

2. Quality of Our Prayer

The quality of our prayer is marked by the fruit it produces in our life; not the feelings we get during prayer.

The fruit that we are speaking of are spiritual fruits. The greatest fruit of prayer is an increasing love of God, followed closely by a love for neighbor. Another common fruit of prayer is peace. Peace is a Fruit of the Holy Sprit and one of Christ's most repeated blessings ("peace be with you"). And then there are the rest of the Fruits of the Holy Spirit; perfections that the Holy Spirit forms in us (CCC 1832). Tradition and Scripture (Gal 5:22-23) identify twelve fruits of the Spirit: charity, joy, peace, patience, kindness, goodness, generosity, gentleness, faithfulness, modesty, self-control, and chastity. Watch for these as you grow in prayer!

3. Quantity of Our Prayer

Quantity of our prayer is measured in time given to God (as opposed to quantity of words or devotions). Our ability to spend time with God will grow as our interior life grows.

Your long-term goal should be at least 30 minutes of daily mental prayer (our immediate goal is 15 minutes). St. Teresa of Avila says: "The person who is fully determined to make a half hour's mental prayer every morning, cost what it may, has already traveled half this journey," (the journey being communion with God).

Many other Saints point towards at least 30 minutes. And our ordinary experience confirms this. It simply takes time to focus ourselves, to express ourselves, to quiet ourselves so that we can hear God.

In this retreat we start with 5 minutes of silence each day and work toward spending 15 minutes in mental prayer. In the last week of the series we will discuss guidelines to increase that time to 30 minutes each day.

Now let's return our focus to fortitude. This is a good place to go with your time of silent prayer. When and how are you challenged with fortitude, consistency or perseverance? When have you had successes? How do you need God to help you in this area of your life?

Please spend 7 minutes in silent prayer; talking with God about today's session.

Let's close in prayer:

Lord Jesus Christ, help me to become ever more aware of Your nearness and Your great love for me. Amen.

Day 12 (Week 2, Day 4)

Pearls from Day 12: Dispositions Part III – Fortitude

Fortitude is one of four Cardinal virtues (along with prudence, justice and temperance). From CCC 1808: "Fortitude is the moral virtue that ensures firmness in difficulties and constancy in the pursuit of the good. It strengthens the resolve to resist temptations and to overcome obstacles in the moral life."

Fortitude is also a gift of the Holy Spirit. We receive a supernatural dose of fortitude with Baptism and Confirmation (the Sacrament by which we lay claim to our faith as a mature adult). As with all virtue we must pray to receive the grace ever more and exercise our will to better partake of the gift of fortitude. We must pray for it and recognize that while we can do nothing without God's grace, we "...can do all things in Him who strengthens us." (Phil 4:13)

The first battle is to be faithful to our times of mental prayer, come what may, according to a definite plan we have established.

Part of this battle is with our feelings. We all come to a point where prayer doesn't "feel" like it's doing anything. Regular and faithful mental prayer, even if it feels of "poor quality" is worth more than inconsistent prayer that feels "sublime."

There is no true love without fidelity.

Mental prayer is a matter of priorities and time with God is our first priority. When we honor our divine appointment with mental prayer, we are trusting that God will order the other commitments in our life so that all is accomplished to His satisfaction.

There is an ordering to Christian prayer. First comes **Consistency** which leads to **Quality** which leads to **Quantity**. Consistency is fortitude in action.

Your Pearls from Day 12

Day 13 (Week 2, Day 5)

DAY 13: PRINCIPLES PART I – PRIMACY OF GOD'S ACTION AND LOVE

> Our first principle focuses on God the Father and the Primacy of God's Action and Love. God is always taking the initiative. God loves us first. This prompts the question - how do we return that love? The answer may surprise you.

Let's open with prayer:

Come Holy Spirit, make of me a fitting dwelling place for the Lord.

YOUR JUNGLE MISSION

You have been learning how important it is to give up your effort to control your circumstances. Actually, you have been learning to give up clutching at the *illusion* of control. Each time you attempt to bend events to suit your narrow plan, things take a turn for the worse. You've come to recognize the reason for this is that as soon as your mind locks on to acting on your plan you forget all about what the Savior has taught you, and you forget to call on His Spirit to guide you.

One of the things that has helped you let go of striving for control is to keep in mind Who is in control. You are not simply handing control over to some mindless, uncaring universe. The Savior has repeatedly explained and reassured you that His Father is shaping reality all around you.

As you journey through the jungle you remind yourself that this is all His creation. When you look up at the night sky and see a billion points of light – all are His. Not only does He order all the stars in the sky, the Savior tells you the Father cares just as much about the smallest details in your own life.

You ask the Savior about all the difficult and tragic things that happen to people. "The Father turns them all to blessings as well. When you are reunited with Him on the mountain, He'll show all of it to you – how He worked all of it for your good."

You ask the Savior, what are you supposed to do for the Father in return? "Let the Him love you."

The Primacy of God the Father

Many years ago, I had an experience in the Atlantic Ocean of getting caught in a strong rip tide and being dragged quickly out into deep waters. The waves were high and there was a wide and powerful current; swimming across it and making my way back to shore would have been difficult if not impossible, at least for me. Fortunately, many lifeguards were patrolling because the surf was so rough, and they soon pulled me in with a tow line. One of the things you figure out quickly when someone is trying to save your life is this – don't make their job any harder. Just go along with whatever they say.

Our first principle of prayer is like this. God is in charge. God created us. God is all-powerful. God is all-loving. There is nothing we can do apart from God. Literally nothing. Our very existence, moment to moment, is dependent on God holding us in existence. St.

Day 13 (Week 2, Day 5)

Paul tells us that it is in God that "we live, move and have our being." (Acts 17:28) And, even in that living, moving and being, "God is the one who, for his good purpose, works in you both to desire and to work." (Phil 2:13)

What all of this means for our interior life is that mental prayer "is not so much about what we do as what God does in us." (Philippe, *Time for God*)

This should be extremely liberating for us. Whether or not our prayer time "feels" good, God is working in us. As Fr. Philippe also points out, "One cannot stand in front of a fire and not be warmed." One cannot spend time in mental prayer and not have his soul enriched. Yes, we can feel the warmth of the fire whereas we don't always feel the "warmth" of mental prayer. Prayer really isn't about feelings. Sometimes God gives us sensible consolation to draw us to Him, but those consolations are secondary, and they must never be confused with being the main thing. Therefore, we need to learn and believe, by faith and reason, that God is enriching our soul during prayer just as the fire warms us. And sometimes, by God's grace, we can "feel" the warmth of prayer in the form of consolations and fruits of the Holy Spirit such as interior peace.

Pope Benedict, writing as Cardinal Ratzinger, tells us, "The love of God, the sole object of Christian contemplation, is a reality which cannot be 'mastered' by any method or technique. On the contrary, we must always have our sights fixed on Jesus Christ, in whom God's love went to the cross for us and there assumed even the condition of estrangement from the Father (cf. Mk 13:34). We therefore should allow God to decide the way he wishes to have us participate in his love." (*On Some Aspects of Christian Meditation*)

And so, our first principle is the Primacy of God's Action. God always initiates, and when we cooperate with Him, He will guide our prayer and see His work in us through to His desired end. Our primary job is to faithfully show up each day and place our trust in God. He takes it from there.

The Law of Love

This flows to the second part of this principle - the Law of Love. God is love. His role in our relationship is to love us. That seems simple enough. What is our role? It is counter to what we are wired to think, which is that to love God back we must *do* something for Him. In fact, our role - how we love God - is to simply receive His love. We love God by letting Him love us.

In this is love, not that we loved God, but that he loved us first. (1 Jn 4:10)

How do we let God love us? How do we receive God's love? By spending time with him in mental prayer and by trusting Him. By having faith in Him. That's why we start with faith and trust as our first disposition.

This requires putting aside our pride, our need to achieve, our need to be in control. To receive God's love, we must let go of our efforts to control our lives and our endeavors to attain our vision of happiness.

We think that we know what will make us happy. "If I can get this person to like me …. If I can get this job promotion … If I do this for my kids …. If I can get past this illness or this emotional hurdle." These may be reasonable desires, but we must trust that God knows exactly what we need for happiness. God knows all the deepest desires of our hearts, even those unknown to us.

We should say with the psalmist:

As for me, I trust in your merciful love.
Let my heart rejoice in your saving help:
Let me sing to the Lord for this goodness to me,
Singing psalms to the name of the Lord, the Most High. (Ps 13:6)

Day 13 (Week 2, Day 5)

And Jesus himself tells us:

Therefore I tell you, do not worry about your life, what you will eat [or drink], or about your body, what you will wear. Is not life more than food and the body more than clothing?
Look at the birds in the sky; they do not sow or reap, they gather nothing into barns, yet your heavenly Father feeds them. Are not you more important than they? (Mt 6:25,26)

That is not to say that we don't also express our love in action, as Jesus tells us to feed the hungry and comfort the widow. But this is our *response* to God's love. First, we must *receive* God's love. We can't give to others what we have not received ourselves.

When we place all our trust and hope in the Lord, then we experience His loving care. Then we are truly able to go into the world and share with others what we have received.

As always, we want to be extremely practical and applied in this retreat. And we must recognize that it can be very difficult to "let God love us," particularly during the trials of life, such as when a loved one becomes gravely ill, or if our children are struggling, or with the loss of a job. Our first instinct is to react, to *do something*. But our first response must be to turn to the Lord and trust in His love and His ability to bring good from hardship. Of course, we go to the Lord with our desires, "Lord, heal my loved one," but even before that our prayer should be "Lord, I trust in your merciful love."

And that's why we start small. When we learn to go trustingly to the Lord with all our small concerns, we are able to do the same when life's big challenges arise.

We also must accustom ourselves to God's blessings. If our ideal of happiness is a mansion and chartered flights to Monaco, we are not going to be able to receive God's gifts of love. God's blessings are peace, joy, meaning, the many small miracles in life, the kindness of a stranger. Most especially, God's blessing is the awareness that God *is*, and that He loves us. When we give ourselves over to this, we find that God provides far more than our limited desires.

This is the primacy of God's love and why we start here. This is where we need to come to God as small children – completely dependent on Him. We express our love by receiving His. Here again, we encounter the passive aspect of prayer.

St. Ignatius of Loyola calls us to enter into God's gaze. To recognize that God is gazing down upon us – God is *always* gazing down upon us. Our part is to simply gaze back upon Him. Have you ever seen an infant gazing up at his parent who is gazing down on their beloved child? There you have it.

The principles of God's Initiative and Love result in prayer that is profoundly simple. God does all the work out of love for us and our job is to let him do it; to let Him love us.

It's a funny thing that it's not so easy to be simple. We naturally complicate things. We expect things to be complicated. We are wary of things that seem too simple, too good to be true. To achieve simplicity in our prayer life takes time and the operation of God's grace to heal and purify us.

Please spend 7 minutes in silent prayer; talking with God about today's session.

Let's close in prayer:

Lord Jesus Christ, help me to be ever more aware of Your nearness and Your great love for me. Amen.

Day 13 (Week 2, Day 5)

Pearls from Day 13: Principles Part I – Primacy of God's Action and Love

Our first principle addresses attributes of God that are most properly associated with God the father.

The Primacy of God's Action reminds us that God is in charge. God created us. God is all-powerful. God is all-loving. There is nothing we can do apart from God.

What all of this means for our interior life is that mental prayer "is not so much about what we do as what God does in us." (Philippe, *Time for God*)

This should be extremely liberating for us - whether or not our prayer time "feels" good – God is working in us.

God always initiates, and when we cooperate with Him, He sees His work in us through to His desired end. Our primary job is to faithfully show up each day and place our trust in God. He takes it from there.

The second part of this principle, the Law of Love flows from the first. God's role in our relationship is to love us. God loves us first.

The unique twist is that our role in the relationship is to receive God's love. How do we receive God's love? We let God love us.

And how do we let God love us? By spending time with him in mental prayer and by trusting Him. By having faith in Him.

To receive God's love, we must let go of our efforts to control our life and our striving to attain our vision of happiness.

That is not to say that we don't also express our love in action, as Jesus tells us to feed the hungry and comfort the widow. But this is our *response* to God's love. First, we must *receive* God's love. We can't give to others what we have not received ourselves.

When we place all our trust and hope in the Lord, then we experience His loving care. Then we are truly able to go into the world and share with others what we have received.

Your Pearls from Day 13

DAY 14: PRINCIPLES PART II – THE HUMANITY OF JESUS AND INDWELLING OF THE SPIRIT

> Yesterday we reflected on God the Father, gazing down upon us. But our heavenly Father desires also to be close to us, as close as can be. He does this through His Son and His Spirit ... and, through an important facet of our own being. We will consider all of this in today's reflection on our second and third principles.

Let's open with prayer:

Come Holy Spirit, make of me a fitting dwelling place for the Lord.

Your Jungle Mission

For many weeks you had been traveling through a lush valley. At first the beauty was startling. That was when the monotony set in and, with it, the opportunity to grow in the virtue and gift of fortitude.

At last the terrain began to change and your path through the jungle was taking you out of the valley. You awoke this morning excited for the day's hike. You would be ascending

Day 14 (Week 2, Day 6)

to higher elevations of the mountains surrounding the valley, and for the next few days you would hike along a ridgeline that gently swung from mountain to mountain. The air would be fresh and clear and there would be tremendous views.

There would also be some challenging mountaineering. The Savior and the more experienced nomads were skilled at finding paths through the rocks that avoided the most treacherous pitches, but the hiking would not be without danger.

Fortunately, the morning hiking was fairly easy and gave everyone time to become accustomed to the new terrain and exertion. But the easy hiking eventually gave way to scrambling up steep slopes. Here and there the steep slopes transitioned to challenging pitches of rock climbing. The experienced nomads were positioned at key locations along these pitches to help the others climb up safely.

You were pleased to find how naturally the climbing had become for you. You were learning to listen to His Spirit, so that He could guide you to the best positions to place your hands and feet. Oscar, who had joined the nomads not long ago with his wife Wendy, was traveling near you. This was his first experience with rock climbing. He was also just learning to listen to the Spirit and was having a tougher go of it, but he was determined to keep pace with the rest of the nomads.

That was when tragedy struck. As Oscar reached up for his next hand hold, the small rock supporting his right foot broke free. Gravity took hold of him and in the blink of an eye he vanished downward. You looked down and prepared yourself for the terrible sight of your companion crumpled upon the rocks below. Instead you were amazed to see him in the arms of the Savior. You don't know how He showed up in just the nick of time, but somehow He had, and had grabbed hold of Oscar. They both tumbled a way down, but the Savior protected Oscar from harm and got them safely settled on a large, sturdy ledge of rock.

You climbed down to join them and were amazed to see that Oscar had barely a scratch on him. You were even more amazed to see the Savior actually had a large and angry gash on his arm and another on His leg.

He was the Savior. He could do anything. Why would He permit Himself to be injured, even if it was to save one of the nomads? Couldn't He have simply saved Oscar without being injured Himself?

What an unusual Savior. What an unusual man.

The Humanity of Jesus

Our first principle is The Primacy of God's Action and Law of Love. The first part shows us that God's activity is primary. God does most of the work, we participate. Mental prayer "is not so much about what we do as what God does in us." The second part shows us that God's work in us is purely loving and the twist is that we return that love by simply allowing ourselves to be loved by God - so that we can receive His love and share it with others.

What is God's greatest expression of love for us?

That question brings us to our second principle - that God gives himself to us through the humanity of His Son. Our faith, as we have said, is inherently incarnational since it is through the incarnation of Jesus Christ that we are redeemed and reunited with the Father.

For God so loved the world that he gave his only Son, so that

Day 14 (Week 2, Day 6)

everyone who believes in him might not perish but might have eternal life. (Jn 3:16)

We live in this reality of a redeemed world and none of us can truly appreciate what that means. What would life be like right now had Christ not come down to Earth and suffered and died for us? People look at the Old Testament, with its brutality and cheapness of life, and say "there is the proof that God doesn't exist." No, it is exactly the opposite! It is proof of the desperate condition of humanity and how much we needed a savior. It shows how cruel and depraved we are without God and when left to our own devices. Israel proves it. They were the chosen ones. And yet, time and again they turned away. Israel is all of us. Without a savior, without someone to stand in the breach for us, we lose our way and are lost.

The ancient Israelites understood this need for a savior. Hence, the Psalmist writes:

When the Lord delivers his people from bondage,
Then Jacob will be glad, and Israel rejoice. (Ps 14:7)

It is the Second Person of the Trinity who delivers us from the bondage of sin and death, and in Him – first and foremost – is where we receive God's love. Recall from Day 5 that this is why our faith is incarnational. And therefore, our mental prayer has a particular focus on Jesus. In the initial stage of discursive meditation, the words and deeds of Jesus are the most suitable object of our meditation. It is by meditating on Jesus that we come to know God: "No one knows the Father except the Son and anyone to whom the Son wishes to reveal him." (Mt 11:27)

We encounter this focus on Jesus in the formula that is at the heart of every Sacrifice of the Mass. "Through him, with him, in him, in the unity of the Holy Spirit, all glory and honor are yours, almighty Father, forever and ever."

And from scripture:

God is one. One also is the mediator between God and men, the man Christ Jesus, who gave himself as ransom for all. (1 Tim 2:5-6)

God gave us eternal life, and this life is in his Son. Whoever possesses the Son has life; whoever does not possess the Son of God does not have life. (1 John 5:11-12)

I am the way, and the truth, and the life. (John 14:6)

Whoever has seen me has seen the father. (Jn 14:8-9)

And a sampling from spiritual masters:

"Fix your eyes on the Crucified and nothing else will be of much importance to you." (St. Teresa, *Interior Castle*)

"Therefore, the primary concern of every Christian should be to live the life that Christ brought to us, to be united with Christ to the point of being configured with him." (Aumann, *Spiritual Theology*)

"It is in union with Jesus Christ that we must perform all our acts, by keeping Jesus before our eyes, in our heart and in our hands." (Tanquerey, *The Spiritual Life*)

Let us return to Jesus' own words. *I am the Way*. Jesus tells us that he is the only way to the Father. He is the Gate. He is the Narrow Path.

I am the Truth. Why the truth? Why aren't we done with *I am the Way*? "To have found the way is not the end; it is the beginning." (Sheed, *Theology for Beginners*). God desires relationship with us. A primary way of knowing God is knowing his Truth. Christ is the fullness of Truth. He is Truth. He is uncreated wisdom. And God's Truth (which includes his laws) helps us to navigate through life's challenges so that we do not lose our way. Laws are not bad, they are not pointless constraints. God's laws, as has been said, are like the banks of a river, without which the water loses its direction, power and purpose.

I am the Life. Christ is the source of supernatural life. This is what fortifies us to follow His way and His Truth. We first receive life in his Spirit at baptism. We continue to grow in the Holy Spirit through grace conferred by living a sacramental life and a life of prayer and virtue.

As you know by now, mental prayer is indispensable in growing closer to Jesus, so that he does indeed become our Way, Truth and Life. The mysteries of Jesus' life are ideal objects of our meditation. "Every aspect of his humanity, each of his characteristics, even the smallest and most hidden, each of his words, deeds, and gestures, every stage of his life from his conception in Mary's womb, to his Ascension, brings us into communion with God the Father if we receive it in faith." (Philippe, *Time for God*)

THE INDWELLING OF THE HOLY SPIRIT

Now we come to our third guide, who travels within us like a GPS implanted in our soul, guiding us every step of the way. This is our third and final principle – the Indwelling of the Holy Spirit.

> *If a man loves me, he will keep my word, and my father will love him, and we will come to him and make our home with him.* (Jn 14:23)
>
> *Do you not know that your body is a temple of the Holy Spirit within you?* (1 Cor 6:19)
>
> "If I had understood, as I do today, that in this tiny palace of my soul, such a great King is living, I would not have left him alone so often." – St. Teresa of Avila

The indwelling is most appropriately associated with the Holy Spirit, because the indwelling is an act of love and the Holy Spirit proceeds from the love within the Trinity (recall that the love between the Father and Son is so perfect, complete, self-giving and fruitful that it is actually a person, the Holy Spirit). But where one person of the Trinity acts, all are present. So, the Father and Son are also present in our souls with the indwelling of the Spirit.

This reality is something we need to accept by faith, fostered by the words of scripture and teachings of the Saints. In many instances God will give the consolation of sensing His presence in our soul and we may become assured of the indwelling through the experience of peace "which surpasses understanding." But whether or not we receive these affirmations of the indwelling we must accept in faith that God is dwelling in us.

But we do, in fact, know the Spirit through our reason and our experience.

One way in which we can relate to the Holy Spirit is through parenthood. Good parents desire the best things for their children. They want their children to be able to "make the most of their gifts". And, good parents work to pass on family traditions and plan for their children's inheritance.

In a similar way, God gave us our marvelous gifts of intellect and will – in His own likeness. But those gifts cannot operate on their own, or at least not to their fullest capacity. Our minds must be illumined and our wills strengthened by the Spirit. This what St. Paul is speaking of in Romans: "I do not do the good I want, but I do the evil I do not want." (Rom 7:19) So, God prepared a way for us to make the most of our gifts. In Romans Chapter 8, St. Paul tells us "But you are not in the flesh; on the contrary, you are in the spirit, if only the Spirit of God dwells in you." (Rom 8:9)

And what of our *spiritual Tradition* – our precious faith – it is the Spirit that unlocks the mysteries of scripture and reveals Jesus (who is Truth). "But when he comes, the Spirit of truth, he will guide you to all truth." (Jn 16:13) And what of our *spiritual inheritance* – Heaven? The Spirit is our guide and counselor in this life so that we can arrive safely to our Heavenly home. Consider Philippians: "I am confident of this, that the one who began a good work in you will continue to complete it until the day of Christ Jesus." (Phil 1:6)

Everyday experiences of the Holy Spirit include the operation of our conscience (that "little voice") and experiences of consolation. We also experience the Holy Spirit through the Body of Christ when we come together in community and experience a deeper connectedness than mere human interaction can explain.

BAPTISM IN THE SPIRIT

No discussion of the Holy Spirit is complete without mentioning *Baptism in the Spirit*. We have discussed that grace is a gift from God, that it is a share in divine life. We also discussed that grace cannot fully operate in us until we accept it. Most often when we are baptized (and if we receive the Sacrament of Confirmation), we are not, at that time, in a position of maturity to fully accept the grace of that sacrament. In this case the grace of the sacrament is said to be "tied" – it is constrained by our lack of mature acceptance. The grace does not operate in us, miracles do not occur; it is similar to how Jesus was not received in his hometown: "Jesus could not perform many miracles because of their lack of faith." (Mt 13:58)

When we come to the point where we can say with our mind and heart "Jesus is Lord" the grace is released. The Spirit enters and flows through us. This is Baptism in the Spirit. Sometimes it unfolds slowly other times quite powerfully and spontaneously at that moment when the soul is truly ready to receive the Holy Spirit. If you have experienced this influx of the Spirit, you would know it. If not, or if you are uncertain, then *pray for the grace*. Pray for the coming of the Holy Spirit.

Baptism in the Spirit releases the theological virtue of supernatural faith in a pronounced way. We realize with a new certainty beyond simple human understanding that God is absolutely real and is absolutely who He says He is.

WE COME HARDWIRED FOR COMMUNION WITH GOD

Finally, recall our spiritual soul. Our soul is spirit. Why did God create man with a spiritual soul? For communion. To be able to share in the communion of the Trinity. In Genesis God breathes His Spirit into man. Our spirit communing with *the Spirit*. This is what we were made for. This is what Jesus desired so much to restore in us. His Spirit dwelling with our spirit. And what does the Holy Spirit do? He reveals Christ: "But when he comes, the Spirit of truth, he will guide you to all truth." (Jn 16:13). And what does Christ do? He reveals His Father: "No one knows the Son except the Father, and no one knows the Father except the Son and anyone to whom the Son wishes to reveal him." (Mt 11:27) It is through our spiritual soul that we are restored to communion with the Trinity.

Please spend 7 minutes in silent prayer; talking with God about today's session.

Let's close in prayer:

Lord Jesus Christ, help me to be ever more aware of Your nearness and Your great love for me. Amen.

Pearls from Day 14: The Humanity of Jesus and the Indwelling of the Holy Spirit

Our heavenly Father is not only gazing down upon us at every moment, He also desires to be close to us, as close as can be. He does this through His Son and His Spirit.

Our first principle was the Primacy of God's Action and Law of Love. God always takes the initiative and loves us first.

This brings us to our second principle - that God gives himself to us through the humanity of Jesus. This is God's greatest act of love. *For God so loved the world that he gave his only Son, so that everyone who believes in him might not perish but might have eternal life.* (Jn 3:16)

Our faith, then, is inherently incarnational since it is through the incarnation of Jesus Christ that we are redeemed and reunited with the Father.

In Christian Meditation we primarily focus on the life of Christ because it is through His incarnation that God has fully revealed His plan for our salvation, which is His plan for reuniting us with Himself. Christ also gives us a model of what it means to be perfectly human.

The third principle is the Indwelling of the Holy Spirit. Jesus tells us that it is better that He departs so that we can receive His Spirit. It is through the Spirit that God dwells *in* us. It is through this indwelling that God heals our fallen nature. *I am confident of this, that the one who began a good work in you will continue to complete it until the day of Christ Jesus.* (Phil 1:6)

No discussion of the Holy Spirit is complete without mentioning Baptism in the Spirit. The graces of baptism and confirmation are tied to our full acceptance. When we come to the point where we can say with our mind and heart "Jesus is Lord" the grace is released. The Spirit enters and flows through us. This is Baptism in the Spirit.

God created man with a spiritual soul to be able to share in the communion of the Trinity. In Genesis God breathes His Spirit into man. Our spirit communing with *the Spirit* - this is what we were made for. This is what Jesus desired so much to restore in us. His Spirit dwelling with our spirit. And what does the Holy Spirit do? He reveals Christ: "But when he comes, the Spirit of truth, he will guide you to all truth." (Jn 16:13). And what does Christ do? He reveals His Father: "No one knows the Son except the Father, and no one knows the Father except the Son and anyone to whom the Son wishes to reveal him." (Mt 11:27)

Thus, it is through our spiritual soul that we are restored to communion with the Trinity.

Your Pearls from Day 14

DAY 15: WEEK 2 – PUTTING IT ALL TOGETHER WITH ASCETICISM

> Welcome to the end of Week 2 of our retreat! This past week we focused on dispositions and principles that help us grow in relationship with God. Dispositions and principles are very much concerned with how we grow our interior life. It is a curious reality that we grow our interior life by becoming small; we must become small so that God becomes big in our life. How do we become small? That is the role of asceticism.

Let's begin with opening prayer:

Come Holy Spirit, make of me a fitting dwelling place for the Lord.

YOUR JUNGLE MISSION

You've been noticing changes in yourself. Physically, you're in better condition than ever before; better than you thought possible for that matter. Your thinking is also much clearer; you are more and more able to assess a situation and determine the best course of action without much or any assistance. What's more, you've gained the confidence to set about your decision without handwringing or delay. You're

Day 15 (Week 2, Day 7)

also finding yourself much more aware of the needs of those around you – perhaps because you've become more confident and capable of taking care of yourself. And you no longer miss the cheap distractions and comforts of your former life. Your daily experiences are so much richer than anything projected on a screen – the relationships and challenges of your jungle mission are deeply fulfilling.

And it's not just you who is noticing the changes. The more experienced nomads have made similar observations about your growth. In fact, the way you relate to the experienced nomads has changed. They're still far advanced to be sure, but they no longer seem impossibly far advanced. You are now experiencing for yourself how they came to the level of experience, knowledge and discipline that they possess. You see yourself following that same Way.

What's more, the newest arrivals are now looking up to you as one of the experienced nomads. Now there's a switch! And a great responsibility....

Without doubt, the aspect of your transformation you find most satisfying is the ability to say "no" to yourself. When you first arrived (and for all your life prior to that) you were a slave to your emotions, desires and weaknesses. How many times would you give in to an impulse only to regret it soon after? There was an inner voice (it was in you, but yet it wasn't really your voice) constantly tugging you down the wrong path. You were trapped on the emotional rollercoaster of doing the things you knew were not good for you and not doing the things you knew were and then beating yourself up about it. Only to repeat the pattern.

The closer you followed the example of the Savior and the

more you called on His Spirit for guidance, the stronger you became at saying "no" to that misleading voice. It was difficult at first, but now that you think about it you realize how natural it has become.

Asceticism and Happiness

Today is the last day of Week 2 and the last day of each week is when we tie everything together. This week we have been looking at dispositions and principles that are particularly effective for advancing our spiritual growth. The dispositions are associated with our nature. They are faith, trust, purity of intention, humility and fortitude. Our three principles are the initiative God the Father and law of Love, the incarnation of the God the Son and the indwelling of God the Spirit. They focus on how we relate to the three persons of the Trinity.

Asceticism is a practice that compliments these dispositions and principles and is indispensable for spiritual growth.

Asceticism. We envision Monte Python skits of people whipping themselves, or people forcing themselves to watch *Ishtar*.

In a more positive vein, we might associate asceticism with St. Paul's comments about "competing well for the faith" and how "athletes deprive themselves of all manner of things."

Indeed, St. Paul's teachings get right to the point since *ascetical* comes from the Greek word meaning exercise or effort. Traditionally asceticism is particularly associated with the first two ages of the interior life – purgative and illuminative – in which we are purifying ourselves and growing in holiness. In most general terms, asceticism is the "science of spiritual perfection" (A. Tanquerey, *The Spiritual Life*). The Catechism defines asceticism as "the practice of penance, mortification and self-denial to promote greater self-mastery and to foster the way of perfection by embracing the way of the cross."

Asceticism is part of our path to holiness. And for us, holiness and happiness are the same thing. The world does not want us to associate asceticism with happiness. But, then again, the world does not really want us to be happy, either.

So let's take a very practical look at how asceticism relates both to happiness in our everyday life and to the sanctification of our eternal soul.

Two Approaches to Spiritual Growth

Our discussions of dispositions and principles repeatedly reference the three enemies of our spiritual growth: our fallen nature, the world and satan and his minions. And we have talked about the poisonous fruit they cultivate, such as fear – the enemy of trust; pride - the enemy of purity of intention and humility; and, irresoluteness, fatigue and boredom – the enemies of fortitude. In a similar way we saw how our three principles (the actions of God the Father, Son and Holy Spirit) reveal God's work to redeem us and free us from the slavery of sin and our fallen nature.

So, there are two sides to the coin. On one side is filling ourselves with God and growing in holiness; on the other is emptying ourselves of sinful attachments and turning from evil.

For the past five days we have mostly focused on the "filling" and the "growing" side of the coin. To be certain, as we do this, we naturally combat sin and evil in our life. For example, growth in humility naturally combats our pride. But that is an indirect way of attacking the enemy. We also have at our disposal a way to make a direct frontal assault, and that is asceticism.

First, we must understand that when we consider the three enemies, there is not much we can do about the world and satan. The world is fallen and will be until Christ's return. And satan is beyond redemption.

But there is much we can do about ourselves. And that is great news, because it turns out of the three enemies, we ourselves are the worst. St. John Cassian, a towering figure from the period of the Desert Fathers, puts it well: "No one is more my enemy than my own heart which is the one of the household closest to me." And similarly, from St. Bernard: "The enemy that dwells with us in the same house injures us most."

Asceticism is how we battle and overcome our fallen nature, destroy our unhealthy attachments and are rid of the "false self" so that we can become fully who God created us to be. As we do this, we're also doing the best things we can to minimize the evil influences of the world and satan, because we no longer collaborate with evil, we no longer give in to the allurements of the world and we take away satan's strongholds in our lives – the places where he worms in with his lies, deceptions and perversions.

As we empty and purify ourselves through asceticism, we make more and more room for God and His goodness (through prayer and good works).

Asceticism is for Everyone

We must understand that asceticism is for everyone. God desires freedom for everyone, not just a chosen few monks and cloistered nuns. And, really – who doesn't want to be free? Of course, the real challenge is embracing the work of becoming free. But there is more than just wanting freedom – that's really just a by-product. We should embrace asceticism because God instructs us to do so. And, if God instructs us to do so, it must be important to our salvation (the disposition of trust).

Jesus says, "Whoever wishes to come after me must deny himself." (Mt 16:24) And He says, "Amen, amen, I say to you, unless a grain of wheat falls to the ground and dies, it remains just a grain of wheat; but if it dies, it produces much fruit. Whoever loves his life loses it, and whoever hates his life in this world will preserve it for eternal life." (Jn 20:24-25)

Jesus is talking about the problem of clinging to worldly things and placing them above the spiritual reality for which we are created. We must die to our worldly attachments if we are to bear fruit. The culprit here, and what we must grow to "hate", is our fallen nature; also referred to as "the flesh".

St. Paul says, "The flesh lusts against the spirit and the spirit against the flesh; the two are directly opposed" (Gal. 5:17).

And so asceticism is necessary for each and every one of us to grow in holiness and experience the transformation we all desire and that God desires for us.

St. John Chrysostom says, "You greatly delude yourself and err, if you think that one thing is demanded from the layman and another from the monk ... Because all must rise to the same height; and what has turned the world upside down is that we think only the monk must live rigorously, while the rest are allowed to live a life of indolence."

And we all suffer from the same effects of original sin. St. Paul says that he sees a principle in himself that "I do not do the good I want, but I do the evil I do not want." (Rom 7:19) We all have that principle in us, and we all endure great suffering because of it. God desires to free us from that suffering: "You will know the truth, and the truth will set you free" (Jn 8:32). Jesus is that truth, and a large part of how we come to Him and his freedom is by leaving our fallen self through asceticism.

So asceticism is for all of us. And, just as with mental prayer, we really can't advance in the spiritual life without asceticism.

Mental prayer is particularly necessary to make God big in our life.

Asceticism is particularly necessary to make ourselves small.

The two work hand-in-hand.

Asceticism is a Great Gift

Asceticism really is the gift that keeps giving.

We are created for God. As we discussed with our three principles – this is why we have a spiritual soul, so that we can commune with God. But due to the fall we look to satisfy that longing with things other than God, and particularly with pleasure, ease and comfort (that is why we are our own worst enemy). The world and satan are all too happy to oblige this disordered thirst with all manner of cheap substitutes for God.

As we often point out, "ease and comfort" look different for everyone. For a workaholic it looks like working 20 hours a day. The world might hold that up as an ideal of discipline and achievement. But, in fact, it's a disordered search for comfort in the success and distraction that comes easily to the workaholic. Here we provide the standard disclaimer – there is nothing wrong with good hard work, the Saints were tremendous laborers *in the vineyard* – and that's the point, we must always be working for God.

All of us have our own areas of brokenness and weakness (our own "core wound" or "predominant flaw") – whether it's greed, gluttony, lust, anger, vanity, sloth or outright pride; we become enslaved to our weakness.

Think of the expressions we use – "I'm powerless against…," "I can't say no to…," "I just fall into…," "No matter what I do I find myself…." More often than not, rather than tearing out these weaknesses at the root, we rationalize them. The enemy is genius at marketing his goods and services and loves to trot out aphorisms to trick us to accept our wounds and enslavement by making us feel "empowered" and "free to be ourselves," because "I am who I am," "it's all good," "everyone else does it," "I don't have to change," and so on. But that is not freedom. It is merely a way of repackaging the fact that we are slaves to our weaknesses. It is not freedom if we can't look at someone without lust. It is not freedom to be powerless at a dessert buffet. It is not freedom to be drawn into gossip and then regret it later.

True freedom is when we have the power to say "no" to any evil inclination and "take it or leave it" when it comes to pleasures and indulgences. Then the world and the enemy have no power over us.

When we gain self-mastery and empty ourselves of attachments we are more available to fill ourselves with God and the things of God.

How it Works

The goal of asceticism is the destruction of what is sometimes thought of as the "false self" or the ego or what St. Paul calls the "old man." This comes forth when we operate from our pride; that determination that "I know best." I know best how to use my time. I know best how to plan for my future. I know best how to help my neighbor. I know best how to arrange for my own leisure and entertainment. I know best that five donuts are far better than one.

The shift that must take place is to seek God's will in all things and follow that path ("I am the Way, the Truth and the Life" .... "Deny yourself, take up your cross and *follow me*"). Yes, we must also use our own God-given intellect, but the goal is that everything we do begins, ends and is carried out with God.

We are very quick to put God aside and move ahead with our own plans.

Ascetical practices counteract that. They push our will aside so we can move ahead with God's plans.

Some or all of this may be familiar ground for you, but we'll start at the beginning for completeness.

In principle asceticism is quite simple. The spiritual masters consistently distinguish between interior and exterior *mortification*, where mortification means to subdue our desires. Exterior mortification purifies our exterior senses (associated with things we watch, touch, listen to and eat). Gluttony and lust are desires that we master with exterior mortification. Interior mortification purifies our interior senses from disordered passions of pride, greed, anger, sloth and envy.

We mortify ourselves by choking off the oxygen to our disordered desires. We often know for ourselves where we should start with our mortification. Where are we weak? Where do we give in and then regret it? If it isn't clear, bring it to prayer.

Let's look at a simple example. Say, we have an oversized sweet tooth and tend to overindulge. We should start with an ascetical practice that is meaningful, but achievable. Perhaps we decide to give up dessert two days a week. That's it, we're done. We stick with that commitment come what may. It will be hard at first, but in time it will come naturally. And then we bring it back to prayer, and we let God lead us from there. God will lead us to either grow that mortification or move to something else.

The same holds with interior mortification. If we are prone to anger, then we want to find a small and achievable way to start managing our anger. Is there a specific situation that routinely rouses our anger? How can we avoid that situation? Enter into these self-assessments in the company of the Holy Spirit – pray for His guidance to show you what to give up or change.

Asceticism is foremost a spiritual practice. Our dispositions are particularly helpful. We enter into asceticism in faith and trust that this is doing good, that God is guiding and working through this (again this is why we start small to get the ball rolling – God will take it from there). Purity of intention – we're not doing this to get something out of it, "I've been doing this for a month now and I haven't lost a pound...", we do it because God desires it. Humility - recognizing we can do nothing good on our own. Everything good is accomplished through God – "With Christ I can do all things." Keep praying for the grace. On the flip side, we have to participate. It is God's grace, but we have to do our part – that is fortitude. We must keep showing up.

Day 15 (Week 2, Day 7)

If we fall ("the spirit is willing, but the flesh is weak"), ask forgiveness and start again. God makes all things new.

Recall from our discussion on humility that Christ warns us, "Amen, I say to you, unless you turn and become like children, you will not enter the Kingdom of heaven. Whoever becomes humble like this child is the greatest in the Kingdom of heaven." (Mt 18:4,5) We "turn and become like children" through asceticism, because we let go of our illusion of control and learn to embrace our littleness and dependence on God.

Again we repeat the importance of starting small and seeing it through. Backsliding in spiritual matters is very counterproductive because we have *three* enemies ready to pounce.

Lastly, asceticism is extremely empowering! As we start to gain mastery in one area we grow in confidence in all areas; similar to how when we grow in one virtue, we grow in all. But beware spiritual pride. If satan fails at keeping you from succeeding in your mortification he will try to rob you of that victory by twisting it to pride. It is all for God's glory!

Closing Comments

Asceticism is a perfect complement to our principles and dispositions; they all work together to help us overcome our fallen nature and unite ourselves to Christ.

Here are some final pearls from scripture:

...he has bestowed on us the precious and very great promises, so that through them you may come to share in the divine nature, after escaping from the corruption that is in the world because of evil desire. (2 Pt 1:4)

But whoever is joined to the Lord becomes one spirit with him. (1 Cor 6:17)

Asceticism is our path to being freed from corruption and joined to Christ. That is how we follow Him in this life. And into the next.

Please spend 7 minutes in silent prayer; talking with God about today's session.

Let's close in prayer:

Lord Jesus Christ, help me to be ever more aware of Your nearness and Your great love for me. Amen.

Day 15 (Week 2, Day 7)

Pearls from Day 15: Week 2 - Putting It All Together with Asceticism

St. Paul points to asceticism with comments about "competing well for the faith" and how "athletes deprive themselves of all manner of things."

In broad terms, asceticism is the "science of spiritual perfection" (A. Tanquerey, *The Spiritual Life*). The Catechism defines it as "the practice of penance, mortification and self-denial to promote greater self-mastery and to foster the way of perfection by embracing the way of the cross." (CCC definition of *Ascesis*)

Asceticism is how we battle and overcome our fallen nature, destroy our unhealthy attachments and are rid of the "false self" so that we can become fully who God created us to be. As we do this, we're also doing the best things to minimize the evil influences of the world and satan, because we no longer give in to the allurements of the world and we take away satan's strongholds in our lives – the places where he worms in with his lies, deceptions, temptations and perversions.

We must understand that asceticism is for everyone. God desires freedom for everyone, not just a chosen few monks and cloistered nuns. St. John Chrysostom says, "You greatly delude yourself and err, if you think that one thing is demanded from the layman and another from the monk ... Because all must rise to the same height; and what has turned the world upside down is that we think only the monk must live rigorously, while the rest are allowed to live a life of indolence."

We are all created for God. We were all created for greatness in this life. But due to the fall we look to satisfy that longing with things other than God, and particularly with pleasure, ease, and comfort (that is why we are our own worst enemy). All of us have our own areas of brokenness and weakness (our own "core wound" or "predominant fault") – whether it's greed, gluttony, lust, anger, vanity, sloth or outright pride; we become enslaved to our weakness.

True freedom is when we have the power to say "no" to any evil inclination and can "take it or leave it" when it comes to pleasures and indulgences. When we gain self-mastery and empty ourselves of attachments through asceticism, we are more available to fill ourselves with love of God and neighbor.

In principle asceticism is quite simple. The spiritual masters consistently distinguish between interior and exterior mortification, where "mortification" means to subdue our desires. Exterior mortification purifies our exterior senses (associated with things we see, taste, touch and hear). Gluttony and lust are desires that we master with exterior mortification. Interior mortification purifies our interior senses from disordered passions of pride, greed, anger, sloth and envy.

We mortify ourselves by choking off the oxygen to our disordered desires. We often know for ourselves where we should start with our mortification. Where are we weak? Where do we give in and then regret it? But if it isn't clear, bring it to prayer. Then settle on a modest, achievable discipline (e.g. skipping dessert twice a week) and stick to it (backsliding is very counterproductive).

As we start to gain mastery in one area we grow in confidence in all areas; similar to how when we grow in one virtue, we grow in all. But beware spiritual pride. It is all for God's glory.

Your Pearls from Day 15

WEEK 3
MEDITATION, OUR STARTING POINT

(each session followed by 10 minutes of meditation)

DAY 16: MEDITATION – INTO THE SILENCE, TO KNOW GOD AND LISTEN TO HIM

> Welcome to Week 3 of our retreat! The musical *The King and I* gave us the wonderful song *Getting to Know You*. You can probably hear the melody as you read these lyrics (if not, you owe it to yourself to pull up the Marni Nixon version):

Getting to know you. Getting to know all about you.
Getting to like you. Getting to hope you like me.

We can't truly like someone we don't know. We can't deeply love someone we don't know. This is where meditation comes in – to better know and love God. And as a bonus – we don't have to "hope He likes us" – He loved each of us perfectly from before the beginning of time. *Where* is it that we come to know God? In silence. And what else happens in that silence? We hear Him.

Come Holy Spirit, make of me a fitting dwelling place for the Lord.

Day 16 (Week 3, Day 1)

Your Jungle Mission

You cannot put your finger on how it changed or when, but it was definitely different. It's one of those things that evolves right before you, but slowly enough that you don't notice the day-to-day changes until something causes you to take stock and recognize it's no longer what it used to be.

When He first saved you from becoming prey to that giant snake, He was so strange and different – He seemed almost unreal. And when you joined up with the other nomads He seemed impossibly far above you. The experienced nomads themselves seemed impossibly far advanced from you, and He was so far above them.

You found it difficult to be in His presence. You were awkward and stiff. Sometimes you were overly formal. Other times, especially when you were tired and wanted something, you were not respectful enough. And you never felt like you were being yourself around Him. The issue, you knew, wasn't Him – He was always perfectly Himself and perfectly welcoming. The issue was you.

At some point that all changed, and that's what you can't exactly put your finger on, but it definitely changed. Amidst all His teaching, all your walks together, all your conversations, all His care for you – somewhere during all of that you had grown to have a real relationship with Him. You had grown to be more yourself with Him (in fact, you had become more yourself with yourself).

Somewhere along the Way, you and the Savior had become friends.

MENTAL PRAYER – A LOVING RELATIONSHIP

Before starting on our mission, or any other significant undertaking, we must prepare. And that's what we've been doing for these past two weeks.

Today we move ahead and take the first formal step on our journey of mental prayer. It may seem like a modest first step – but make no mistake, today is monumental! The greatest adventures begin with that first step. Think of whatever is the most significant experience in your life – your marriage, birth of a child, overcoming a great challenge, whatever it is – think back to the very first step that put you on that path. At the time you probably didn't even realize the significance of that first step. It may have seemed like a very ordinary first step. Now you recognize it was the start of something extraordinary.

That is what today is all about.

And with our first formal step into Christian meditation we are going to look from a very high level at the approach you'll be taking. We want to see the entire landscape of your session of Christian meditation. Then, for the rest of the week, we will look at separate elements in detail.

Recall from Day 2 that mental prayer is distinguished as meditation and contemplation. We play a much more active role in mediation, whereas in contemplation we are almost completely passive.

Meditation is the mode of prayer with which we begin. It is also the mode of prayer for the purgative age of our interior life. Contemplation is the mode of prayer that God may lead us to if we are among the fortunate few who arrive at the unitive age in this life. In between (the illuminative age) we transition from the most active meditation (discursive meditation) to a more passive meditation (affective meditation or affective prayer) and finally to the initial stage of contemplation.

In meditation we use our faculties of thought, imagination,

Day 16 (Week 3, Day 1)

emotion and memory, and focus them through sacred scripture and spiritual reading to open our minds and hearts to the Lord; to better know Him and His will for us and to better love Him and our neighbor. Meditating on God and His Truth is akin to spending time with a friend and getting to know them. You learn how God cares for you when you meditate on Christ's healings and the details of what He said and did with someone as He healed them. You learn God's road map for holiness in this life when you meditate on the Sermon on the Mount. You learn what God looks like when you meditate on Christ's words that if you see Him you see the Father.

Meditation is generally distinguished between two types: "discursive meditation" and "affective meditation". Discursive implies moving from one idea to another. In prayer, we allow one truth to lead us to other ideas and truths. We don't "force" it. We let the relationship unfold. We let the Holy Spirit lead us. This is counter-intuitive because of how we typically learn a new subject. We want an outline, a syllabus. *Cliff's Notes* would be nice.

But that is how you learn geometry. That is not how you fall in love with someone. You let the relationship unfold. So too with God. Today you might meditate on the nativity. Tomorrow the Spirit might lead you to the last supper. Each day is a new adventure, a new discovery. Through discursive meditation we deepen our understanding and belief of the mysteries of the faith; particularly the mysteries of the life of Christ (the Rosary can be a powerful meditative prayer in this regard).

As we become more convicted of the great Truths of Christianity, meditation becomes simpler and quieter (this may occur over many years). This is distinguished as *affective meditation* (or simply, *affective prayer*). In this case the heart is engaged more than the mind. We are no longer able to engage in extended periods of discursive meditation. Now, simple expressions of devout affections dominate our prayer (simple expressions of praise, thanksgiving, or petitions for

Grace such as "Lord, help me to better love you"). This focus on our affections for God is, of course, the source of the term *affective* prayer.

We again emphasize that expressions like "devout affections" aren't just flowery talk. As we meditate more and more on the life of Christ, we come to experience for ourselves the words of St. John: "The way we came to know love, was that he laid down his life for us." (1 Jn 3:16) Through meditation we come to truly understand the depth of self-sacrifice of Jesus, personally, for us. We meet Jesus, as God who also became true man – like us in all ways except sin. He *willed* himself to fully experience, and suffer, all the things that we experience and suffer. Why? Yes, to save us, but also to show and teach us what a perfectly human life looks like.

What do you say to someone who has done a great kindness for you? "I'm at a loss for words..." and "Thank you' doesn't even begin to cover it!" This is the point we come to with Christ in our meditation – a point where we become so aware of Christ's love for us (through discursive meditation) that thoughts and words become wholly insufficient and we are left with simple expressions of wonder, remorse, gratitude, humility, and love. This is the transition to affective prayer, and ultimately to contemplation.

We find, once more, Christian meditation and contemplation are fundamentally different from eastern varieties of meditation (yoga, Buddhism, mindfulness, etc.). In Christian mental prayer we open ourselves up to the Triune God so that He can do His work in us. To the extent that we quiet ourselves and endeavor to empty ourselves (especially of distractions from our lower faculties), it is so we can be filled by the Triune God.

The Catechism provides the following insights (CCC 2705-2708):

"Meditation is above all a quest. The mind seeks to understand the why and how of the Christian life in order to adhere and respond to what the Lord is asking. The required attentiveness is difficult to sustain. We are usually helped by books,

Day 16 (Week 3, Day 1)

and Christians do not want for them: the Sacred Scriptures, particularly the Gospels, holy icons, liturgical texts of the day or season, writings of the spiritual fathers, works of spirituality, the great book of creation, and that of history the page on which the "today" of God is written.

To meditate on what we read helps us to make it our own by confronting it with ourselves. Here, another book is opened: the book of life. We pass from thoughts to reality. To the extent that we are humble and faithful, we discover in meditation the movements that stir the heart and we are able to discern them. It is a question of acting truthfully in order to come into the light: "Lord, what do you want me to do?"

There are as many and varied methods of meditation as there are spiritual masters. Christians owe it to themselves to develop the desire to meditate regularly, lest they come to resemble the three first kinds of soil in the parable of the sower. But a method is only a guide; the important thing is to advance, with the Holy Spirit, along the one way of prayer: Christ Jesus

Meditation engages thought, imagination, emotion, and desire. This mobilization of faculties is necessary in order to deepen our convictions of faith, prompt the conversion of our heart, and strengthen our will to follow Christ. Christian prayer tries above all to meditate on the mysteries of Christ, as in *lectio divina* or the rosary. This form of prayerful reflection is of great value, but Christian prayer should go further: to the knowledge of the love of the Lord Jesus, to union with him."

As noted in the Catechism and discussed last week, there is no single method of mental prayer that is *the* approach to mental prayer. Rather, there are universal guiding dispositions and principles which we learned about last week.

St. Teresa of Avila, as we have said, spent very little time on method. She reinforced that what is most important is to grow in virtue and resist everything that is not of God: "If you would progress a long way on this road and ascend to the Mansions of your desire, the important thing is not to think much, but to love much."

OUR INITIAL APPROACH

Be that as it may, we must start somewhere, and the Saints and other spiritual masters have repeatedly pointed to methods for beginners with similar fundamental steps. As it happens these methods can be summarized with words starting with "R" and you will see these methods outlined with anywhere from three to five R's.

Here we will work with five R's: Recollect, Read, Reflect, Relate, Resolve. Again, you will find many versions of this approach to Christian meditation, sometimes with different names, different order or with different steps combined, but all work to the same end. Most importantly, all these methods point to the priceless R-word - RELATIONSHIP. Always have in mind that mental prayer is about growing in *relationship* with God ("the One who we know loves us"), and everything else will fall into place.

We will briefly introduce the five steps here and spend more time with them over the next few days.

Recollect: Take a few minutes to bring yourself into the presence of God. St. Ignatius of Loyola describes this as entering into His gaze. God is already there with you, gazing down upon you (He also dwells within you). This is a time for you to turn your gaze from worldly things to God. You might find it helpful to think of yourself as physically turning toward Him. You might also call to mind that God dwells within you. Or, call to mind times when you were particularly aware of God (moments of grace and even small miracles in your life) is remarkably effective; you can "taste" those moments again.

Read: Enter into Sacred Scripture or other good spiritual reading. This is decidedly a case of quality over quantity; you may only end up reading a few sentences. The simplest and best place to start is with the life of Christ in the Gospels or with the Psalms.

Day 16 (Week 3, Day 1)

Reflect: Now is the time to enter into deeper meditation with your reading. Reflection is the first formal step of meditation (recollection and reading are preparation) and is primarily an activity of the intellect. As you read, when something captures your attention, pause and sit with it. Invite the Holy Spirit to bring you *light* and *insight*. Savor the small details. Place yourself into the particular passage. If it's a scene in the Gospel, put yourself in it. What are the sounds, smells, sights and activities going on about you? Consider the circumstances of the passage – who, what, when, where, why and how? Why did the Holy Spirit guide you to that specific passage? What is God, in His love for you, specifically and personally saying to you?

Relate: This is the highpoint of meditation and when we are most fully engaged in conversation with God. This is primarily an act of the will. Our reflection stirs our heart – over time with increasing love for God. Speak with Christ about what has been stirred in your heart and give time, in silence, for Him to respond.

Resolve: As you come to the end of your meditation it is appropriate to give thanks to God for his goodness. Thank God simply for the gift of spending time with Him and for the revelation He has given you through this time of meditation. Even if meditation "felt" dry, have utmost faith that it *was* fruitful – just in ways unknown to you at the moment. Thanksgiving should flow into a specific resolution (another important R-word). Determine one concrete action you can take with you for the rest of the day to put into practice what was revealed to you by the Holy Spirit. For example: perhaps you are inspired to be mindful to say a short prayer for anyone who frustrates you or tries your patience. If you can't come up with a specific resolution, then take a phrase, thought or image from your reflection and repeat it throughout the day.

Resolution should also include *Reconciliation*. We are often shown a specific shortcoming as part of our reflection. Resolution is a good time to ask the Lord's forgiveness (and to determine to bring it to the Sacrament of Reconciliation). This self-awareness can also be a good source for the specific resolution you carry with you for the day - focused to counteract the specific shortcoming.

SACRED SILENCE

It is with precision that today's session is titled "Into the Silence – To Know God and Listen to Him." Mental prayer is necessarily *silent* prayer. Christ teaches us this. Christ was fully divine – He was one with God the Father. But Christ *willed* himself to be fully human. In Christ's humanity He experienced everything we do (except sin). Happiness, sadness, frustration, fear – all of it. Including fatigue and distraction. And so Christ would seek solitude – in the desert, the wilderness, on a mountain top – so that He could join with the Father in prayer. Christ was teaching us how to meditate.

The virtue of solitude is silence. Sacred silence. We are not simply removing ourselves from the noise and distraction of the world. We are removing ourselves from the noise and distraction of the world so that we can draw close to God. So that we can meditate on Him and hear His "still, small voice." From Mother Teresa:

> "We need to find God, and He cannot be found in noise and restlessness. God is the friend of silence. See how nature - trees, flowers, grass - grows in silence; see the stars, the moon and sun, how they move in silence. ... The more we receive in silent prayer, the more we can give in our active life. We need silence to be able to touch souls. The essential thing is not what we say, but what God says to us and through us. All our words will be useless unless they come from within - words which do not give the light of Christ increase the darkness."

That really is the whole point of our time of meditation. As a general rule, meditation is not about petitions or discerning major decisions. Our general petitions and intercessions should be offered separately – this could certainly be *added* at the end of our time of

Day 16 (Week 3, Day 1)

meditation – but petitions and intercessions should never be the focus of our time of meditation.

It is the same with discernment (e.g. Should I marry this person? or, Should I change jobs?). We should absolutely strive to make all decisions with and in the Lord, and we should absolutely set aside dedicated prayer time to discern major decisions. But that should generally be separate from our meditation time. Our meditation time is about God's agenda, not ours. It could be that the Lord will redirect our meditation time to the issue we wish to discern – but in that case it's the Lord's initiative not our agenda.

So it is in Sacred Silence (silence in the company of God) that we come to know Him and hear him speaking to us.

Today you should extend your time in silence to 10 minutes. But today you will be entering into that silence with the assistance of the 5 R's. You can pull up any of the 'guided meditations' on the *Interior Life* app to assist you with your time of meditation. This will be our approach to meditation for the remainder of this retreat. From there it will evolve; along with your life-long relationship with God through daily mental prayer.

Let's close in prayer:

Lord Jesus Christ, help me to become ever more aware of Your nearness and Your great love for me. Amen.

.

Pearls from Day 16: Into the Silence – To Know God and Listen to Him

All great undertakings require careful preparation. That is what we have been doing for the past two weeks. We now turn our attention from preparation to proceeding with Christian mental prayer.

By way of review, Christian mental prayer transitions from meditation to contemplation as we move through the purgative, illuminative and unitive stages.

We start with discursive meditation. Discursive simply means that we move from concept to concept. The point of meditation is to grow closer to God and to convict ourselves of the great truths of God, in particular the life of Christ. It is by meditating on these great truths (for example Christ' passion), in the presence of the Holy Spirit, that we come to truly know and love God and listen to Him.

In discursive meditation our activity predominates – we use our intellect, imagination and memory to bring the object of our meditation to life. There is no one method or technique for meditation. Human nature, however, needs a place to start and many Saints and spiritual masters have developed approaches for their students, all of which are similar. We will use an approach of "five R's": Recollect, Read, Reflect, Relate and Resolve.

Recollect: Take a few minutes to bring yourself into the presence of God. St. Ignatius of Loyola describes this as entering into His gaze. God is already there with you, gazing down upon you.

Read: Enter into Scripture or other good spiritual reading. This is decidedly a case of quality over quantity; you may only end up reading a few sentences. The simplest and best place to start is with the life of Christ in the Gospels.

Reflect: Now is the time to enter into deeper meditation with your reading. Reflection is the first formal step of meditation (recollection and reading are preparation) and is primarily an activity of the intellect. As you read, when something captures your attention, pause and sit with it. Invite the Holy Spirit to bring you light and insight. Savor the small details.

Relate: This is the highpoint of meditation and when we are most fully engaged in conversation with God. This is primarily an act of the will. Our reflection stirs our heart, increasingly over time with love for God. Speak with God about what has been stirred in your heart and give time, in silence, for Him to respond.

Resolve: As you come to the end of your meditation it is appropriate to give thanks to God for his goodness and ask forgiveness for any shortcomings that have been raised. Determine one concrete action you can take with you for the rest of the day to put into practice what was revealed to you by the Holy Spirit.

The purpose of Christian meditation is getting to know God and to listen to Him. Christ teaches us by example that this requires silence, sacred silence. As a general rule, petitions, intercession and discernment of major life decisions should be done during a separate time of prayer.

Mental prayer is a school of Sacred Silence. We are not simply removing ourselves from the noise and distraction of the world. We are removing ourselves from the noise and distraction of the world so that we can draw close to God. So that we can meditate on Him and hear His "still, small voice."

Your Pearls from Day 16

DAY 17: CHRISTIAN MEDITATION
STEP 1 - RECOLLECTION

> Before an undertaking of grand scale, we take a moment to pull ourselves together, to remind ourselves of all we have done to arrive at this moment and then we take that step ... into the unknown future. That is the process of recollection – pulling ourselves together. And what undertaking is grander than a daily appointment with the Creator of the Universe?

Let's open with prayer:

Come Holy Spirit, make of me a fitting dwelling place for the Lord. Amen.

YOUR JUNGLE MISSION

Before setting out for the day you first spend time with the Savior. He always likes to meet with the nomads one-on-one (how does He make the time?)

You greet one another. He always asks how you slept, how you are feeling and what you'd like for breakfast.

You discuss the plan for the day; what you are likely to encounter and how you should prepare for it. Perhaps it will be an easy walk through the savannah. But the high grass could conceal snakes or other predators, so you will need to make plenty of noise to flush them out. Or, the day's journey may take you through hill country and you will need to plan for arduous hiking, taking your time with plenty of rest breaks so that you are not overcome with fatigue. The Savior has taught you that the jungle is not the place of careless mistakes.

The Savior then goes off to spend time with other nomads. It's going to be a full day and you return to your tent to pull together your gear for the day. As you do so you remind yourself of all the things He's taught and shown you in the past. And you call to mind His reassurances that He'll be there whenever you need Him.

IMMEDIATE PREPARATION FOR PRAYER

This first step of being recollected is also called the *immediate preparation* for our meditation. It is referred to as immediate because it is what we do at the moment we start meditation. There is also a *remote* preparation, which is everything else we do prior to our time of meditation; we will learn more about that in a few days.

Your immediate preparation in prayer includes your setting. We discussed this on the first day of the retreat. To recap, you should create your own oratory (place of prayer), a quiet, reverent, peaceful, comfortable place. Your setting should include a crucifix and other devotional items that are meaningful to you (such as a statue of Our Lady or image of the Sacred Heart). Your sitting position should be comfortable but not so comfortable that you are likely to doze off. You should choose a time of day that lends itself to prayer (when you're alert and free from disruptions) and stick with that time (it may need to be different on the weekends, but set a fixed time for the weekends as well). Once you get this aspect of your immediate preparation settled you do not need to revisit it; it simply becomes part of your prayer discipline.

STEP 1: RECOLLECTION

Recollection is your daily *immediate preparation* of your meditation.

One of our Lord's disciples demonstrates recollection:

Jesus was praying in a certain place, and when He had finished, one of His disciples said to Him, "Lord, teach us to pray just as John taught his disciples." (Lk 11:1)

The disciple was with Jesus. He must have been watching Jesus pray. Something stirred in his heart to move him to approach Jesus. The disciple is modeling recollection; he pulled himself together and approached Jesus.

We also need to be present with Jesus and approach Him to begin our meditation. As with any other conversation, it would be awkward for us to simply sit down and try to start deep meditation on scripture. Likewise, it would have been awkward for the disciple to just run up out of nowhere and ask Jesus to teach him to pray; the disciple was there waiting on Jesus. You are entering into conversation with God (who is also Creator of the Universe as well as Creator of You). It is appropriate to take a few minutes to clear your mind, approach God and greet Him properly.

If that last sentence seems a bit surreal to you, it should! We are talking about you, sitting down for a conversation with the Lord of Heaven and Earth, just the same as if you were sitting down to chat with your neighbor. In this life we will never be able to fully comprehend how both truly real and truly extraordinary this is, but we must always battle against the temptation to think that we are just sitting by ourselves or that God isn't truly and fully present with us.

On a side note, this calls to mind one of the endless tactics the enemy can try to use against you – to make you think to yourself "let's face it, I don't really believe God is sitting here with me right now." It is true that it can take much time, effort and prayer to accept the amazing reality of God's ever-presence. We must pray for the grace and use our faculties to exercise that grace. And it is exactly so that we will grow in our realization that God is always with us that we need to spend daily time in prayer with Him. So, don't let the enemy derail your good intentions and rob you of your time with God. Exercise your faith (our first disposition) and pray for more – "Lord, increase my faith!"

This is all part of being recollected, or placing ourselves in the presence of God. There are many ways to do this, and in time you will find what fits most naturally with your personal relationship with God. Here are several approaches, which can be used individually or in combination.

1. Remind yourself that this time of prayer is a conversation with God and is every bit as real as speaking with a friend (it's actually more real – God is reality itself and knows you better than you know yourself).

2. Don't be distracted or discouraged by the fact that your faculties (thoughts, impulses, imagination, memories) may tend to stray in different directions. Recall our session on human anthropology – our faculties are naturally disordered, and it will take time, discipline and patience to reign them in. Even then, take comfort in knowing the greatest Saints continued to struggle with distractions in prayer, but still received tremendous graces from their prayer. We will talk more about distraction later this week, it suffices for now to point out that we must simply do our best to keep drawing our mind and heart back to God. St. Bernard offered the following prayer: "Intentions, thoughts, desires, and my whole interior, come let us ascend the mountain, let us go to the place where

Day 17 (Week 3, Day 2)

the Lord sees or is seen. Cares, solicitudes, anxieties, labors, pains and external duties wait here for my return."

3. ACTS Prayer. ACTS is an acronym for Adoration, Contrition, Thanksgiving, Supplication (in their general order of importance). You can briefly touch on all four modes as you entire into recollection. As a simple example: "God you are so great" (Adoration); "I apologize for anything I've done that wasn't as loving as it should have been" (Contrition), "Thank you for your great love and being here with me now" (Thanksgiving); "Please come to my aid, help me in this time of prayer" (Supplication). Or, try praying Psalms 95 or 100, which are among the standard "Invitatory" psalms of the *Liturgy of the Hours*.

4. From our first principle: remind yourself, as a simple act of faith, that God is everywhere. God's sustaining presence is in all of creation (otherwise everything would cease to be). You might envision God the Father gazing down upon your right now.

5. From our second principle: call to mind the humanity of Jesus in whatever way is most familiar to you. In your imagination, place yourself in the presence of Jesus. Imagine yourself with him in a Gospel scene (perhaps as depicted in a movie or classic painting). Or, imagine Christ with you, sitting next to you.

6. From our third principle: remind yourself, as a simple act of faith, that God the Spirit is within you. This isn't simply His sustaining presence – He sustains aardvarks and sunflowers, but He doesn't *dwell* in them. The Triune God literally dwells in your soul.

7. Call to mind God's public miracles. Become very familiar with a few of God's great miracles – either from the Gospels or from public miracles that have been approved or found worthy of consideration by the Church such as the Fatima miracles, the Shroud of Turin, miraculous healings by the Saints, or the numerous Eucharistic miracles. Turn to these to revive your

faith and wonder. The ancient Israelites would continuously retell God's great deeds. For example, try praying with Psalm 77.

8. Call to mind past experiences of the presence of God and his goodness. These are the "pearls" we collected on Day 8. This could be from powerful life moments like your wedding day, the birth of a child or a tender moment at the passing of a loved one. Perhaps there was a time when you felt certain God orchestrated a fortuitous "coincidence" in your life. Perhaps God revealed himself to you in a powerful way while on a retreat. Perhaps you have encountered your Guardian Angel (it happens more often than most people realize).

9. Call to mind God in the Tabernacle or being in His presence in Eucharistic adoration.

It is also particularly suitable at the start of meditation to recognize our unworthiness and acknowledge that we are incapable of praying without God's grace and call upon the Holy Spirit to assist us: "God, come to my aid, make haste to help me!" and "Lord, teach me to pray!"

This first step of relating to God may only take a few minutes. However, a golden principle of the spiritual life is to follow consolation. If in your recollection you are strongly drawn to Him, stay with that. For example, perhaps you relate to God by envisioning Christ walking on water. But today He seems even more real and present and you have a sense of Him calling you out of the boat. The last thing to do is disengage from that experience of Christ because it's time to move onto your spiritual reading. In fact, if you end up spending your entire time of meditation close to God in recollection (for example, remaining with Christ on the water), that is an excellent meditation session. Praise God!

This returns us to our dispositions and principles. Recall Disposition #3 – humility. We must be ever smaller and God ever larger. "I must decrease that He might increase." This goes hand-in-hand

Day 17 (Week 3, Day 2)

with Principle #1 – the Primacy of God. God is infinite whether we recognize it or not. But He can't do His good work in us unless we acknowledge His primacy and follow His lead – if He wants to stay with you in recollection – then that's where you are meant to be.

In closing, the whole point of recollection is to lift ourselves to God, Who is already there, waiting on us.

Please spend 10 minutes in meditation either reflecting on today's session or today's Gospel reading (which you can pull up in the *Interior Life* app).

Let's close in prayer:

Lord Jesus Christ, help me to be ever more aware of Your nearness and Your great love for me. Amen.

Pearls from Day 17: Christian Meditation Step 1 - Recollection

Entering into prayer is to place yourself in the presence of God, who is also Creator of the Universe as well as Creator of you. It is appropriate to take a few minutes to clear your mind, approach God and greet Him properly.

It can take much time, effort and prayer to fully come to the amazing reality of God's ever-presence. We must pray for the grace and use our faculties to exercise that grace. And it's exactly so that we will grow in our realization that God is always with us that we need to spend daily time in prayer with Him.

This is all part of being recollected (or, placing yourself in the presence of God). There are many ways to do this, and in time you will find what fits most naturally with your personal relationship with God. Here are several approaches which can be used individually or in combination.

1. Remind yourself that this time of prayer is a conversation with God and is every bit as real as speaking with a friend (and it's actually more real – God is reality itself and knows you better than you know yourself).

2. Don't be distracted or discouraged by the fact that all your faculties (thoughts, impulses, imagination, memories) will tend to stray in different directions. Recall the session on human anthropology – our faculties are naturally disordered, and it will take time, discipline and patience to reign them in.

3. Pray the ACTS prayer – Adoration, Contrition, Thanksgiving, Supplication (see Psalm 100).

4. From our first principle: remind yourself, as a simple act of faith, that God is everywhere. You might envision God the Father gazing down upon you right now.

Day 17 (Week 3, Day 2)

5. From our second principle: call to mind the humanity of Jesus in whatever way is most familiar to you. In your imagination, place yourself in the presence of Jesus. Imagine yourself with him in a Gospel scene (perhaps as depicted in a movie or classic painting). Or, imagine Christ with you, sitting next to you.

6. From our third principle: remind yourself, as a simple act of faith, that God dwells within you. This isn't simply His sustaining presence – He sustains aardvarks and sunflowers, but He doesn't dwell in them.

7. Call to mind past experiences of the presence of God and his goodness. These are your personal "pearls" collected on Day 8.

8. Reflect on God's public miracles from Sacred Scripture or accepted modern miracles, such as Fatima, the Shroud of Turin, Eucharistic miracles, or miracles of the Saints (see Psalm 77).

9. Call to mind God in the Tabernacle or being in His presence in Eucharistic adoration.

A golden principle of the spiritual life is to follow consolation. If in your recollection you are strongly drawn to Him, stay with that. In fact, if you end up spending your entire time of meditation close to God in recollection, that is an excellent meditation session. Praise God!

Your Pearls from Day 17

DAY 18: CHRISTIAN MEDITATION STEPS 2 AND 3 – READ AND REFLECT

> My wife and I have this habit that when one of us reads something that really grabs us we will interrupt the other and share it. That same dynamic is at work with your meditation *reading* and *reflection*. Rest assured that God has a piece of Good News that He wants to share with you.

Come Holy Spirit, make of me a fitting dwelling place for the Lord.

YOUR JUNGLE MISSION

When you first entered into the jungle it seemed a place of constant noise and activity. In fact, it was overwhelming - foreign, confusing, and chaotic. In a strange way, it reminded you of your prior life in the world – full of noise and hustle and bustle.

But as soon as you fell in with the other nomads and started following the Way, you came to recognize that there was a definite rhythm of life and orderliness to the jungle. You slowly gave yourself over to that rhythm. The daily life of the nomads was attuned to it. Waking up with the sunrise. Taking a rest during the heat of the day. Being attentive to the patterns of the jungle. Settling in for the night as the sun went down.

One of the patterns that quickly emerged was spending regular times each day with the Savior and His Spirit. In the morning and evening and many points in between. And then there was always a good deal of alone time – while hiking, or when taking a rest, or when preparing things at camp. These were the times when you could reflect back on things the Savior said and did. There was always so much hidden in even His simplest actions that you always discovered something new when you took the time to reflect on it.

From Yesterday

In yesterday's session we focused on *recollection*. With recollection we remind ourselves of God's ever-presence. We can do this by thinking of Jesus, perhaps in a scriptural scene that connects with us (such as feeding the multitudes). Or we can reflect on one of our pearls, or any of the other approaches from yesterday.

Now that you've quieted yourself as best as you can (some days this will be easier than others) and have brought yourself into God's presence, you can move more deeply into your meditation. And today we look at steps 2 and 3.

Step 2: Read

The main point of the spiritual reading is to give your intellect something to discuss with God. Returning to our analogy of meeting with a friend, you begin your time together with a warm greeting and perhaps some small talk, but then you move to whatever really needs to be discussed. Perhaps your friend is having difficulty in a relationship, or you are considering a change in your career. Likewise,

Day 18 (Week 3, Day 3)

the spiritual reading is the grist for meaningful conversation in your time with God.

During the early phase of spiritual life (the purgative age), spiritual reading is particularly effective to deepen our faith and strengthen our convictions for the Truth that God has revealed to mankind. This often becomes an intellectually active time in our spiritual life - when we start to hunger for God's truth. What is Jesus really teaching us in the beatitudes? When and why does Jesus weep? When does He get angry? Why does He sometimes command even His apostles to tell no one what they have seen or heard?

When selecting spiritual reading, preference is given to the life of Christ in the Gospels. This is because scripture is the Living Word of God, and the Gospels are the height of scripture.

> *Indeed, the word of God is living and effective, sharper than any two-edged sword, penetrating even between soul and spirit, joints and marrow, and able to discern reflections and thoughts of the heart.* (Heb 4:12)
>
> *Whoever is of God hears the words of God.* (John 10:27)
>
> *And for this reason we too give thanks to God unceasingly, that, in receiving the word of God from hearing us, you received not a human word but, as it truly is, the word of God, which is now at work in you who believe.* (1 Thes 2:13)

These passages of scripture are themselves excellent for meditation, especially when we consider that "Word of God" refers first to Jesus Christ, then Sacred Scripture.

The reading should be relatively short, usually just a few paragraphs, because it needs to be something on which we can meditate - taking it in with a "single gaze" without jumping around and going back to reread sections, which runs the risk of introducing distraction. Before starting, you can offer a short prayer (an aspiration) to the Holy Spirit to guide your reading with gifts of light and insight.

When a certain passage, event or conversation grabs your attention, stop and reflect on it. The point here is not to "get through" all your selected reading, but to settle on a brief passage or concept that you can bring to the Lord, for Him to open up for you. Trust that the Holy Spirit is bringing your attention to that passage and converse with God about what it might hold for you.

An Ignatian take on selecting your reading material is the concept of repetition (another R-word). If a passage is particularly fruitful in meditation, St. Ignatius advises that we return to it. Spend the next day's meditation session digging for ever deeper riches.

A final thought on recollection and reading. You may find it counterproductive to interrupt your time of recollection with reading. You are perfectly free to start with just a brief time in recollection – simply to direct your mind to God. Move to your spiritual reading. And then continue with a few minutes of recollection before moving to reflection.

Step 3: Reflect

It is good to continue to offer brief aspirations of prayer to the Holy Spirit to guide your time of reflection, which should flow naturally from the reading. As you read, something will typically grab hold of your attention, and you should stay with that.

If you get through the entire passage and nothing has really grabbed your attention, then simply pick whatever part of the reading stood out the most. This is one more small way to practice faith and trust – that the Holy Spirit is there with you, guiding you and producing fruit from every aspect of your meditation.

In our reflection we engage our intellect and related faculties such as imagination and memory, to deepen our understanding of the subject of our reading. How to go about the reflection is very much up to the individual but there are several principles that provide helpful starting points.

Day 18 (Week 3, Day 3)

1. Invite the Holy Spirit to guide your time of reflection, to bring gifts of light and insight, and to draw your mind to the knowledge and insights the Lord desires for you.

2. Explore the circumstances of the passage (who, what, how, why, when, and where). This approach is particularly appropriate when the subject is the life of Christ (as opposed to an abstract subject like the virtue of patience). This is not meant to be a tedious exercise. Not all six circumstances must be entertained, some will be more appropriate than others for a given subject.

3. Engage the imagination. This works both for historical passages (e.g. the life of Christ) and abstract subjects such as virtues and sacraments. If the subject is an event in the life of Christ, our imagination serves to make it real – what do people in the passage sound and look like? What is the setting? What is the weather? What is Jesus wearing? What is He doing? For abstract subjects, like virtues, the imagination can be used to bring concrete examples to mind (for example the virtue of patience could bring imagery of Christ carrying His cross). As with all things in meditation, this should not be taken to the extreme of becoming a burden or distraction. Some people don't have particularly active imaginations (St. Teresa of Avila wrote of having a very limited power of imagination). The point is to use your imagination to enrich your prayer (and keep your imagination from straying to random subjects) and let it run its natural course.

4. Self-examination. It is particularly useful to place yourself into the passage of your reflection. If it is a scene from Christ's life or other scripture, who are you in that scene? For abstractions, what is your own personal experience of the subject (again, if the subject is the virtue of patience, use your experiences of success and failure in that virtue).

Reflection should not be rushed, especially for those new to meditation and in the purgative age of the spiritual life. Enough time should be spent to allow the intellect to fully penetrate the subject matter. Do not stop on the very first insight; inevitably there is deeper fruit which the Spirit desires for you, and this will provide richer inspiration for the next step - relating to God through prayerful conversation.

As you can see, all of this unfolds in the company of the Holy Spirit. And once again, these steps of meditation should not get in the way of meditation itself. Maybe there are days that you don't need reading material for meditation as you already have a passage of scripture in your mind (but whenever you can, go back to the actual scripture because it is God's Living Word). Some days your imagination may be very effective at bringing scripture to life, other days, not so much.

What matters most is that you endeavor to give the best of yourself to your reading and reflection. God will take it from there.

A final thought about scripture and meditation. The anonymous author of the *Cloud of Unknowing* has this to say about the Living Word of God as a mirror for our spiritual soul:

"God's word, either written or spoken, can be compared to a mirror. Spiritually, the eye of your soul is your intellect; your conscience is your face in spiritual terms. And just as you can see that if there is a spot of dirt on your bodily face, your bodily eye cannot perceive that spot or know where it is without a mirror or instruction from outside itself, so it is spiritually... So you can see that no thinking can be fully achieved by beginners and those making progress unless reading or listening comes first, and no prayer can be achieved without thinking."

In other words, Sacred Scripture, when we meditate with it, reveals our soul to us, just as a mirror reveals our face. At the same

Day 18 (Week 3, Day 3)

time Sacred Scripture is revealing Christ, who is perfectly human. It is this marriage of self-revelation and Divine revelation, occurring within our soul, that is the source of the transformation we hope for. This is where our broken humanity is healed bit by bit and made new in His image.

Please spend 10 minutes in meditation either reflecting on today's session or today's Gospel reading.

Let's close in prayer:

Lord Jesus Christ, help me to become ever more aware of Your nearness and Your love for me. Amen.

Pearls from Day 18: Christian Meditation Steps 2 and 3 – Read and Reflect

In the analogy of meeting with a friend, recollection is when we greet one another and get "caught up." The conversation then moves to deeper sharing– this is analogous to Reading and, especially, Reflection, which are Steps 2 and 3 of our approach to Christian Meditation.

STEP 2 - READ

Reading and reflection are primarily an act of the intellect.

The purpose of the reading material is to give our intellect something to discuss with God. Particularly in the purgative age of our spiritual life, the reading material helps us to know Jesus and strengthen our convictions in the great truths of our faith.

Scripture, particularly the life of Christ in the Gospels, is given preference in reading material because scripture is the living Word of God.

Invite the Holy Spirit to bring you gifts of light and insight to guide your reading.

The reading should be short enough that you can take it in "in a single gaze," typically a few paragraphs. When you come to something that strikes your attention you should stop there and move to reflection. The point is not to "finish" the passage. If nothing is particularly striking, then you should trust in the guidance of the Holy Spirit and select an excerpt that is most fitting for reflection.

Day 18 (Week 3, Day 3)

Step 3 – Reflect

Here you bring all your mental faculties to bear. Invite the Holy Spirit to guide the time of reflection to the knowledge and insights the Lord desires for you.

Explore the circumstances of the passage (who, what, when, why, where).

Engage your imagination. What is happening in the passage? Where are people standing? What is the weather? Who is Jesus looking at? If the passage is a concept (like a beatitude) rather than an event, you can still engage your imagination to explore the concept by applying to your life.

Personalize the reflection. Meditation is not a purely intellectual exercise. The point is not to identify some clever insights. The purpose is to learn and know what God desires from that passage for you, in the here and now of your life.

Do not rush the reflection. We typically think to stop at the first "aha" that comes to us. Often, there is something deeper that the Spirit desires to reveal. Go deeper.

Sacred Scripture, when we meditate with it, reveals our soul to us, just as a mirror reveals our face. At the same time Sacred Scripture is revealing Christ, who is perfectly human. It is this marriage of self-revelation and Divine revelation where our broken humanity is healed bit by bit and made new in His image.

─── Your Pearls from Day 18 ───

DAY 19: CHRISTIAN MEDITATION STEPS 4 AND 5 – RELATE AND RESOLVE

> Why do we need friends? Why is it gratifying when we can share something with an old friend, with someone who "gets it"? Because that is how we were created. We were created for communion with others. The One who created us desires nothing less than that kind of sharing with us. This includes sharing in meditation, and the deepest part of that sharing is when we *relate* our meditation to Him.

Let's open with prayer:

Come Holy Spirit, make of me a fitting dwelling place for the Lord.

YOUR JUNGLE MISSION

A few days ago you were hiking up some steep slopes. A pattern emerged that the base of the slopes were covered with gravel and small stones (the Savior called it scree and talus). As you climbed to the upper elevations the surface of the slope transitioned to hard, solid rock (He called this competent rock).

The Savior had alerted you ahead of time that it would be much easier to climb the hard rock than to trudge through the soft, shifting sand and gravel. Even though the rock surfaces might be a little steeper, they were firm and reliable, whereas the sand and gravel would quickly shift and easily take your feet out from under you. He also pointed out how similar this was to life – that it was much better to set yourself on what was solid and lasting.

That certainly made sense to you. What He said next stuck with you. He pointed out that the sand and gravel at the base of the slope had once been part of the competent rock at the top. Time and nature worked together to wear down the rock. The loose and unreliable gravel had once been hard and solid rock. He told you, "Everything in this world is passing away."

You had been reflecting on these things since. You were reflecting on your prior life and the passing and fleeting things that you once clung to for stability. And you were reflecting on your own personality – the parts of yourself that you thought made you important and of worth to others. It came to you that your true source of worth and dignity was that His Father created you, and He loved you and His Spirit was guiding you in sharing that love with others. It was becoming more and more clear that you were not made for this world. There was nothing in this world that would endure over time – all of it would eventually fall away and leave you empty. No, you were not made for this world; you were made for what awaited you at the mountain top.

All of these thoughts were flooding into you. You couldn't wait to see the Savior this evening and share these with Him. And listen to what He had to say about all of it.

Day 19 (Week 3, Day 4)

From Yesterday

Yesterday's meditation activities, Read and Reflect, were exercises of the mind. We contemplated our reading using our intellectual powers, doing our best to understand what the reading tells us about God and what it means to us in our spiritual life and our life in the world.

Today we turn that primarily intellectual exercise into a loving conversation with God. As always, those aren't just sentimental words. God loves you. He loves you perfectly. God speaks with you in your spiritual soul. That is why he created you with such a soul; to commune with Him. Put those two things together - God loves you *and* He speaks with you in your soul - and you have *a loving conversation with God*.

Step 4: Relate

Let's go back to having lunch with your friend. On the way to lunch, you might be thinking ahead to your time together. Maybe something is weighing on your mind. Or, perhaps you know your friend is carrying a heavy burden. Before you even sit down with them, you are focused on your friend and thinking through these things. However, you are not yet in conversation with your friend. That is closer to the activity of step 3, your meditation *reflection*. While it is part of your relationship with God, and you certainly called on the Holy Spirit to be present and guide your time of reflection, it is mostly an individual activity.

Now you sit down with your friend. *Now* you are in conversation as opposed to just thinking about the conversation. So too in prayer, now you turn the fruits of your reflection over to God in conversation with Him. This is the highpoint of meditation and when we are most fully engaged in prayer. The considerations and insights we derived from reflection should rouse our *affections*. Some points to consider:

1. Recall that whereas the *reflection* is more an act of the intellect

(thinking about God), *relating* is more an act of the will (expressing what has been roused in our heart).

2. Affections are stirrings of the heart spurred by the reflection, such as faith, hope, love, admiration, praise, thanksgiving, remorse for one's sins, and so forth. This is a healthy use of our feelings and passions, this is what they were made for. This is part of how we reorder them to God.

3. Speak with God as openly, honestly, and simply as you can. Tell Him what you love about Him. If you have questions and concerns, ask Him.

4. Give time to listen to God. From time to time you may hear Him answer in an inner voice. Most times there will simply be silence, but rest assured God is working in your soul.

5. Change your pronouns. If the subject of your reflection is the life of Christ, during the reflection you may have been considering Christ in the third person (He did this... He said that...). Change to the second person (Jesus, You did this for me .... You said that to me). Or if your reflection is on a concept, like "Blessed are those who feed the hungry," it would become something like "Blessed am I when I feed the hungry."

6. Reflection *shows* us the way. Relating to God *leads us along* the way. If we stop only at the reflection without relating to God, we may gain intellectual knowledge, but we will advance truly little in love and holiness. The analogy used is that of a needle and thread. Sewing with a needle but no thread is a futile exercise. The needle leads the way, but the thread accomplishes the goal. Similarly, if we only reflect, it is like sewing without thread. It is the relating that accomplishes the goal, which is deepening our relationship with God.

The key is to remember that this is a time of conversation with God. You are speaking to Him of the things that are stirred in your heart from your reflection. God is speaking his love into your soul. St. Teresa of Avila tells us in *The Way of Perfection*: "Do you suppose that because we cannot hear Him, He is silent? He speaks clearly to the heart when we beg Him from our heart to do so... Soon after we have begun to force ourselves to remain near the Lord, He will give us indications that ... He heard us." In Week 4 we will see how we receive those indications that God hears us and is responding.

You may find yourself moving back and forth from reflect to relate. That is perfectly fine and why we are not rigidly confined to a process or method.

Step 5: Resolution

The fifth and final step of our meditation is the Resolution. By this, we mean resolution in both a general way (bringing the meditation to a close) and resolution in a particular way (deciding on a specific action to carry through until tomorrow's meditation).

At some point we sense our conversation with God winding down. Never rush your time relating to God. If you are having a lively conversation don't bring it to a close just because you might be coming to the end of your allotted time. Similarly, if your time of relating to God is particularly dry and arduous, don't stop it early; out of generosity and fortitude stay with your reflection and relation until your allotted meditation time is complete, trusting that God is there working with you and pouring unseen grace into your soul. St. Teresa of Avila also says, "success at prayer is assured," whether we feel it a success or not. As our meditation ends it is proper to offer contrition, petitions, make a firm resolution and end with gratitude.

Contrition: We are often shown specific areas of our sinfulness during reflection and relation. We should offer appropriate contrition for any such revelations. We should receive this with tremendous gratitude. Have you ever had the experience of making the same mistake over and over and at some point, asking a friend "why didn't you tell me not to do that?" God loves us too much to leave us in our sinfulness. One of the major graces of mental prayer is that it reveals where sin has a hold on our life so that we can, by God's grace, conquer the sin and grow in virtue. Confess your sins to God as you would in the sacrament of reconciliation (note that this is not a substitute for regularly receiving the sacrament, which is a vital necessity for Catholics). If you're not Catholic, offer a suitable act of contrition (an example is provided in Day 28).

Petitions: We are often shown things we desire and need for ourselves and others. We should offer these petitions with great faith and confidence. In addition to the specific petitions that arise from the meditation, the *dispositions* that were discussed last week also provide excellent petitions – pray for an increase in faith, trust, purity, humility and fortitude (and, of course, charity). Note that as we said at the beginning of the week, our general petitions and intercessions should be set aside for a separate time (you can include them as part of the close of your mental prayer so long as you establish that as part of your routine *and* it doesn't detract from your time in meditation).

Resolution: Here lies a particularly powerful dynamic of daily mental prayer – the mechanism for true transformation of mind and heart. Says Rev. Dom Vitalis LeHodey (*The Ways of Mental Prayer*), "Meditation, without a resolution, is an army maneuvering at random and without an object, and it consequently cannot hope to gain the victory." The reverse is also true (and explains why so many New Year's Resolutions go nowhere): "But often also to make resolutions without praying is to attempt to fly without wings." And from St. Vincent de Paul, "The principal fruit of mental prayer consists of making a good resolution, and a strong one too."

We should make a resolution based on the graces received in the meditation. If you've been made aware of a particular inclination to sin (e.g. a tendency to gossip), then your resolution that day could be to call on the aid of the Holy Spirit any time you might be drawn into a situation that lends itself to gossip. The resolution should be very concrete – specific and actionable – so that you can readily put it into practice that day. You may find yourself returning to the same resolution for several days in a row (which can be very effective). Or, you may find yourself moving to a different resolution each day. Follow the promptings of the Spirit on this. Over time you will find a rhythm in forming and carrying out your resolution. On days when a specific resolution does not present itself you can return to the prior day's resolution or take a phrase from prayer and repeat it throughout the day to help maintain your focus on God.

Gratitude. And finally, complete your meditation with gratitude. Thank God for the gift of this time with him. If you spend your meditation in the presence of a crucifix you might kiss the wood of the cross. Finish by blessing yourself and continue with your day but keep the graces of your meditation close to your heart.

Example Meditation Session

Say that you've selected Mathew's narrative of the Sermon on the Mount. Since the entire sermon is much too long for reflection you find yourself drawn to the passage on anger (Mt 5:21-26). Before you start reading you take a few minutes to quiet yourself and remind yourself that you are in the presence of God. Maybe the birth of your first child is a strong reminder of God's goodness, so you go back to that moment and then remind yourself that God is just as present with you now as He was in that moment. As you draw closer to the Lord you pray to the Holy Spirit to come to your aid and to guide your time of meditation with gifts of light and insight. Now you begin to read the passage:

You have heard that it was said to your ancestors, "You shall not kill"; and whoever kills will be liable to judgment. (Mt 5:21)

And as you continue, Jesus' next words particularly grab your attention:

But I say to you, whoever is angry with his brother will be liable to judgment, and whoever says to his brother, "Raqa," will be answerable to the Sanhedrin and, says whoever says, "You fool," will be liable to fiery Gehenna. (Mt 5:22)

You have heard these words before, but this time you hear them differently; something inside of you is stirred. Even though you haven't finished the reading, this is a time to pause and sit with this passage (Remember, if you complete the entire reading and nothing particularly stands out to you, just pick whatever seems most fitting and trust completely that the Spirit is guiding you).

Now for the reflection. In this example you were struck by Jesus' teaching that simply being angry with your brother is akin to the sin of killing. First you start to explore the circumstances of this passage: who, what, how, when, where and why. As you do this, you engage your imagination. Where is this set? What does "the mount" look like? Maybe it happens to look like the small hill of your backyard. Maybe you envision photographs you have seen of the Holy Land. Where is Jesus standing? What is he wearing? Who else is there? Note that you don't have to explore each of the circumstances, only the ones that are most fitting and helpful to bring you more deeply into the passage.

Now your mind can start intellectually turning over the passage. Is it really as bad to have angry thoughts and emotions as it is to kill someone? What is Jesus getting at? What is it that makes a thought or emotion evil? Is all anger evil? And so on.

As you ponder the passage you place yourself into it. Who am I angry at? What is that anger doing to me? What is it doing to them? What is it doing to God? As you ponder you ask the Holy Spirit to guide your thoughts. You continue to turn this over in your intellect until you sense that you are running out of new ways to think about it.

Now it's time to relate back to God. It may start as simple as "Lord, I love you." "Lord, thank you for constantly forgiving me instead of being angry with me." "Lord, I'm confused? How does this passage apply to my relationship with _____?" "Lord, help me in my anger with my loved ones." You share with God whatever is on your heart from your reflection. Then offer a time of silence for God to respond.

You may receive certain promptings. Perhaps the Lord places the name of someone on your heart with whom you need to reconcile. Perhaps you fear the Lord's anger for your sins and in response to this the Lord simply affirms His great love for you. Or there may simply be silence (as is most often the case), but over time you will come to grow in your trust and knowledge that it isn't "just silence." Listen again to St. Teresa of Avila: "Do you suppose that because we cannot hear Him, He is silent? He speaks clearly to the heart when we beg Him from our heart to do so... Soon after we have begun to force ourselves to remain near the Lord, He will give us *indications* that ... He heard us."

When most people commit themselves to prayer, they begin to experience those "*indications.*" They find the hardships of life become more bearable, even meaningful. They experience relationships long frozen over beginning to thaw. They recognize God's hand in "chance happenings."

Your resolution should flow from your reflection. If, for example, the Lord did place on your heart the name of someone who tends to stir your anger, you might resolve to pray to the Holy Spirit before you have any interactions with that person. Or, you might offer up small sacrifices for that person during the course of the day.

Closing Comments

The method described above is quite simple and beautiful in how each step builds on the one prior. Let's look at it one final time in the broadest strokes:

Step 1 – Recollect. We place ourselves in God's presence so that the rest of the meditation is a loving dialogue with God.

Step 2 – Read. This isn't ordinary reading. Now that we have placed ourselves in God's presence, we are reading with God, in trust that He will lead us to the appropriate subject for our reflection.

Step 3 – Reflection. Now that God has brought us to the subject of our reflection, we bring all that we have to bear on it, so that God can reveal Himself to us through the subject.

Step 4 – Relate. Our new insights into God, from our reflection, move our heart to love Him more. We express this back to God and leave time for Him to respond in the depths of our soul.

Step 5 – Resolve. Our time in reflection and relation with God will also prompt us with insights about ourselves. Based on this, we create a resolution to carry with us through the day and this provides a concrete way in which we grow in holiness.

This completes your session of meditation. We spent four full days introducing this method and there is a great deal of information here, and we are still only scratching the surface! Having all of this piled on you at once may make this approach to meditation feel clunky and artificial. If so, be assured that is the furthest from what meditation should be (and it is also why mental prayer can't be distilled down into a single method). The rigid steps described above are meant to be fluid and alive. As you work with this approach you will start to make it your own and it will become very natural because it will become your conversation with the One who you know loves you.

Please spend 10 minutes in meditation either reflecting on today's session or today's Gospel reading.

Let's close in prayer:

Lord Jesus Christ, help me to become ever more aware of Your nearness and Your great love for me. Amen.

Day 19 (Week 3, Day 4)

Pearls from Day 19: Christian Meditation Steps 4 and 5 – Relate and Resolve

Why do we need friends? Why is it gratifying when we can share something with an old friend, with someone who "gets it?" Because that is how we were created. We were created for communion with others. The One who created us wants to share in our meditation and the deepest part of that sharing is Step 4, when we *relate* our meditation to Him, to God.

As with any conversation with a friend, we don't abruptly end it. We say our farewells and we plan for when we will next visit. This is Step 5, *resolution*.

STEP 4: RELATE

Reading and Reflection are primarily an activity of the intellect. In our friend analogy, before the visit you might be thinking ahead to your time together and what you want to discuss with them. That is closer to the activity of our meditation reflection (Step 3).

When you and your friend meet and talk in person, that is closer to *relating* to God. Relating turns our prayer into a loving conversation with God. As always, those aren't just sentimental words. God loves you. He loves you perfectly. God speaks with you in your spiritual soul. That is why he created you with a spiritual soul; to commune with Him. Put those two things together - God loves you *and* He speaks with you in your soul - and you have a loving conversation with God.

The considerations and insights we derived from reflection should rouse our *affections*. Some points to consider:

1. Affections are stirrings of the heart spurred by the reflection.

This is a healthy exercise of feelings and passions; this is part of how we heal and reorder them to God.

2. Speak with God as openly, honestly and simply as you can. Tell Him what you love about Him from your reflection. If you have questions, ask Him.

3. Give time to listen to God. On occasion, you may hear Him answer in an inner voice. Most times there will simply be silence, but rest assured God is working in your soul.

4. Change your pronouns. If the subject is the life of Christ, during the reflection you may have been considering Christ in the third person (He did this... He said that...). Change to the second person (Jesus, You did this for me... You said that to me...).

5. Reflection *shows* us the way. Relating to God *leads us along* the way. By a sewing analogy, reflection is the needle, but relating to God is the thread that makes the sewing effective.

Never rush your time relating to God, if you are having a lively conversation don't bring it to a close just because you might be coming to the end of your allotted time. Similarly, if your time of relating to God is particularly dry and arduous, don't stop early. Never backslide in your prayer commitments.

STEP 5: RESOLUTION

The fifth and final step of meditation is the Resolution. By this, we mean resolution both in a general way (bringing the meditation to a close) and resolution in a particular way (deciding on a specific action to carry through until tomorrow's meditation).

At some point we sense our conversation with God to be winding down. As our meditation comes to a close it is proper to offer contrition, petitions, make a firm resolution and end with gratitude.

Contrition: We are often shown specific areas of our sinfulness during reflection and relation. Ask God's forgiveness for these sins.

Petitions: We are often shown things we desire and need for ourselves and others. We should offer these petitions with great faith and confidence.

Resolution: Here lies a particularly powerful dynamic of daily mental prayer – the mechanism for true transformation of mind and heart. Says Rev. Dom Vitalis LeHodey (*The Ways of Mental Prayer*), "Meditation, without a resolution, is an army maneuvering at random and without an object, and it consequently cannot hope to gain the victory."

We should make a resolution based on the graces received in the meditation. The resolution should be very concrete – specific and actionable – so that you can readily put it into practice that day. You may find yourself returning to the same resolution for several days in a row (which can be very effective). Or you may find yourself moving to a different resolution each day. You should follow the promptings of the Spirit on this. Over time you will find a rhythm in forming and carrying out your resolution. On days where a specific resolution doesn't present itself you can return to the prior day's resolution or take a phrase from your reading and repeat it throughout the day to help maintain your focus on God.

Gratitude. And finally, complete your meditation with gratitude. Thank God for the gift of this time with him. If you spend your meditation in the presence of a crucifix you might kiss the wood of the cross. Finish by blessing yourself and continue with your day keeping the graces of your meditation close to your heart.

Your Pearls from Day 19

DAY 20: DEALING WITH DISTRACTION – IMMEDIATE RESPONSES

> Today and tomorrow we tackle the great hobgoblin of silent prayer – distraction! Sometimes it seems we are always at war with our lower nature. We want to lose weight but food *tastes so good*. We want to get in shape but strenuous exercise *hurts*. We know we should forgive someone, but we don't *feel* like forgiving. And, we want to pray, but there are all these *distractions*. Yes, the same fallen part of our nature that makes food taste too good to pass up, exercise too difficult to start up, and forgiveness too painful to offer up, also brings us distractions. It is a very rotten gift that keeps giving. But we have great hope – we call them our *lower* faculties for a reason. Our *higher* faculties allow us to tap into God's grace, and God's grace can conquer anything, even those pesky (and sometimes not-so-pesky) distractions. `

Let's open with prayer:

Come Holy Spirit, make of me a fitting dwelling place for the Lord.

Your Jungle Mission

You continue to have many self-revelations and there is so much you want to discuss with the Savior. So many things about your past life that have come into focus. You want to learn all you can from that and apply it to your life now. And there are so many insights you now have into the world around you. So many of the things the Savior had told you about Himself and His Father and His Spirit you now see in a new light. And so many of the things that the Savior had told you about yourself and what you were created for have taken a new meaning.

Today's hike is easy, but long, and the nomads are all spread out along the trail. You are lagging toward the back of the caravan because your mind is on your reflections; you are trying to get it all straight in your head as you hike along, so that you don't forget any of it when you sit down with the Savior in the evening.

There is still a long way to go before making camp. You're not particularly tired, but you've found yourself in a nice setting to take a rest. You've come into a clearing with a stream and a great view of a mountain waterfall. You collect a few stones to skim along the top of the water. Oh, there's a nice one, but too pretty to lose to the water, you put that in your pocket. That get's you thinking about stones and rocks and gravel and all of the insights you wanted to share with Savior. Now, what were all of them? You'd better be getting on your way.

But isn't that Oscar and Wendy over there? You haven't spoken with him since he took that nasty fall. Some of the other nomads are with them cooling their feet in the water. It would be nice to spend some time with them.

Day 20 (Week 3, Day 5)

Minutes turn into hours and suddenly you realize the sun is getting low in the sky and you still have a ways to go to get to camp. You grab your pack and hustle double time. You arrive at camp late for dinner and bone tired - too tired to visit with the Savior, you just want to crawl into your bed.

When morning comes you realize you never got to share your reflections with the Savior. Your brain is still foggy with sleep as you go to greet Him, feeling badly that you're struggling to remember all the things you wanted to share with Him. But when you meet Him and He gives you a long, warm embrace, it all comes flooding back.

Distraction

Distraction is a constant companion to the human condition. This is certainly true for prayer – but also true for all efforts that require focus. You will find much about combating distraction from psychology researchers, self-help promoters, eastern meditation gurus and so on.

But you are now armed with vital information that they don't have, unless they are among the fortunate few who understand Christian anthropology and spirituality.

We know from Christian anthropology that the human mind is gifted with powerful faculties of memory, imagination, and instincts. Unfortunately, these faculties have been corrupted by the fall and often work against us by creating distractions and anxieties. And we know there are enemies of our human nature that are actively at work to distract us from prayer and the reality of God and His plan for our life. We must exercise our intellect and will to call on the power of God to guide us back to the task at hand. On a side note - this is a primary purpose of all authentic Christian art – to provide music, imagery and writing that lift our mind to Christ and Godly things.

The saints were well aware of the challenge of distraction; no less than St. Augustine reflected on his struggles with routine distraction during prayer. Dealing with distraction is just another facet of growing in the discipline of prayer. As in all things, let it not be a discouragement. God is greater than your distractions!

First, we need to distinguish between distraction and aridity. Distractions act in opposition to our intellect. Aridity opposes our will. Distractions turn our *mind* away from thinking of Godly things. Aridity (dryness) inclines us to emotional obstacles such as boredom, discouragement, and fatigue, and saps our will to continue our time of prayer. There can certainly be some overlap between the two, but understand that when our mind gets carried away, we are talking about distraction.

Are you still with me?

Distraction can then be distinguished as voluntary and involuntary. Our primary focus is involuntary distraction. These are thoughts and images unbidden that work to turn our mind from meditation. Any of these thoughts and images can also be voluntary if we willfully call them up and entertain them. If so, these are actually venial sins because they are offenses against our commitment to God.

For now, we will assume our distractions are involuntary. We will divide involuntary distractions into four categories: transient, impulsive, worries, and, pain and suffering. This is not definitive nor exhaustive and there will certainly be overlap between these categories. Today we deal with the *immediate* response to distractions, which is to say, how to handle them when they occur during prayer. Tomorrow we will talk about the *remote* preparation for prayer and how all the other activities of our day relate to distractions.

Day 20 (Week 3, Day 5)

Transient

The start of your prayer session (Recollection) is a time of transition, just like the start of an exercise session. You don't jump right into strenuous exercise; you ease your body into it with warmups. So too, your mind must transition into prayer from your prior activities and it will be natural to have lingering thoughts and images. For example, if you were just helping your children with an activity, you are going to have that on your mind as you transition into prayer. Allow these to play out, while at the same time bringing yourself into the presence of God.

Impulsive

For most of us, impulsive and fleeting thoughts are the most persistent and pernicious source of distraction. Imagination, memories and passions are part of our lower nature. They are also very potent. Today's media is finely tuned to engage our imagination and passions (desires and emotions). Sophisticated imagery and reward mechanisms are used to manipulate us to crave entertainment, products, services and experiences.

Left unchecked, our over-stimulated imagination and desires overwhelm our intellect and will (our higher faculties). Our mind impulsively wanders to various thoughts and images impressed on it by secular media, and it wanders as well as to related memories and daydreams.

What to do:

1. **Focus on the Big Picture.** Medical science shows that when we focus our mind on our long-term goal we gain a sense of control, dopamine is released and motivation increased. So return to *recollection* if needed and remind yourself why you're praying and Who you're praying with.
2. **Perseverance.** Train your will and your intellect like an

athlete training his body. Be aware, and as your mind starts wandering, will yourself back to God's presence, again and again.

- a. *Get back in the house.* When Jesus begins teaching in parables (to chastise the Pharisees and Sadducees) he takes to preaching to his disciples "in the house." He reserves his simplest and clearest teaching for his devoted disciples. When you catch your mind wandering with distractions it is as if you stepped out of the house for a moment. Imagine that Jesus is inside with the disciples, speaking to them, and you're missing out. Get back in the house – don't miss a thing!

- b. *Get back in the boat.* Or, think of the 12 apostles with Jesus in the boat. When you find your mind drifting with distraction, imagine you have fallen out of the boat. Climb back in!

3. **Pay attention.** What are your distractions? Are they repeatedly coming from the same sources (work, TV, news, social media)? This will help you get to the root of many of your distractions.

4. **Share with God.** Turn your distractions into a positive. Make them part of your relationship with God. Invite Him into the topic of your distraction. Yes, this might be a little uncomfortable or downright disturbing depending on the nature of the distraction – but that's the point – to be as real as you can with God. Again, you may also find it helpful to "reset" your prayer by returning to *recollection* – reminding yourself of the presence of God.

5. **Renounce them.** (see the following discussion of *the work of the enemy*)

6. **Get to the root of the distractions.** The actions below are not immediate responses (we don't do them at the time of prayer), but they are worth mentioning while we are on

Day 20 (Week 3, Day 5)

the topic of impulsive distractions (more will be said on this tomorrow):

a. Write it down. Our brain isn't meant to hold things and loathes unresolved issues – these create "rehearsal loops" and "open loops" – and "loops" are bad. Organize your life outside of your prayer time – something as simple as a to-do list and planner (or try the *Getting Things Done* system) will relieve quite a bit of distraction.

b. Get rid of the junk food. What are you feeding your mind? Binge-watching secular TV and movies, soaking up cable news and talk radio, getting absorbed in video games, spending hours on social media – all these things will only "feed the beast." If you want real spiritual growth you must cut these things out (just like if you want real health gains you need to cut out the junk food).

c. Load up on health food. Replace the junk food with good spiritual nourishment. Watch good Catholic programming (try EWTN and *Formed* online streaming). Read spiritual classics (see the retreat Reference lists). Read great Christian literature. If that sounds boring, it is only because you are still addicted to the junk food. You may have to force yourself to exchange the junk for health food, but after a while it will become natural.

d. Follow your own natural rhythm. If you are the kind of person who can jump right into the deep end of the pool – good for you! Go ahead and cancel your Facebook subscription and be done with it! If you are the kind of person who needs to slowly wade into the water – good for you! Come up with a plan on how you will steadily reduce and eventually remove the junk food from your diet. Make it concrete – write it down and stick to it.

7. **Train your brain.** Remember from Christian anthropology that your mind is greater than simply your brain. Your brain

is only the material stuff between your ears (which we share in large part with animals). Your mind includes your spiritual powers of intellect and will – at some point these are more than just the firing of neurons. Science is even beginning to confirm this. We need to train our lower mental functions. As noted above, we do this by getting rid of the junk food, loading up on healthy food and exercising our mind and will in perseverance. Whether we're aware of it or not, our brains are already being trained by everything we take in – especially entertainment and social media (as we'll discuss tomorrow). We need to combat that with positive training. Will this completely remove impulsive distractions? No. Our brains will always remain distractible, just like our bodies will always be prone to sickness and deterioration. It is an unavoidable aspect of our fallen nature. But the steps above will go a long way to bringing peace in prayer and all other aspects of life.

Worries

Christ, St. Paul, Doctors of the Church, the Saints, spiritual masters, they all tell us that a primary tactic of the enemy is to use the future against us. Fears, worries, concerns, anxieties – we see these at work in ourselves and everyone around us and becoming ever more pervasive. Fear is the enemy of Faith and Hope in God. Our worries rob our peace and can be a great impediment to prayer.

What to do:

1. **Pay attention.** What are your worries? Keep track of them. Write them down (have a notepad handy when you pray). Assess your worries over time. What patterns emerge? Worries about money? Worries about relationships? As you name and corral your worries, you are using your God-given faculties of intellect and will to master them.

2. **Bring them to God.** We don't want to rely solely on our own

faculties. The most important thing is to bring your worries to God. Make them part of your prayer. Include them in your closing petitions – "Lord, release me from the fear of _____." If needed, dedicate a separate session of prayer to particularly persistent worries.

3. **Trials.** Some worries stem from severe troubles in life – particularly when we or our loved ones are amid a great trial. This is associated with suffering (discussed next). Here we rely on virtues of faith, hope, and fortitude to encourage our self that God will bring good from the present trial, and to restrain our self from fruitless worrying about the future.

4. **Turn to Scripture.** Read and re-read Matthew 6:25-34 ("Can any of you by worrying add a single moment to your life...").

5. **Find encouragements.** Call to mind the many past fears that never materialized. Some of them, in fact, probably turned out far better than you dared imagine. This is what the ancient Israelites repeated in prayer through many of the Psalms (try Psalm 33 or 77, and make yourself the subject of the Psalm).

6. **Attachments.** Repeated worries often reveal an area of attachment that needs to be healed by God (for example an unhealthy reliance on money over God's providence). Work with God so that he can reveal and heal the source of the worry and replace it with His sovereignty.

7. **Be not afraid!** Trusting in God vanquishes worry. The future is in God's hands. Most worries never materialize, and whatever may come, God is bigger than any challenges we may face.

Pain and Suffering

Emotional suffering and chronic physical pain are great crosses to bear and will understandably occupy much of our prayer time. The Catholic faith offers a response to suffering that is unparalleled in its beauty and power (and is yet another area of important departure from harmful teachings of eastern mysticism). Catholicism reveals the redemptive power of suffering - our ability to join our suffering to that of Christ. "Now I rejoice in my sufferings for your sake, and in my flesh I am filling up what is lacking in the afflictions of Christ." (Col 1:24)

This is extremely holy ground. "If the angels were capable of envy, they would envy us for two things: one is the receiving of Holy Communion, and the other is suffering." (*Diary of St. Faustina*).

In all gentleness and all truth, prayer is the preeminent place to bring our pain and suffering. The unique revelation of redemptive suffering teaches us that rather than an impediment to prayer, prayer transforms our pain and suffering into something life-giving and meritorious.

What to do:

1. **Accept.** We must accept the reality of our pain and suffering without becoming embittered. "We accept good things from God should we not accept evil?" (Job 2:10) God *permits* evil and will bring good from it. The greatest good (the resurrection) came from the greatest evil (the crucifixion). Christ Himself encourages us to embrace our crosses, because we draw particularly close to Him when we do so.

2. **Don't just accept - *pray* for acceptance.** It is not easy to accept evil in our lives and trust that God will work good through pain and suffering. We must pray for that grace.

3. **Look to Jesus.** Jesus Christ sanctified suffering, most perfectly on the Cross. We can join our suffering to his. "By his passion and death on the cross Christ has given a new meaning to suffering: it can henceforth configure us to him and unite us with his redemptive passion." (CCC 1505)

4. **Offer your pain and suffering.** "Offer it up" has become something of a catch phrase, but it reveals a great truth. Christ told us that some things can only be accomplished through

prayer and suffering (or fasting). When we offer our suffering to God it becomes meritorious, a source of grace. Try offering your pain and suffering for loved ones or for the Church and be consoled in knowing that you are, by God's grace, transforming your pain and suffering into miracles in someone else's life.

The Work of the Enemy

Recall that there are three enemies that we face: our fallen nature, the fallen world, and satan and his minions. While we are fully capable of distracting ourselves with our own disordered mind, in many cases distractions are brought about through the harassment of demons. Satan is at war with humanity and is always trying to drag us down. Just as we have a Guardian Angel working to protect us and draw us to God, there are demons constantly prowling about and attempting to derail our efforts to grow in holiness. These evil spirits typically work by introducing pain and regrets from the past, anxieties about the future and any impure thoughts, images and memories our minds have available to them. A tactic to use in prayer is, in that moment, renounce the spirit of whatever distraction you are facing in the name of Jesus (that is the key). "In the name of Jesus, I renounce all spirits of envy", or "...of lust", or "...that keep drawing my mind to _____". You may be surprised how quickly this will bring relief and a sense of peace. This will be discussed further tomorrow and in next week's session on Spiritual Combat. For today, we simply must remember that ours is not a battle against flesh and blood but against principalities and powers (which is to say, fallen angels).

Closing Comments

Other tried and true meditation aids can be applied to mental prayer. You can spend a moment focusing on taking a few deep breaths (but do not be drawn into the "body scan" methodology of mindfulness). Envisioning your distractions as a *PowerPoint* presentation and advancing the slides to the end can help some people move distracting thoughts from their mind. Maintaining a regular sleep schedule and healthy diet helps maintain circadian rhythms and metabolism, all of which helps with our power to focus and discipline our mind. It can also be effective to simply pour out all your concerns to God – whatever is weighing on your mind at the start of the session, envision yourself giving all of that over to God. And we previously looked at of St. Bernard's prayer, "Intentions, thoughts, desires, and my whole interior, come let us ascend the mountain, let us go to the place where the Lord sees or is seen. Cares, solicitudes, anxieties, labors, pains and external duties wait here for my return."

What needs repeating is that distractions are part of the human condition. We have two eyes, opposable thumbs, we walk upright, and we have brains that are hardwired to be distractible. Therefore, to a certain extent we simply must accept the annoyance of distractions as a fact of life this side of Heaven.

St. Teresa of Avila says it is exactly this lack of self-realization that causes frustration with distraction because "we do not understand our wounded condition, and we expect ourselves to be what we are not." (Fr. Thomas Dubay, *Fire Within*) St. Teresa suffered with severe distraction in prayer for many *years*. Her distractions continued even when she advanced to the heights of mystical contemplation. She notes that in a certain way the distractions increased because of the simplicity of contemplation – the absence of the active reflection and its tendency to focus the mind.

St. Alphonsus Liguori (*12 Steps to Holiness and Salvation*) teaches that "As long as you strive to preserve the proper attention at prayer, you need not be disturbed by involuntary distractions, provided you do not consent to them, they can do you no harm." St. Teresa goes so far as to say that distractions can be profitable when, by faith and love for God, we persevere through them.

Thus, our most powerful weapons against distractions are:

1. **Love.** We pray out of love of God and neighbor. Our time of prayer is one of the most precious gifts that we can offer God.

Our time in prayer is also how we grow in holiness so we can best help and intercede for our brothers and sisters.

2. **Trust.** God perfects our prayer. All we must do is make our best effort to be with him during our time of mental prayer. Even if the entire time was wracked with distraction, we must have faith and trust that it was a very fruitful time of prayer.

3. **Perseverance.** The enemy wants to discourage us because he knows that mental prayer is one of the most powerful ways for us to grow in holiness and build the Kingdom of God on earth. The worst thing we can do is give in and give up. We must pray for the grace to maintain our mental prayer, especially when it is difficult.

A final comment on *voluntary* distractions. All that we have said about involuntary distractions applies to voluntary. But because voluntary distractions are an act of the will (choosing to dwell on the thoughts, images and feelings) they are sinful. You should seek God's forgiveness, particularly in the sacrament of reconciliation. Note that if you're undergoing severe hardships in life it's only natural and spiritually healthy for you to bring this to the Lord – but you should still make an effort to trust that hardship to God and make room for Him to open other doors for you during your time in meditation.

If certain distractions become more than a passing issue, if you find yourself obsessed with certain memories or thought patterns you should seek the guidance of an experienced spiritual director.

Distractions are a very real enemy of prayer – but they're not the last word. God is. "I can do all things through Christ who strengthens me." (Phil 4:13) You can even overcome your own distractible brain.

Please spend 10 minutes in meditation either reflecting on today's session or today's Gospel reading.

Let's close in prayer:

Lord Jesus Christ, help me to become ever more aware of Your nearness and Your great love for me. Amen.

Pearls from Day 20: Dealing with Distraction – Immediate Responses

Distraction is a constant companion to prayer. This is due to our fallen nature and we will never completely escape it. Even the likes of St. Teresa of Avila and St. Augustine wrote of their battles with distraction.

But we need to do our best to respond to distraction and to not compound the problem.

Distraction is different from aridity. Distraction opposes our intellect – our ability to focus and think about Godly things. Aridity (dryness) opposes our will – feelings of fatigue and boredom sap our will to sustain our time of prayer.

Distraction is distinguished as voluntary and involuntary. Voluntary distractions are those that we intentionally enter into during prayer. This is like pulling out your cell phone while speaking with someone. Involuntary distractions are those that come unbidden. Here we focus on involuntary distractions.

We categorize involuntary distractions as transient, impulsive, worries and pain/suffering. This is an informal categorization.

Transient: Our minds are filled with the events of the day prior to our meditation. It necessarily takes time for these thoughts to play out and our minds to settle down. This is one reason why we have a time of recollection.

Impulsive: Our lower mental faculties (imagination, memory, instinct) are very powerful. They are over-stimulated by today's media saturation and can completely overwhelm our time of prayer. We need fortitude to repeatedly draw ourselves back from daydreams. We should pay attention to patterns that reveal common sources of distractions (e.g. politics or gossip). We also need to severely limit

Day 20 (Week 3, Day 5)

the amount of secular media we consume (so that we don't "feed the beast").

Worries: The enemy is constantly trying to divert us with worries about the future. We should pay attention to the source of our worries and bring these issues to God. Read Matthew 6:25-34 again and again (*Can any of you by worrying add a single moment to your life...*). Find encouragement in past worries that never materialized – or even worked out better than hoped.

Pain and Suffering: Physical and emotional pain, watching a loved one suffer, these are great crosses and will understandably occupy much of our time of prayer. Catholicism offers the only true response to pain and suffering – that it can be redemptive. If we "offer up" our suffering by joining it to Christ on the cross, it becomes meritorious – grace is released in our life and in the world.

Our battle with distraction is actually part of our relationship with God. As in all things – invite God into your distractions. And our battle with distraction is part of the larger battle with the enemy. The enemy is always working to derail our efforts to grow in holiness. St. Teresa of Avila points out that it is our lack of self-realization that causes frustration with distraction because "we do not understand our wounded condition, and we expect ourselves to be what we are not." (T. Dubay, *The Fire Within*)

Distractions of themselves are not evil (so long as we don't willfully seek and entertain them). We need only to do our best to avoid distraction and to bring our mind and heart back to God when they occur.

Your Pearls from Day 20

DAY 21: REMOTE PREPARATION FOR PRAYER

> Yesterday we looked at common sources of distraction in our prayer. Today we will look at one of the deepest roots of the obstacles to our spiritual life – our environment. Our environment matters. Spend time in the company of people who are prayerful and positive, it will rub off on you. Spend time in the company of people who cuss and gossip, that stuff rubs off too. Yes indeed, our environment matters.

Let's open with prayer:

Come Holy Spirit, make of me a fitting dwelling place for the Lord.

YOUR JUNGLE MISSION

You've had so much revelation in the past few weeks. About the Savior and His Father and Spirit. About the world around you and the Way to the Mountain Top. About your past life. About who you are and what you are created for.

But it's one thing to *know* all of these things, it's another to *act* on them.

There are still many of your old ways and patterns that you

find yourself attached too, even though you know they're not good for you.

There are new habits and patterns that you want to establish in your life.

It's a lot to hold and sort out and prioritize in your mind at once.

And then you heard one of the other nomads talking about her *plan of life*. Even without knowing the particulars, you knew in an instant that was what you needed, and that was what you'd be discussing with the Savior in the evening.

REMOTE PREPARATION FOR PRAYER

Our time in mental prayer is a distinct activity but it is not meant to be isolated from all the other aspects of our life. And in fact, it can't be. St. Teresa of Avila reminds us again and again that growth in mental prayer goes hand-in-hand with growth in virtue. Mother Teresa was (and the order she founded remains) a living example of this. Christ exemplified this perfectly in His life – His prayer in solitude and His public ministry of healing and redemption were bound together as one complete act of self-giving love.

Just so, all the rest of our life effects our mental prayer. And our mental prayer effects all the rest of our life. They are bound together.

In this session we are going to look more closely at the "all of the rest of our life" part of things.

First, let's consider this in the context of our jungle mission. With an undertaking as dangerous and demanding as a journey through a jungle, everything we do will either build us up for success or weaken and hinder us from achieving our goal (the far-off summit). Before setting off on our mission we should train, study and prepare. Once

Day 21 (Week 3, Day 6)

on our mission, everything we do each day counts. One of the most important things for our mission is to avoid mortal dangers. We need to beware of poisonous creatures particularly in the high grass and thick jungle. We should give a wide berth to the mating and feeding grounds of deadly predators. Along with avoiding sources of certain death, we need to pay careful attention to everything else that we do in the jungle. It matters whether we get enough rest and eat properly. It matters whether we plan for each new day and stay focused during that day's hike. It matters whether we keep our gear in good working condition. Every little thing is either advancing or hindering our success.

The graphics below depict this dynamic in our spiritual life (color versions are available in the ebook and mobile app for this retreat). So, we repeat, all the rest of our life effects our mental prayer. And our mental prayer effects all the rest of our life. They are bound together.

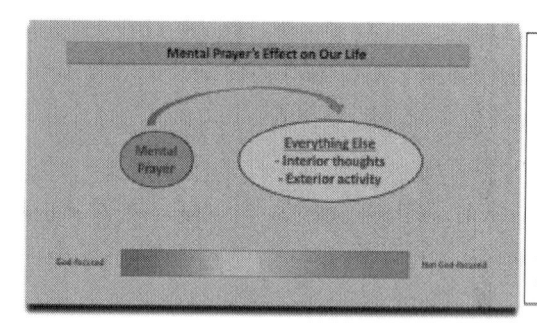

Mental Prayer's Effect on Our Life	
[diagram: Mental Prayer → Everything Else (Interior thoughts, Exterior activity); God-focused ↔ Not God-focused]	Recall our discussion of our interior and exterior life. Here we're going to simplify it a little. We're going to look specifically at mental prayer (meditation and contemplation) and all the other aspects of our life (our interior thoughts and exterior action). Ideally our mental prayer elevates all of the other aspects of our life.

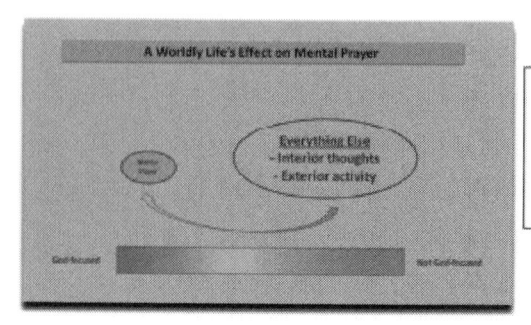

A Worldly Life's Effect on Mental Prayer	
[diagram: Everything Else (Interior thoughts, Exterior activity) → Mental Prayer; God-focused ↔ Not God-focused]	However, the rest of our life also impacts our mental prayer. Everything we do in life effects our relationship with God, and so it directly effects our prayer life.

With that summary of the symbiotic relationship of our mental prayer and the rest of our interior and exterior life, let's look at a hypothetical evolution of the spiritual life.

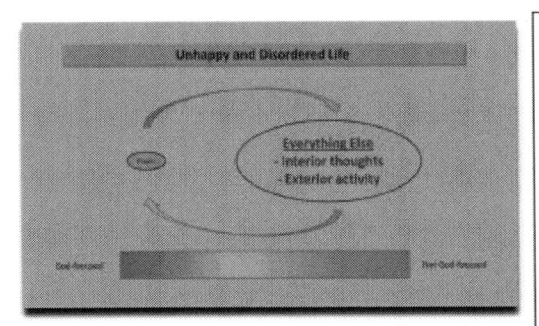

Unhappy and Disordered Life

Looking at this two-way relationship between our mental prayer and the rest of our life, if we live a very worldly life, what little prayer we have will be anemic and unable to elevate the other aspects of our life - this is reflected in the Parable of the Sower, "As for what was sown among thorns, this is he who hears the word, but the cares of the world and the delight in riches choke the word, and it proves unfruitful."

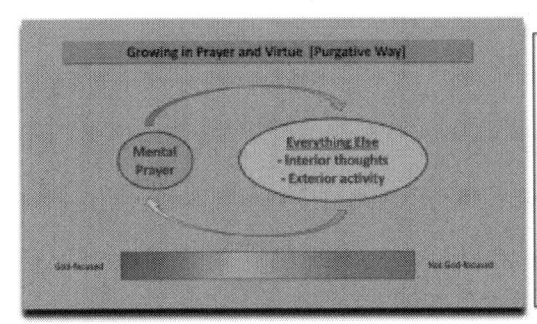

Growing in Prayer and Virtue [Purgative Way]

When we begin to detach ourselves from the world, prioritize our prayer life and bring God more and more into all areas of our life we are coming into the Purgative Way and growing in holiness (and happiness). Now the other areas of life are ceasing to be an impediment to prayer and actually support our prayer life.

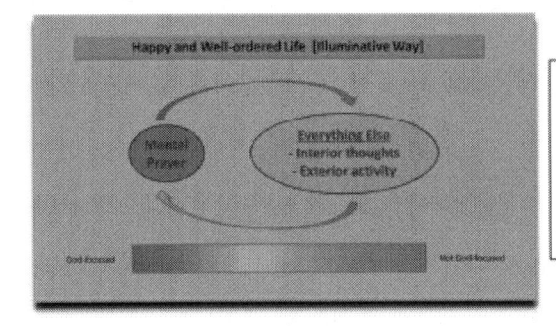

Happy and Well-ordered Life [Illuminative Way]

As we transition to the Illuminative Way all aspects of our life are becoming harmonized. We have rid ourselves of serious sin and our lower nature is coming under command of our spiritual powers as we grow in virtue and love for God.

Day 21 (Week 3, Day 6)

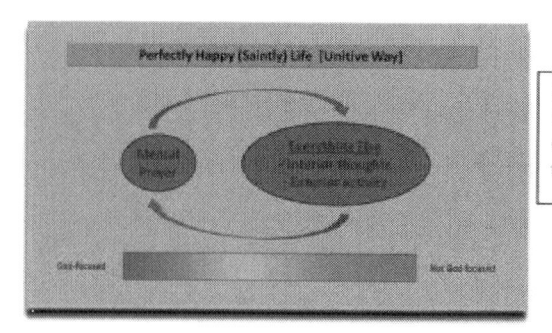

> In the Unitive Way all of our nature is ordered to God. This is the source of true happiness, as modeled by the great Saints.

Plan of Life

It is tremendously useful in any human endeavor to have a plan. Yes, life happens, and best laid plans change and change again. But the effort of planning and having a plan to work from is universally valued. As attributed to President Eisenhower, "Plans are worthless, but planning is everything."

A Plan of Life will help you focus by starting at the highest level (getting to Heaven) and drilling down to the small details (should I say yes or no to another request for volunteers at my child's school?).

The following outline offers one approach (based on a hierarchy of relationships); you can come up with many other ways to do this. Some items below might be new to you (e.g. rosary, spiritual direction). next week we will be discussing many of these additional aspects of our spiritual life.

The overarching theme of your plan of life is this: what is your vocation - what are you called to sacrifice for? Christ tells us that the purpose of our life is to lay it down for God and neighbor. It is that sacrificial aspect of your life that powerfully connects you with Christ and gives your life meaning, purpose and fulfillment. It is what makes you most alive. Your plan of life will help you take command of how you spend your time so you can give the best of yourself to God and the people He places in your life.

1. **God.** Our first priority is our relationship with God (the first and greatest commandment) and working out our salvation.

    a. Prayer Life – This includes the totality of prayer, particularly our Sunday Mass obligation (liturgical prayer), daily mental prayer and any specific devotions (e.g. daily rosary, daily examen and intercessory prayer).

    b. Sacramental Life – When received worthily the Sacraments confer a share in the divine life of the Trinity. You should be receiving the Eucharist weekly and reconciliation once a month. For non-Catholic Christians, your Church probably recognizes some type of "spiritual markers" (such as Baptism, Marriage and Communion) that are similar to the Sacraments. There is more on the role of Sacraments in our spiritual life in Day 28.

    c. Spiritual Formation – The more we know God and our Faith the better we will love God and others.

        i. Faith Formation – This includes a solid knowledge of scripture and the tradition of the Church.

        ii. Spiritual Formation – Commitment to mental prayer and regularly going on retreat. A wise and experienced spiritual guide is indispensable. If you don't have a spiritual director, pray for one.

        iii. Growing in Virtue – Our efforts of prayer and faith formation should be borne out in a life of great virtue, living out faith, hope, love, prudence, justice, fortitude and temperance.

        iv. Devotion to Mary – Mary leads us to her Son. One of the principal ways that God works is through others. How many times has God worked in your life through the people around you? God's greatest work through a human being was through Mary, and he continues to work through her.

Day 21 (Week 3, Day 6)

2. **Vocation.** After God, our highest duty is to others through our vocation.

   a. Marriage – Most of us are called to married life. Our single greatest priority is getting our spouse and our children to heaven. *Everything else* is at the service of this duty to our family.

   b. Religious – Consecrated life is a unique and beautiful calling; if this is your calling may God richly bless you for giving your life to Him in such a powerful way.

   c. Single life – This is different from people who are called to married or religious life but have yet to take the vows appropriate to each calling. These are individuals who have discerned they are consecrated to single life, which brings its own beautiful and unique gifts to the world and related commitments and responsibilities.

3. **Body of Christ.** After our personal relationship with God and our duties to our vocation, come our duty to the body of Christ and to all peoples of the world. This is the call to give generously of our time, talent and treasure (which includes tithing – giving at least 10% of our gross household income).

   a. Providing for the needs of the Church – Actively participating in our local Church and providing for its needs.

   b. Providing of the less fortunate – Giving generously of our time, talent and treasure to provide for the material and spiritual needs of others.

   c. Spreading the Gospel – We must strive to share Jesus Christ with the world in all that we do.

4. **Work.** We are all called to work be it gainful employment or managing the home. Because it takes up so much of our time and is important for our worldly existence, work can often overwhelm the other facets of our life. That is the exact

opposite of how it should be, and it is why work comes toward the end of your plan of life. Our work should be much more than simply a source of income or professional achievement or personal satisfaction. Our work is another mission field in which we should sanctify ourselves and spread the Gospel. St. Jose Maria Escriva, the Saint of Saints when it comes to the role of work, spent his life teaching about the importance of work for our spiritual life and salvation. He also taught "For all that, you should put your professional interests in their place: they are only means to an end; they can never be regarded — in any way — as if they were the basic thing." The "basic thing," of course, is love of God and neighbor. Thus, this great Saint also says, "Before God, no occupation is in itself great or small. Everything gains the value of the Love with which it is done." When we approach our work with this mindset it becomes a truly noble undertaking.

5. **Self.** Of course it is important that we love and take good care of ourselves. This includes recreation, hobbies and personal development. Life is richest when this aspect of your life becomes a natural extension of your other relationships and endeavors.

SPIRITUAL HISTORY

As part of developing your Plan of Life, and also to uncover potential sources of distraction, it is useful to take stock of your spiritual history to better understand how it influences your interior life now. What was the religious and spiritual environment of your youth? What were key moments that either moved you closer to God or further from Him? Do you recognize particular spiritual strengths or weaknesses in yourself? Are there any patterns in your life that have led you to this point in your spiritual journey? These days it is also important to consider whether you were ever exposed to the occult (palm or tarot readings, Ouija, etc). These are also all good things to discuss with a spiritual director (see Day 27), particularly any experiences with the occult.

What to Get Rid Of

Yesterday's session focused on distractions. Most distractions are caused by noise, clutter, and bad information in our brains. Our minds are wonderfully sticky (until you need to remember where you left the car keys). Most everything we take in gets stored somewhere. Now think hard about all the stuff that flows into your brain each day. Advertisements. Mindless television. Idle chit-chat and gossip. Think especially about that two-headed purveyor of intellectual empty calories – the internet and social media. And, as we all know, there is much worse out there than just empty calories.

In addition to the information that we take in there are the activities of family life, work, recreation and so on.

You should start by comparing what you do and what you take in against your Plan of Life.

You will find it is easy to weed out the purely superfluous "stuff" – especially that which is delivered by pixels.

But quite a bit of it will get trickier. We create all manner of reasons why we need to spend time on "informative" websites (we have to "stay current", it's important to be an "informed member of society", we want to know what's going on in the world to be able to interact with others, and so on). We create all manner of reasons why it is important to log onto Facebook, Twitter, Instagram and other social media ("it's how we stay connected and build relationships...").

Here we must take a long and sober look at all of this. Let's take "informative" websites – mainstream news, lots of different self-help sites, podcasts and on and on. How critical are these to our daily functions and responsibilities? Let's look at news as just one example. What are our specific responsibilities as related to news and current events? For example, we have the responsibility to vote. How much news do you have to consume to know who to vote for in November? Next to none. Beyond that, what is the necessity of "news?" How does it impact your daily life? How does it further your relationship with God? How does it advance your vocation? How does it further your relationship with your family and others? Does it help you have meaningful conversations with people? If some of it does, then fine. But balance that against the time it takes from your other responsibilities. Does it also serve to agitate you and make you angry towards people that don't think like you? What impact does it have on your prayer life? Is it even accurate and intellectually beneficial?

Social media deserves a particularly careful review. It is very easy to try to justify social media with a few "healthy" anecdotal uses. But think long and hard on this one. Is social media promoting healthy, meaningful relationships? Do you really need to be tracking trivial details of a long-lost middle school friend? To everything in life there is a season. Many relationships are meant to run their course and come to a natural end. As for people you really do need to stay connected with, could the incidental contact made on Facebook be better replaced with a meaningful phone call? To the extent that you do have meaningful activities on social media are you able to login for just a few minutes without being drawn click-by-click into the soul-sucking vortex of posts, images and video clips? Social media is designed to be addictive – search "social media dopamine" for starters. Treat it with the same caution you would treat any other addictive substance. Quite simply, your life would be better without Facebook, Twitter, Instagram and whatever else is bound to come floating down the never-ending social media river of drivel and sewage.

It should also go without saying, but in our current culture it bears repeating – everything remotely immoral must be discarded. Most magazines in the supermarket checkout lane are pornographic and wildly immoral in countless other ways. Many popular novels are out-right filth (think *Fifty Shades of Grey*) or at least not worthy of your precious time (life is too short to read second rate books).

Day 21 (Week 3, Day 6)

Almost nothing from Hollywood and on mainstream network and cable TV belongs in your brain nor anyone else's. Imagine Christ or our Blessed Mother is watching TV with you. It makes you shudder – right? Almost all pop music must go. Have you ever actually listened to the lyrics – whether you know it or not your subconscious is taking it all in.

Similarly, you can review where the rest of your time goes. Recreation, sports, other social activities – are they in settings and with people that are lifting you up or bringing you to near-occasions of sin?

What to Keep and What to Bring on Board

Ridding ourselves of worldly clutter makes room for all that is good, true, and beautiful.

Start with God and family. Lavish your time and attention on them. Hold nothing back.

And then spend more time on your other closest relationships. Don't settle for Facebook. Get out and do something together, even if it's simply a phone call.

Read good books - spiritual classics and great literature. Listen to good music – classical music, sacred music, and some contemporary Christian. Watch good programming – try *Formed* and *EWTN*. Find a few good news and information websites (preferably Christian) and have a hard and fast limit on the time you spend there.

Any activities related to your Church, faith formation and, especially, service and charitable work are worthy uses of your time and talents. St. Teresa of Avila teaches that if we want to grow in prayer we should grow in virtue (especially by serving others). It simply becomes a matter of prayer and discernment so that God can lead you to a much more fulfilling life.

Specific Considerations for Mental Prayer

If you currently consume a great amount of secular news, entertainment, and social media, you will be amazed how much more peaceful your life becomes without it. You will be amazed how little you miss it once you get over the initial withdrawal. Simply removing this clutter from your life will also help with distractions in mental prayer. This will not happen overnight because so much of it is imprinted in your brain, but you will find over time it is easier and easier to recollect yourself and separate from the world.

A good regimen of spiritual reading and faith formation (such as bible and catechism studies and good spiritual reading) will serve to fuel your mental prayer. Particularly in the purgative age, as you are growing in faith through discursive meditation, spiritual reading and faith formation provide you with the mental material, the "grist", for your reflection.

Because spiritual reading for your daily meditation is necessarily short – no more than a paragraph or two – it should be supplemented with additional daily spiritual reading. The two (your mediation reading and other daily spiritual reading) can be related. Perhaps you read a few chapters of the Bible as your daily spiritual reading. If a particular passage grabs your attention, make note of it, and go back to it as the reading for your daily meditation.

Your spiritual reading can also be a time to follow up on questions that arise during meditation. In our prior example we used Jesus' teaching on anger in the Sermon on the Mount. A number of questions were raised during our hypothetical meditation (e.g. "Surely not all anger is bad, like Jesus' cleansing of the temple. What is the difference between good and bad anger?") Don't just leave these questions unanswered - it's time well spent to follow up on them.

Day 21 (Week 3, Day 6)

Mental Prayer and an Integrated Life

As stated in the first week of this series, we are a single person. We have many roles and responsibilities in life, but we have just one life. We are body and soul – spirit and matter – but we only have one nature, our human nature. Everything we are and do is integrated. The spiritual realm of our life is higher, more exalted, than the material realm, yet we exist in both realms and what we do in each matters to both.

The natural order mirrors the spiritual order and can work to reinforce it. All things that create a balanced life in the natural order will promote a healthy spiritual life. Eating a healthy diet. Getting regular exercise and a good night's sleep. Having balance between all our responsibilities, including relaxation and recreation. All of these will positively impact our spiritual life.

And the reverse holds true as well. As we give ourselves more and more to following God's rhythm of life, by developing our interior life through mental prayer, living a sacramental life, serving our neighbor, investing ourselves in the liturgical seasons of the year (Advent, Christmas, Lent, Easter and Ordinary Time) we will find order, peace and simplicity flowing into all aspects of our life.

The 20-second Tactic and the Grace of the Present Moment

Here's a simple habit tactic that can be effective to purge the bad and promote the good – make bad habits 20-seconds harder and good habits 20-seconds easier. It works like this: If you want to break the habit of constantly looking at your phone it is good to schedule when you'll look at it (e.g. "I'll give myself 5 minutes at the top of the hour"). To help yourself from cheating, make it a little harder to look at your phone by not just putting it away, but by also turning it off. Now if you're tempted to look at it, you have to wait for it to power on and that gives you a few seconds to pray to the Holy Spirit for self-control (the grace of the present moment). Creating a 20-second-ish barrier to an unwanted habit is an effective way to give yourself time to intervene and train your brain to say "no" to the impulse.

The opposite is true for promoting good habits – remove the barriers and annoyances so that they are easier to maintain. If you want to start a habit of morning prayer (a very good habit), set yourself up for it before you go to bed. Have your bible and any other spiritual reading by your bedside and set to the proper page. If you need coffee to be able to pray, set your coffee maker the night before, and so on.

Practicing the Presence of God

Brother Lawrence, a simple and holy man in the 17th century, lived and shared this practice and captured the essence of it in a few brief letters and notes (see References). To practice the Presence of God is to cultivate a loving awareness that God is with us every moment of the day. As we mature in this practice, we arrive at a very dynamic place in which we are attuned to God in the present moment – both receiving from, and responding to Him. This presence with God in no way distracts us or diminishes our availability to the people and tasks at hand, in fact it heightens and perfects all that we do.

Closing Comments

If today's session seems like a heavy-handed attack on "everything modern" and "having a little fun" that is because it mostly (but not entirely) is. There is simply no way to pussyfoot around this topic. *You* are too important to me and to God to waste time with watered down "it's all good" language and half measures.

You may be familiar with the heresy of Gnosticism. If not, and in brief, Gnostics believe in a form of dualism in which only things of the spiritual realm (such as our soul) are good and everything of the material realm (our bodies and all physical creation) is evil. Christianity rejects this. God made the world to be good. Yes, it is fallen and much that is in the world can draw us into evil. But when properly ordered, the things of this world are good, promote human happiness and draw us to God. The point of this session is NOT to peddle a puritanical view that we can't have fun and enjoy the good things of the world. But let's face it – the world has enjoyed decades of unfettered indulgence – and thus calls for no small measure of restraint.

Our current secular culture is awash in immorality that is literally engineered to worm its way into your life. If you are not consuming media, *they* are not getting your attention, your money, your vote, or whatever they are after – which is ultimately your soul. Seriously. Precious little that is produced by leading sources of media and entertainment is compatible with a healthy Christian spiritual life.

This session may also sound like it is taking all the fun out of life. Far from it! It is simply a matter of reconditioning our minds to what authentic fun is all about. It is becoming very popular these days to go on "detox" diets, getting rid of all processed foods, additives, artificial ingredients and so on. If you talk to anyone who has gone through this, they will tell you that once their body has been purged, detoxed and reordered to healthy food they can no longer enjoy junk food. The body is repulsed by it because it has been cleansed and now senses the junk food for what it is. I used to drink diet soda like water. These days I cannot go near it. My body senses the cocktail of chemicals and wants nothing to do with it. The same principle holds with modern media and entertainment. Once you purge, detox and reorder yourself to healthier options you will find life is filled with simple pleasures, fun and good humor that far outshine the flashy but shabby counterfeits the world offers in place of authentic Christian living.

Might this be difficult? Does it take sacrifice? *Yes* - certainly, it does! But what do we say in any other area of life - no pain no gain … the power of delayed gratification … you get out what you put in.

So it is in our spiritual life. I say all of this with great humility and gentleness, but also with all Truth and all conviction. God is so pleased that you are making the effort with this retreat. As we said at the outset, God does not ask anything of us that we're not prepared nor able to give, and He will always give us the grace to see it through. Bear in mind that the transformation we are talking about in this retreat is the work of our lifetime, not the work of just these 30 days. Some of the lifestyle changes may be very difficult indeed, but with God all things are possible and can happen with surprising speed.

And, by God's grace – it doesn't have to be all that hard. As with most things, taking the first step is the hardest part. Once you start purging your life of secular entertainment and social media you will experience the benefits for yourself and it will become much easier to progress.

Here is one last example of how this all works, for the visual learner.

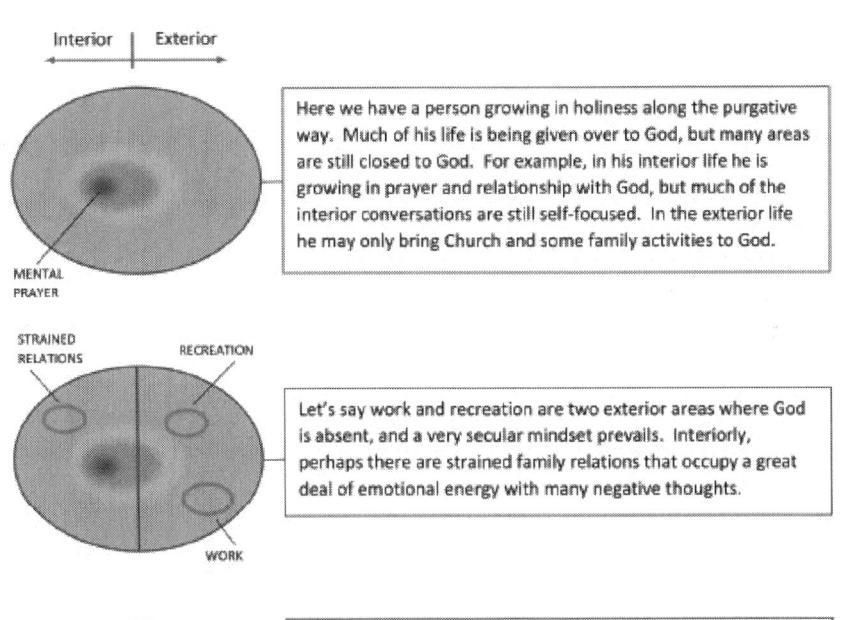

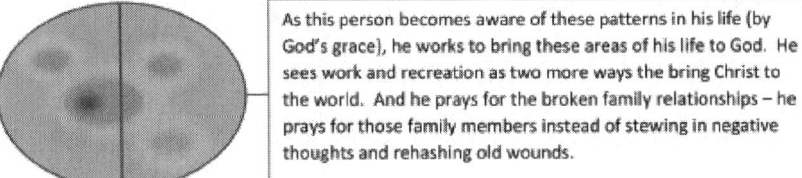

Interior | Exterior

MENTAL PRAYER

Here we have a person growing in holiness along the purgative way. Much of his life is being given over to God, but many areas are still closed to God. For example, in his interior life he is growing in prayer and relationship with God, but much of the interior conversations are still self-focused. In the exterior life he may only bring Church and some family activities to God.

STRAINED RELATIONS   RECREATION

WORK

Let's say work and recreation are two exterior areas where God is absent, and a very secular mindset prevails. Interiorly, perhaps there are strained family relations that occupy a great deal of emotional energy with many negative thoughts.

As this person becomes aware of these patterns in his life (by God's grace), he works to bring these areas of his life to God. He sees work and recreation as two more ways the bring Christ to the world. And he prays for the broken family relationships – he prays for those family members instead of stewing in negative thoughts and rehashing old wounds.

Day 21 (Week 3, Day 6)

On Day 6 we looked at how our interior life is intended to transform our entire life, and we returned to this theme in our charts at the start of today's session. The Day 6 chart of our interior and exterior (active) was idealized. We can look a little more realistically at different areas of our life, as follows.

Bear in mind the above diagrams are purely conceptual, schematic, illustrative and hypothetical; they are not in any way a rigorous mapping of the human person. That said, it is intentional in the third figure that the work, recreation and family relationships are now in contact with the core relationship with God. As we begin to sanctify different aspects of our lives we find that they are brought into our interior life and our conversation with God.

Examine your life in the context of your Plan of Life, and in the company of the Holy Spirit, and determine what next step you are called to take to remove distractions and add or adjust things in the areas of your relationship with God, your vocation, the people in your life, your service, and your work. It's that simple. Take that next small step and God will work wonders through that offering.

Please spend 10 minutes in meditation either reflecting on today's session or today's Gospel reading.

Closing Prayer:

Lord Jesus Christ, help me to be ever more aware of Your nearness and Your great love for me. Amen.

Pearls from Day 21: Remote Preparation for Prayer

"Remote Preparation" for prayer simply refers to everything you do in life apart from your time of mental prayer. Everything else that you do impacts your prayer life just as your prayer life impacts all other aspects of your life.

Our prayer life should elevate every other aspect of our life. But, if our prayer life is too immersed in the responsibilities, worries, noise, distractions and allurements of the world, or if our prayer life is too small, detached and unintentional, instead of our prayer life elevating all aspects of our life it will be dragged down to the level of the world. It will be lifeless.

A *Plan of Life* is a roadmap for our life that helps us achieve balance. Our Plan of Life maps out our responsibilities and activities in four areas: God, Vocation, Neighbor and Work.

Our relationship with God must come first (attending Mass, living a sacramental life, personal prayer, going on retreat, etc.) This is the first great commandment. When we place God first, all other aspects of life will thrive.

Our vocation is a close second to God. This is the specific responsibility that God has given us in this life. For most of us this is family life, and our responsibility is to lead our spouse and children to Heaven.

Serving our neighbor fulfills the second great commandment and this includes the corporeal and spiritual works of mercy – providing for the physical and spiritual needs of others.

Work is an important part of our worldly and spiritual life, but it can tend to overwhelm other facets of life. Work must always be at the service of God, vocation, and neighbor.

And it is important that we love and take good care of ourselves.

Day 21 (Week 3, Day 6)

This includes recreation, hobbies and personal development. Life is richest when this aspect of your life becomes a natural extension of your other relationships and endeavors.

When we are alert and aware in our prayer life, we will start to keep track of the worries and distractions that most disturb us. We can then compare these against our plan of life and determine where to make changes to bring our life into balance.

In this modern age, one of the most important areas to make changes is the consumption of modern media. Most worries, distractions and temptations take root in the messages the world feeds us through media. The Saints repeatedly teach us of the need to ruthlessly separate ourselves from the clutches of the world. Jesus speaks directly to this in the Parable of the Sower, "The seed sown among thorns is the one who hears the word, but then worldly anxiety and the lure of riches choke the word and it bears no fruit." (Mt 13:22)

We must take a brutally honest look at where we prioritize our time and everything that we allow into our brain and determine whether it is of God (and accept it) or not (and reject it). The vast majority of modern secular media, particularly social media and entertainment, should be rejected. In some areas of our life this can be particularly challenging. God is imminently patient and gentle with us – we need only to keep trying to make small strides forward. In all things we must rely on God in whom all things are possible!

Your Pearls from Day 21

DAY 22: WEEK 3 – PUTTING IT ALL TOGETHER – KEEPING IT SIMPLE.

> God is often associated with masculine attributes. God, however, is pure spirit and thus doesn't have a gender. But there are good theological and philosophical reasons for the masculine associations found in scripture. Perhaps the most fitting masculine attribute to associate with God is simplicity (the simple fact is that men are pretty simple).

We can say this without a trace of heresy or irreverence because it turns out that God really is perfectly simple, and this is very important for our prayer life.

Let's begin with opening prayer:

Come Holy Spirit, make of me a fitting dwelling place for the Lord.

YOUR JUNGLE MISSION

You've been working on your plan of life. And you've been particularly focused on your daily routine, for example by pruning out habits that distract you from quality time spent with the Savior and the other nomads.

And you've been spending time reflecting on the events and insights of each day so that you can share them with the Savior in the evening.

And you've been focusing on making good daily resolutions based on your discussions with the Savior.

And you've been thinking about what it means to be human and who the Savior really is.

It all sort of makes sense, and you are developing a good routine to your day. But it also feels a little disjointed, it isn't natural. For example, the other day one of the nomads needed some help first thing in the morning, and you were happy to lend a hand, but it put you outside your new routine and the whole day was thrown off track. You weren't able to step back into your routine.

You look at the more experienced nomads and their routines. They easily adapt new situations into their plan for the day and larger changes into their plan of life. Their life looks so simple and orderly. It seems like second nature to them. In fact, it doesn't seem like second nature – it seems like it has become their very nature. That realization gives you a great deal of relief and hope, because you are following along the same Way.

The Savior affirms as much and regularly reminds you to simply remain faithful to your time with Him, to your resolutions, and letting His Spirit guide you – and the transformation you hope for will follow naturally.

Day 22 (Week 3, Day 7)

Order and Chaos

In the first week of this retreat we turned our attention to the nature of God and the Trinity. God is infinite, eternal and is Three Persons with one Divine Nature. Philosophy also tells us that God is perfectly simple. This simplicity is related to God's infinite nature. If God had "parts," like we do, He would cease to be infinite. If God had parts, one of the parts could, in theory, be taken away, or break down and then God would no longer be infinite. Thus, God must be "part less." God is indivisible – He cannot be divided into any small pieces. God *Is*. "I Am Who Am."

The closer we get to God the closer we get to perfection, and thus the simpler things become. We see this in everything around us. Look at innovation in design. Old cars were Rube Goldberg machines – different parts cobbled together. But look at what they have become. You can often tell the sophistication of design by how sleek, simple, and minimalist it becomes. Look at cell phones – the newer the design, the simpler the operation. Look at relationships. Seriously. We previously talked about older couples, how simple their relationship becomes; how much they can share in a loving glance or gentle touch.

Marvel at the stunning simplicity of $E=mc^2$. Designer, inventor, and futurist R. Buckminster Fuller proclaimed, "When I am working on a problem, I never think about beauty but when I have finished, if the solution is not beautiful, I know it is wrong." Beauty, purity, order, harmony, *simplicity* – these are hallmarks of God.

The enemy always works in opposition to simplicity and order. The mark of the enemy is complexity, confusion, disorder, anarchy, division and chaos. The Greek word diabolos (the root of diabolical) can mean *one who divides* (and, fittingly for the devil, *one who slanders*). We see this throughout history. After the fall, Adam and Eve are confused and scurrying about with fig leaves, hiding from God. We see it in the Tower of Babel – confusion and anarchy are the price to pay for turning from God. We see this in the long-suffering history of the Israelites – repeatedly turning from God and then falling into ruin. We see this in the Gospels leading up to the passion – Christ's enemies sowing division and His disciples falling away. And then the passion itself – a crescendo of disorder and chaos with the apostles scattered, the crowds calling for blood, and Pilate darting in and out of his chambers unsure what to do.

But at the center of it all is Christ – the sole point of peace, elevated above the chaos, in complete self-control.

And then what happens? The Resurrection and then Pentecost. Suddenly order begins to return to the world. The apostles come back together along with Mary. The Church begins to form. There is peace and harmony among the first Christians ("they had everything in common").

Where God is, there is order.

Bear this in mind as we take a brief walk through the past three weeks of this retreat.

The Terrain We've Traveled

Let's step back into our jungle and see how far we've come. In our jungle mission, it is as if we come to a clearing on a high bluff, or plain, or Mesa. We have a better vantage point to see our far-off destination, the mountain top. We can also turn around and look behind us and see how far we have come. When we were down in the thick of the jungle it was difficult to gage our daily progress. Now, as we take a moment to look back, we recognize just how far we have come and how much we have accomplished.

We set out on our mission in Week 1, and traveled through the following terrain about the basics of Christian mental prayer and our relationship with God:

- Mental prayer is about relationship with God. The greatest purpose of our life is to grow in love with God, so that we will spend eternity with Him in Heaven. The second greatest purpose is similar to this, to grow in love for our neighbor and to help bring as many people to Heaven as we can. We can only achieve this purpose by having a deep relationship with God. And we can only have a deep relationship with God by spending time with Him in daily mental prayer - meditation and contemplation.

- Our life is integrated: our interior life (mental prayer, interior thoughts and aspirations, etc.) and our active life (our relationships with other people and activities in the world) are bound together. Without a healthy interior life (relationship with God) our active life suffers.
- As human beings we are a combination of body and spirit. Mental prayer engages all our faculties particularly our highest faculties (our spiritual faculties) of intellect and free will, but also our lower faculties of perception, cognition, imagination, memory and passions (our bodily, or sensual faculties).
- The Catholic faith provides the fullness of Christian spiritual tradition and teaching on mental prayer. The Catholic faith embraces Christ, the riches of scripture, as well as the teaching and example of many great Saints and spiritual masters. We rely heavily on all these sources to grow in faith and virtue.
- Scripture and Catholic tradition teach that we move through three spiritual stages – purgative, illuminative and unitive.

  o Purgative – discursive meditation and purging unhealthy behaviors and inclinations

  o Illuminative – affective meditation transitioning to infused contemplation and closely modelling our life after Christ

  o Unitive – infused contemplation and living in mystical union with God

In Week 2 we set out deeper into our mission, learning about the dispositions and principles of Christian meditation and living.

- We reflected that mental prayer is about relationship. It's not about method. We don't have a method for the other relationships in our lives. Yes, we have basic approaches and principles for getting to know others and getting along them, but we can't distill our relationships to a one-size-fits-all method. The same is true for our relationship with God.
- There are universal dispositions that facilitate our relationship with God, particularly faith, trust, purity, humility, and persistence. Faith and trust – God is at work in our life (and literally in us), even if it doesn't feel like it. Purity – blessed are the pure of heart, for they shall see God. We need to have undivided hearts, and hearts that are not distracted and chasing after the empty promises and diversions of the world. Humility – the powerful antidote to the pride that chokes off our faith and charity. And perseverance – the heroic fortitude and discipline that we require to advance in prayer even when it becomes difficult, for nothing great is ever achieved without determination and sacrifice.
- There are three guiding principles. These principles are associated with Persons – the three persons of the Trinity, and they are our "guides" if you will, on our mission. The first principle is the primacy of God and of love. The "work" of mental prayer is really God's work in us. Everything is God's initiative, we simply make ourselves fully available to Him and allow Him to love us (we receive that love by trusting Him). The second principle is the incarnation of Christ. Our faith is necessarily incarnational. God's great act of love was to become man and then give His life for us – it is through this relationship, with Jesus Christ, that God redeems us. The only way back to the Father is through the Son. And the third principle is the in-dwelling of the Spirit (and thus the Trinity). Jesus gives us His Spirit. Anyone in a state of grace literally has

Day 22 (Week 3, Day 7)

the Spirit of God dwelling in their soul, and this is the source of the power of Christian mental prayer. God is not a cold, distant deity. God is closer to us than we are to ourselves.

- Asceticism is a natural part of spiritual growth. The purpose of our interior life is to fill ourselves with God – which, then, overflows to all our relationships and activities in the world. We will have little room for God if we're filled with self and worldly activities and desires. Our three enemies are satan, the world and our fallen nature. Satan is beyond redemption and there is little we can do to change the world. But we can change ourself. We can purge ourself of our attachments to unhealthy habits and desires. When we do this, satan and the world no longer have a hold on us. We do this through asceticism – small acts of self-discipline and self-denial, so that we rid ourself of the "old man" (the false self of our fallen nature) and allow God to build up the "new man" in us (our true self – as we were created to be).

And now, in Week 3, we have entered fully into Christian mental prayer as we learned the basics of meditation.

- It is true that mental prayer is about relationship, not method. But we all need a starting point and many saints have advised methodologies for discursive meditation, all sharing similar characteristics (discursive meaning that we move from subject to subject and apply our intellect and reason to understand the subject of our meditation). We are using a method of five R's (some methods combine steps so there are 3 or 4 R's).
- Meditation Step 1: Recollect. By recollection we place ourselves in the presence of God.
- Meditation Step 2: Read. Spiritual reading (life of Christ in the Gospels is ideal), to give our intellect material to relate to God.
- Meditation Step 3: Reflect. An act of the intellect. We ponder a particular passage, interiorizing it and better knowing God through it.

- Meditation Step 4: Relate. An act of the will. We share with God what is on our heart and listen for His response.
- Meditation Step 5: Resolve. We express gratitude and repentance. And, take one concrete action to carry with us until our next mental prayer session.

Lastly, we spoke about distractions. We looked at four types: transient, impulsive, worries, and, pain and suffering

Distractions will always be a part of mental prayer because of our fallen nature. What we can control is how we respond to them and what we let into our brain that could be feeding them. How we respond to distractions is generally fourfold. First, perseverance. We keep bringing our mind back to God. Second, keep track. Become aware of what is most often causing distraction – are there particular worries or subjects that your mind goes to? Third, keep bringing them to God, since He can and will heal whatever needs healing. Fourth, we can and should limit the amount of distracting material that we allow into our brain.

This fourth point is key in our culture. Recall that our brain is different from our mind. Our brain is simply the material "stuff" in our skull that we share with animals. Our *mind* includes spiritual capabilities of reason and will. We must strengthen our mind to overcome the natural inclination of our brain to distraction. We must be brutally honest about how we spend our time and what we allow into our brain. Social media, television, news, the vast majority of what is peddled by Hollywood is poisonous for us. We must choke it off.

The analogy of a purging diet is very appropriate. Most people, once they purge themselves from fast food, processed food, caffeine, artificial sweeteners and the like, can never to back to consuming that stuff. Their body now recognizes it for what it is – poison. In the same way once we purge ourselves from the information and entertainment of the world, even things that we can't conceive giving up at

Day 22 (Week 3, Day 7)

the moment, and replace that with wholesome God-focused material, we will never want to go back.

But we must be patient with ourselves. God is infinitely patient. Follow your natural rhythms and just take that next step in separating yourself from unhealthy attachments. But keep moving forward and, as always, beg for the grace. "Lord, help me to give up ___!"

That brings us back to today.

You have certainly noticed, and probably grown tired of how many times I've said, "we'll talk more about this in a few days." Or, in the same vein, repeated occurrences of "as we discussed in the past." Everything we are doing on this retreat is intimately tied together, because it is all bound up in a simple, loving relationship with God. If, at the moment, any of the material from the past three weeks seems like a bunch of disjointed things that you have try to remember and practice, have no doubt that over time it will all coalesce to that same simple, loving relationship – not an awkward, Frankensteinian assembly of parts.

This is how St. Augustine could proclaim – "Love, and do what you will." As we grow ever closer to God and love ever more perfectly, it really doesn't matter what we do. Because whatever we do will automatically be right in the center of God's will. This is similar to the state of "flow" or "being in the zone" – when you're able to do something (like play a sport or an instrument) at a high level and not think about it – you just do it. This is what prayer becomes.

It's very important that you don't let the volume of information in this retreat become an impediment to your prayer life. If parts of this retreat help you advance in prayer – great, continue to go deeper with them. If parts of this retreat do not seem to help at the time – put them to the side. Maybe the Spirit will draw you back to them at some point, maybe not, but now you know where to find it when you need it.

As we pointed out before, all that is necessary to become a world class person of prayer is: (1) you be you, (2) you make an act of faith to pray with God each day, and (3) you make a genuine effort to grow in virtue (love of God and neighbor and denial of self). If you are faithful to these points you will advance in prayer.

Next week we will touch on several important aspects of the spiritual life, each one of them additional gifts from God to draw us to Him.

Please spend 10 minutes in meditation either reflecting on today's session or today's Gospel reading.

Let's close in prayer:

Lord Jesus Christ, help me to be ever more aware of Your presence and Your great love for me. Amen.

Day 22 (Week 3, Day 7)

Pearls from Day 22: Week 3 - Putting It All Together

Philosophy tells us that God is perfectly simple. This is related to God's infinite nature. If God had "parts" like we do, He would cease to be infinite.

Beauty, purity, symmetry, harmony, balance, simplicity – these are hallmarks of drawing close God. The enemy always works in opposition to simplicity and order. The mark of the enemy is complexity, confusion, chaos, disorder, anarchy, and division.

We should bear this in mind as we progress in mental prayer. Particularly at the beginning we can be easily overwhelmed by the information and lose site of the mission – relationship.

If, at the moment, some of the material from the past three weeks seems overwhelming or disjointed, have no doubt that over time it will all coalesce into a simple, loving relationship – not an awkward assembly of parts.

This is how St. Augustine could proclaim – "Love, and do what you will." As we grow ever closer to God and love ever more perfectly, it really doesn't matter what we do. Because whatever we do will automatically be right in the center of God's will. This is what prayer becomes.

It is particularly important that you do not let the information in this retreat become an impediment to your prayer life. If parts of this retreat help you advance in prayer – great, continue to go deeper with them. If parts of this retreat do not help – put them to the side for now. Maybe the Spirit will draw you back to them at some point and you will know where to find them.

As we pointed out before, all that is necessary to become a world class person of prayer is: (1) you be you, (2) you make an act of faith to pray with God each day, and (3) you make a genuine effort to grow in virtue (love of God and neighbor and denial of self). If you are faithful to these points you will advance in prayer.

Day 22 (Week 3, Day 7)

Your Pearls from Day 22

WEEK 4
PUT OUT INTO THE DEEP

(each session followed by 15 minutes of silent prayer)

DAY 23: CONSOLATION, DESOLATION AND SPIRITUAL COMBAT

> Have you ever had the feeling that something seemed harder than it ought to be? Maybe at work, "if we just didn't have this one competitor breathing down our neck all the time." Obviously in sports, "if there we had no competitor, we could just run up the score." Or managing the household – "if only our family budget was a little bigger," or the universal longing in busy times - "if only there were a couple more hours in the day." It can feel the same in the spiritual life as well – that it is harder than it ought to be. If you have that feeling, it is because that's the way it is. We have an incredibly determined opponent in the spiritual realm.

But we know who our opponent is, we know his petty tricks and tactics, and we have a superstar on our side.

And that is why it is important that we have particularly good communication with our Guides – the Trinity.

Let's begin with opening prayer.

Come Holy Spirit, make of me a fitting dwelling place for the Lord. Amen.

Day 23 (Week 4, Day 1)

Your Jungle Mission

Your journey has taken you back into dense undergrowth of the jungle.

You are reminded of your situation when you first encountered the Savior. The jungle was a dark and dangerous place for you then. If the savior hadn't arrived, you would have soon fallen prey to that snake. And if somehow you evaded the snake it wouldn't have been long before your life was claimed by one of the endless perils of the jungle.

But things are completely different now. With the right Guide and companions, the jungle can be navigated safely. It was just a matter of staying alert and following every command.

It had taken a little time to become confident in following the Savior's hand signals. Was he telling you to move ahead or fall back? Or, don't move a muscle? You'd look to see what the other nomads did and do likewise.

More recently you were becoming accustomed to the promptings of His Spirit. These instructions were much subtler; you had to listen carefully. But they are powerful because you are coming to recognize that His Spirit is always with you.

It has come to the point where you wonder how you were ever able to take a step without Him and His Spirit.

Communicating with God

We know that our mental prayer is a loving conversation with God. But how exactly does God communicate to us? There are many, many ways. First, He communicates with us in the silence. This is the most profound communion of God with our spirit and is the most subtle and illusive for us to come to appreciate. As we have discussed, this is not an empty, sterile silence. It is a listening and trusting silence.

God often communicates to us through ordinary means, through the people and circumstances in our life. Once our spiritual eyes are opened we see God's providence working through these natural causes – the chance meeting, the event that works out better than we could have hoped, the great blessing that emerges from what first seemed to be only disaster, and how smoothly our lives run when we live according to God's plan rather than our own.

God may speak to us more explicitly in our prayer; we may have a name "placed on our heart" or a clear impression of a certain course of action the Lord desires for us.

And God very often speaks to us through movements of spiritual *consolation* and spiritual *desolation*.

Consolation and Desolation

Consolation calls to mind comfort, warmth, encouragement. Desolation calls to mind the opposite, such as loneliness, emptiness, discouragement and even despair. We experience these things in the ordinary course of life, in our relationships with others, and our activities in the world. Whether we know it or not, we also experience *spiritual* consolations and *spiritual* desolations.

Whenever we distinguish something as spiritual, it means that it is explicitly related to our relationship with God. One could argue that everything we do relates to our relationship with God – and that is true in the sense that God is "all in all." But here we distinguish things that are directly and immediately related to our relationship with God. Examples would be our prayer life, activities most closely related to our vocation, worship and sacraments, spiritual commitments such as ministries and service work.

Day 23 (Week 4, Day 1)

In the rest of this discussion when we use the terms consolation and desolation, we are specifically referring to spiritual consolation and spiritual desolation. Examples that follow will better distinguish what we mean by spiritual.

In our discussion of consolation and desolation we are turning to the teaching of St. Ignatius of Loyola (from here on simply St. Ignatius, though not to be confused with St. Ignatius of Antioch – another spiritual giant). St. Ignatius is the preeminent guide on this matter. His masterpiece *Spiritual Exercises* includes his teaching on Discernment of Spirits, which is embodied in "14 Rules." We will turn to that topic in a few days, but for today we are simply going to look at Rules #3 and #4 in which St. Ignatius gives very useful definitions of consolation and desolation. We will start with a direct translation of the third rule (consolation):

> The Third Rule: Of Spiritual Consolation. I call it consolation when some interior movement in the soul is caused, through which the soul comes to be inflamed with love of its Creator and Lord; and when it can in consequence love no created thing on the face of the earth in itself, but in the Creator of them all.
>
> Likewise, when it sheds tears that move to love of its Lord, whether out of sorrow for one's sins, or for the Passion of Christ our Lord, or because of other things directly connected with His service and praise.
>
> Finally, I call consolation every increase of hope, faith and charity, and all interior joy which calls and attracts to heavenly things and to the salvation of one's soul, quieting it and giving it peace in its Creator and Lord.

Thus, the third rule gives a name and description to something most everyone has experienced but few people ever recognize for what it is. When you have that "uplifting of heart" (sometimes to the point of tears) at the experience of something genuinely good, true, or beautiful, it is the Good Spirit moving in you to draw you to God.

Spiritual consolation can flow from ordinary consolation. For example, we might be vacationing on a beach and look out at a beautiful sunset over the ocean. This will give us feelings of ordinary (or natural) consolation. We think how glad we are to be on vacation. How beautiful the beach is, the warm sand, the rhythm of the waves rolling to shore. Perhaps one evening, after watching sunsets for the past few days, something is different. Now our *mind* is lifted to thoughts of God and we start to think "this is all a gift from God."

With this uplifting of the mind we start to realize how good God is, how good God has been to us, and how grateful we are to God, and now our *heart* is lifting up to God as well. This *affective* response – an uplifting of heart, a sense of well-being and realization of God's love – this is spiritual consolation. By *affective* we mean a response that can be felt (it is sensible – we perceive it through our senses, through feelings of peace, warmth, and joy) and it engages our emotions.

This, by the way, is an extremely healthy exercise of our emotions – this is what they were created for!

The fourth rule presents desolation:

The Fourth Rule: Of Spiritual Desolation. I call desolation all the contrary of the third rule, such as darkness of soul, disturbance in it, movement to things low and earthly, the unquiet of different agitations and temptations, moving to want of confidence, without hope, without love, when one finds oneself all lazy, tepid, sad, and as if separated from his Creator and Lord. Because, as consolation is contrary to desolation, in the same way the thoughts which come from consolation are contrary to the thoughts which come from desolation.

Desolation discourages us and saps our will to turn to God and weakens our resolve to engage in holy endeavors. Desolation can also be natural – everything from simply having a bad day to the heavy cross of clinical depression. And natural desolation (e.g. depression) can lead to spiritual depression, if left unchecked. For example, if we are going through trying times at work, long hours and discouraging results, this will lead to spiritual desolation if we allow it to derail our mental prayer routine because we are too tired and feel too disheartened.

Spiritual desolation is permitted by God to strengthen us in faith and fortitude. When we overcome desolation, we emerge stronger – just as hard exercise and discipline strengthen our body and mind.

Great care must be taken because of the equal but opposite principle. When we give into temptation it paves the way for further defeats. St. John of the Cross is a great teacher on the topic of how and why God permits desolation, and we are meant to grow from it.

It is important that we learn to attune ourselves to consolation and desolation and understand how to respond to these movements – we follow consolation and we turn to God and persevere through desolation until it passes. We will talk about this more in a few days with the topic of Discernment of Spirits. For today, we simply introduce the concepts.

Spiritual Combat

Finally, draw your strength from the Lord and from his mighty power. Put on the armor of God so that you may be able to stand firm against the tactics of the devil. For our struggle is not with flesh and blood but with the principalities, with the powers, with the world rulers of this present darkness, with the evil spirits in the heavens. (Eph 6:10-12)

There you have it. The true battle in this life is not against any*one* or any*thing* on earth, it's against the devil and principalities and powers. Principalities and powers refer to choirs of fallen angels – they are ranks of demons.

Our well-known three enemies are the world, the flesh and satan. We understand our fallen flesh from Week 1 – our bodies decay, our intellect is darkened, our will weakened, and our passions disordered and inclined to sin (i.e. *concupiscence*). Just as we are a combination of sacred (spiritual soul) and fallen (the flesh), so is the world. God created the world and called it good, and much of creation reveals that sacred nature. But because of the fall, the world is subject to decay and filled with all of us fallen creatures who tend to come together and hatch stupendously bad ideas that do far more harm as a collective than we could ever accomplish individually.

The fall makes the world and each of us vulnerable to the workings of satan and his minions.

Satan knows this and consequently we are in a constant state of combat. Our hearts are continually under siege.

Now this may all be familiar to you. But, if this is new to you it may seem too much to take seriously. It may sound like a poorly contrived combination of horror movie and conspiracy theory. It is, in fact, quite like the movie *The Matrix* and its plot device of an alternate reality; an alternate reality that is actually controlling our perceived reality, and of which very few are aware.

The spiritual reality beneath the surface of the physical world is always influencing our perception of reality and is a constant battleground for our souls. In fact, the spiritual reality, imperceptible but playing out all around us (the actions of angels and demons and the working of God in our soul), is greater than the physical reality that we take in through our senses.

Since this is a *spiritual* battle, we must defend ourselves with *spiritual* weapons. Ephesians Chapter 6 goes on to list weapons of truth, righteousness, readiness for the Gospel, faith, scripture, and constant prayer. This is why we must be able to communicate

Day 23 (Week 4, Day 1)

closely with our Guides. For the rest of this week we will be looking at the various means our faith gives us to grow in holiness and defend ourselves in battle.

A few closing comments are fitting at this point. Our greatest battle is for our own heart. We cannot redeem satan – he is irrevocably damned to hell. Nor can we redeem the world; at best we can try to bring light to the world where God leads us. But we can master ourselves. And the more we master ourselves, the more we take away the enemy's ability to tempt and derail us. When we perfectly master ourselves, the enemy literally has no place to gain the slightest foothold against us.

Yes, the enemy can still harass us with everything from inconveniences to genuine tragedies (think of the Book of Job), but these are all external, the enemy cannot disrupt our soul or turn us from God.

How do we master ourself? By growing in relationship with God and disciplining (or *mortifying*) our fallen nature through asceticism so that we increasingly turn our will over to doing His will. This is why we end our daily meditation with a concrete resolution that we carry through to our next prayer session.

Fr. Lorenzo Scupoli (1530-1610) authored the classic guide – *Spiritual Combat*. It is believed that St. Francis de Sales (another spiritual giant) carried this book in his pocket for 18 years as his go-to guide for navigating the spiritual life. He has this to say:

> The essence of the spiritual life ... consists in nothing else but the knowledge of the divine goodness and greatness, of our own nothingness and proneness to all evil; in the love of God and hatred of self; in entire subjection, not only to God Himself, but for the love of Him, to all creatures...

Fr. Scupoli uses the term "hatred of self" in the same way that Jesus tells us we must "hate our father and brother," which is to say, that God must absolutely come first in our life. But he also uses the term in the same way that St. Paul talks about hating ourselves, in that he is talking about a particular aspect self – *the flesh*. This is the fallen aspect of our nature. This is the aspect of human nature that is not of God's original design. St. Paul is referring to the flesh when he says, "For the flesh has desires against the Spirit and the Spirit against the flesh; these are opposed to each other, so that you may not do what you want." (Eph 5:17) It is through this fallen aspect of our nature that the enemy gets its hooks into us. So, the more we discipline and detach ourselves from our fallen desires, the closer we grow to God and the less hold the enemy can have on us, as we have noted before.

Self-denial (fasting or other offering) is also a powerful way to intercede for others when combined with prayer. Jesus drove out a demon when His disciples failed to and explained "This kind can only come out through prayer and fasting." (Mk 9:29)

This tradition of self-mastery is very much passed on to us by the Desert Fathers. It is not unlike military training. The rigorous preparation of elite military forces is first and foremost to master themselves so that in the heat of battle they won't cave into their lower nature and impulsively flee (and get shot in the back!).

How does Fr. Scupoli recommend that we engage in Spiritual Combat?

> "You must provide yourself with four very safe and highly necessary weapons ... ***distrust of self, trust in God, spiritual exercises, and prayer***."

You'll find instruction on how to wield each of these weapons in this retreat:

Distrust of self was introduced in Week 1, when we learned about our fallen nature and how unreliable are our disordered passions, our weakened will, and our darkened intellect.

Trust in God was covered in week 2 - faith and trust are our first disposition. We must trust God in all things. In fact, as we saw, this is how we love God – by trusting ourselves to him.

Prayer was specifically covered in week 3 and is the focus of this entire retreat.

What of ***spiritual exercises***? That is the topic for the rest of this week. But first we needed to learn a little more about how God speaks to us (e.g. consolation and desolation) and the battle we face (spiritual combat).

It really is a jungle out there. But we are in the best of hands.

If you are able, increase your meditation time to 15 minutes, either reflecting on today's session or today's Gospel reading.

Let's close in prayer:

Lord Jesus Christ, help me to become ever more aware of Your nearness and Your great love for me. Amen.

Pearls from Day 23: Consolation, Desolation and Spiritual Combat

Spiritual consolation and spiritual desolation are consolations and desolations that either draw us to or away from God. Here are partial definitions from St. Ignatius of Loyola's spiritual exercises:

"Finally, I call consolation every increase of hope, faith and charity, and all interior joy which calls and attracts to heavenly things and to the salvation of one's soul, quieting it and giving it peace in its Creator and Lord."

"I call desolation all the contrary of the third rule, such as darkness of soul, disturbance in it, movement to things low and earthly, the unquiet of different agitations and temptations, moving to want of confidence, without hope, without love, when one finds oneself all lazy, tepid, sad, and as if separated from his Creator and Lord."

There are many ways that God communicates with us, but the ebb and flow of consolation is particularly important to navigating the spiritual life. We follow consolation, and we turn to God and persevere through desolation until it passes

It is critically important that we recognize that we are in a state of constant warfare in the spiritual realm. St. Paul puts it this way:

Finally, draw your strength from the Lord and from his mighty power. Put on the armor of God so that you may be able to stand firm against the tactics of the devil. For our struggle is not with flesh and blood but with the principalities, with the powers, with the world rulers of this present darkness, with the evil spirits in the heavens. (Eph 6:10-12)

"Principalities" and "powers" are choirs of fallen angels; they are ranks of demons.

Recall that our three enemies are satan, the world and ourselves.

Day 23 (Week 4, Day 1)

We understand satan is evil. Just looking at the world around us confirms that it, too, is fallen. And we must recognize that we are our own enemy, that is to say, *our fallen nature* is our own enemy. Fr. Lorenzo Scupoli (1530-1610), in *Spiritual Combat*, identifies how we are to deal with our fallen nature:

"The essence of the spiritual life ... consists in nothing else but the knowledge of the divine goodness and greatness, of our own nothingness and proneness to all evil; in the love of God and hatred of self; in entire subjection, not only to God Himself, but for the love of Him, to all creatures..."

Fr. Scupoli uses "hate" as Jesus does when he tells us we "must hate our father and brother" – it means we can put nothing above God – even our earthly family. But, Fr. Scupoli is also referring to hating ourselves in the context of hating the fallen aspect of our nature – the part of us that is not of God, that is not how God design us to be. St. Paul also frames this perfectly:

For I know that good does not dwell in me, that is, in my flesh. The willing is ready at hand but doing the good is not. For I do not do the good I want, but I do the evil I do not want. (Rom 7:18,19)

The point here is that satan can't be redeemed – he is irrevocably damned to hell. Nor can we redeem the world; at best we can try to bring light to the world where God leads us. But we can overcome our fallen nature, and this is critically important. It is through our fallen nature that the devil tempts us to turn toward the world and our own desires for pleasure and control – and thus turn away from God. If we master our fallen nature (what St. Paul calls "the flesh") satan no longer has any power over us. This is also when we come to that goal of complete harmony as we are no longer at war with ourselves internally.

This then is Spiritual Combat, the battle to master ourselves so that the devil and the temptations of the world hold no power over us. And only then are we free to love God and choose His will. We can only do this by the grace of God. And our primary means of tapping into that grace is mental prayer.

Your Pearls from Day 23

DAY 24: GROWING IN VIRTUE AND CONQUERING YOUR ROOT SIN

> We are naturally attracted to harmony. We know this with music – what if one member of a barbershop quartet is off key? We instinctively know when a team is working in harmony, be it in sports or in the workplace. And, we certainly desire harmony in our homes – parents understand the truism that you are only as happy as your least happy child and we've all heard "if momma isn't happy, nobody's happy".

This is modeled after the harmony of the Trinity; three infinite persons sharing *one* divine nature. What one does, they all do. But exterior harmony is difficult to achieve. Ever try having two cooks in the kitchen? And interior harmony, even more so. That is where virtue enters in.

Let's open with prayer:

Come Holy Spirit, make of me a fitting dwelling place for the Lord. Amen.

Your Jungle Mission

You have been working hard to develop good habits in the jungle. You've discovered your greatest weakness is sensuality – you are naturally attracted to relaxation, comfort and pleasure. It has been difficult for you to embrace the physical challenges of the jungle and you miss many of the creature comforts of your prior life.

Jungle life and self-denial seems to come easy to many of the other nomads. Of course, you're coming to understand that they have their own challenges like pride or vanity, that can often take them off track.

You've noticed an interesting correlation between your attachment to sensuality and your relationships with others. The more you give in to your desires, the more it distances you from the others. Not just from the other nomads, but from the Savior and His Father and Spirit. It's subtle (and sometimes not so so sublte), but when you focus on yourself and arranging for your own comfort and pleasure you find that you miss out on the simple pleasures and satisfaction that come from giving the best of yourself to the activities around you.

Just the other morning you ended up sleeping late. You could have been up at your usual time but just didn't feel like it; it was drizzling outside and you were so comfortable in your tent. By the time you got up and going the other nomads had already finished their morning routines – they had kept their spirits up despite the rain and were ready to set out for the day. You had to rush to catch up and weren't able to prepare for the day ahead the way you like to.

But the opposite is also true. The more you practice self-control and moderation the better your time with your fellow nomads. And especially, you find it much easier to listen and follow the directions from the Savior and His Spirit.

A Life of Virtue

We have said again and again that prayer is relationship – it is *not* about method or technique. That is absolutely true. No exceptions. But growth in our spiritual life is marked by growth in good behaviors and habits. Recall our discussion that everything we do in our life effects our prayer (just as our prayer effects everything else that we do in our life).

This leads to the question – how are we supposed to live our life? Are there better ways to live our life? The answer, of course, is *yes*! A good life, a life of interior harmony, harmony with others and harmony with God is a *virtuous* life. When someone is exceptionally good at something, we call them a *virtuoso*. We want to become a virtuoso at living the life that God gave us. This is the role of virtue.

Our dispositions from week 2 (faith, trust, purity, humility and perseverance) are virtues that are particularly effective for growing our prayer life; which is why we place a special emphasis on them. But there are many other virtues that help elevate all the other facets of our life.

Virtue is, thus, especially important. But because of the fall, virtue does not come easily. Here is what the Catechism has to say:

> "It is not easy for man, wounded by sin, to maintain moral balance. Christ's gift of salvation offers us the grace necessary to persevere in the pursuit of the virtues. Everyone should always ask for this grace of light and strength, frequent the sacraments, cooperate with the Holy Spirit, and follow his calls to love what is good and shun evil." (CCC 1811)

So, it does take effort on our part to grow in virtue and it especially requires God's grace. A good place to start is a brief review of how our spiritual tradition explains virtue, similar to our discussion from Day 10 regarding the theological virtues (faith, hope and love) and cardinal virtues (prudence, justice, fortitude and temperance). The theological virtues have God as both their object and end. Cardinal virtues have God as their end, but the object is either us (prudence) or things external to us (justice, fortitude, and temperance).

The four cardinal virtues are also known as human, natural or acquired virtues. This is because we can acquire them, to an extent, on our own. However, we can never grow into the perfection of these virtues without God's grace. "Human virtues are firm attitudes, stable dispositions, habitual perfections of intellect and will that govern our actions, order our passions, and guide our conduct according to reason and faith." (CCC 1804) This is exactly what we've been talking about – that our higher, spiritual faculties of intellect and will must be exercised over our lower, sensitive faculties such as memory and imagination. The better we do this the greater will be our inner harmony.

The cardinal virtues are encountered throughout scripture and specifically named in Wisdom 8:7, "If anyone loves righteousness, Wisdom's labors are virtues; for she teaches temperance and prudence, justice and courage."

The Catechism gives the following definitions of the cardinal virtues (CCC 1806-1809):

> <u>Prudence</u> is the virtue that disposes practical reason to discern our true good in every circumstance and to choose the right means of achieving it.
>
> <u>Justice</u> is the moral virtue that consists in the constant and firm will to give their due to God and neighbor.
>
> <u>Fortitude</u> is the moral virtue that ensures firmness in difficulties and constancy in the pursuit of the good.

Day 24 (Week 4, Day 2)

<u>Temperance</u> is the moral virtue that moderates the attraction of pleasures and provides balance in the use of created goods.

The three theological virtues, faith, hope and love are *infused* virtues. They must be infused into our soul by God; we cannot acquire them by any natural means. We receive these virtues with the gift of sanctifying grace at baptism and we must pray for an increase in them. We can also grow in these virtues by practicing them. As with all gifts from God, they become active and fruitful in our life when we accept them by living them out. "The human virtues are rooted in the theological virtues, which adapt man's faculties for participation in the divine nature …. The theological virtues are the foundation of Christian moral activity, they animate it and give it is special character." (CCC 1812, 1813)

We also encounter the theological virtues throughout scripture, "So faith, hope, love remain, these three; but the greatest of these is love." (1 Cor 13:13) Love (also known as charity) is the greatest because in Heaven we will no longer need faith and hope because we will be with God and will see Him as He is; all that will remain for us is to live in His love. Love is also the greatest virtue because all others depend on it. Love is how we turn our will to God's will. Love is how we welcome the Holy Spirit into our soul. If we choose against love in the extreme by engaging in serious sin, the Holy Spirit will depart from us. Faith and hope, while still in us, will be lifeless, until and unless we repent and turn back to God through the sacrament of reconciliation.

The Catechism gives the following definitions of the theological virtues (CCC 1806-1809):

<u>Faith</u> is the theological virtue by which we believe in God and believe all that he has said and revealed to us. (CCC 1814)

<u>Hope</u> is the theological virtue by which we desire the kingdom of heaven and eternal life as our happiness. (CCC 1817)

<u>Charity</u> is the theological virtue by which we love God above

all things for his own sake, and our neighbor as ourselves for the love of God. (CCC 1822)

The theological virtues of faith, hope and love are elevated and oriented to supernatural reality.

Faith gives us the supernatural ability to believe in God and His revelation. This is precisely why you can never talk, argue, or convince a person into believing in God. Yes, by giving good arguments and, more importantly, showing genuine Christian love, you can help pave the way for someone to believe - and in this way you are being an instrument of actual grace. However, for a person to receive that *deep inner conviction* that God is real is a supernatural gift.

We all hope for good things. And the greatest good we can hope for is, in fact, a supernatural good – God himself. The hope that we can attain eternal life with God gives the supernatural ability to endure hardship and trial in this life because even the greatest hardship is nothing compared the eternal happiness we hope for.

Charity, at it's purest, is love that contains no self-interest. We love God completely for His sake, because we recognize His complete perfection. Charity best unites our soul to God; our intellect through its esteem for God's perfection and our will out of a desire to conform ourselves to His perfect will. And thus charity is the virtue in which all other virtues are found, because charity is the virtue by which we come to know and act as God knows and acts.

The challenge we face in growing in virtue comes from our fallen nature and inclination to sin.

First, let us look at sin in general. The Catechism describes sin as "an offense against reason, truth, and right conscience; it is failure in genuine love for God and neighbor caused by a perverse attachment to certain goods." (CCC 18490) When we sin, we turn away from God by placing things and ourselves above Him and His plan for our life.

Our spiritual tradition distinguishes seven capital sins (much of this teaching is attributed to Pope St. Gregory the Great and St.

John Cassian, who was associated with the Desert Fathers, in the 4th century). The root of all sin is pride, just as the source of all virtue is charity. Pride is the ultimate turning from God to self. Our Lord tells us this, "For out of the heart come all evil thoughts." (Mt 15:19) It is in our heart, our willfulness, where we turn from God. But charity and the Spirit of God also reside in our heart and when we welcome and cooperate with them, they are more than capable of banishing sin.

Here we need to focus on the cardinal virtue of temperance. While we tend to associate temperance with countering gluttony and drunkenness (which it does), it is more generally the virtue that opposes *all* sin. Recall that the definition of sin is a disordered attachment to created goods. Temperance moderates our passions and desires for the things of the world, including the opinions and admiration of others. Temperance is the cardinal virtue in which is found all other sub-virtues that oppose specific sinful inclinations. Below is a list of the seven capital sins and the virtues that vanquish them. Note that all the virtues are contained in the cardinal virtue of temperance. Each of the capital sins can have subtle variations and shadings and so you may see different virtues sometimes identified to counter each sin, but the following list gives a general idea of how this plays out.

Capital Sin	Conquering Virtue
Pride	Humility
Greed (Avarice)	Generosity, Trust in God
Lust	Chastity
Anger	Meekness
Gluttony	Temperance as such (e.g. discipline, moderation, sobriety)
Envy	Kindness
Sloth	Diligence, Magnanimity

OUR ROOT SIN

Recall our three enemies – satan, the world and our own fallen nature (the flesh). We can't change satan or the world, but we can change ourselves. We change ourselves by first understanding how the fall specifically and individually affects us.

An important teaching in Catholic spiritual tradition which has been lost in modern times is the understanding that each of us suffers from a root sin, sometimes called a predominant fault. Just as we all have human characteristics that are unique to us, such as our fingerprints and unique mix of gifts and talents, we also must grapple with our own unique tendencies to sin. Each us of has one or two areas where we are most inclined to fall into sin.

Our root sin may be any one of the capital sins. Some spiritual masters simplify the list to three potential root sins (which incorporate several of the capital sins) - *pride* (pride and sloth), *vanity* (envy, anger and avarice), and *sensuality* (lust and gluttony). This is based in part on St. John, "For all that is in the world – the lust of the flesh (*sensuality*) and the lust of the eyes (*vanity*) and the pride of life (*pride*) – is not of the Father but is of the world." (1 John 2:16)

Often our root sin is a perversion of a particular strength. Someone who is naturally empathetic and gifted at hospitality and providing comfort to others may fall into sensuality. A person who is particularly capable at accomplishing great things in the world, instead of doing them for God can be turned to do them for their own glory (vanity or *vainglory*).

It can be extremely helpful to think of our root sin as a "core wound." Here we recognize that we are all wounded by original sin. It is like a disease passed down to us from our original parents.

The key issue is our free will. In our conscience we know when we are falling deeply into sin. If we deaden our conscience and refuse to turn to God, we go down a very dark path indeed. But as soon as we move toward God, His grace enters. In God we see our disordered

Day 24 (Week 4, Day 2)

inclinations not as a sin to be indulged but a wound to be healed and a weakness to be mastered (by God's grace).

Our core wound is often exacerbated by woundedness in the world. If a person who has a core wound of pride is not shown unconditional love from their parents and, especially, not introduced to the love of God, their natural inclination toward pride will be increased by the need for worldly achievement.

It is a major effort to identify, root out and heal our core wound, our predominant fault. Especially as we advance in the spiritual life, the manifestation of our woundedness can be very subtle.

For the purpose of this retreat, and as a starting point if this is new to you, we turn to the "two P's" - Pray and Practice. *Pray* for the grace of self-knowledge of your root sin and the grace to overcome it.

Where does *practice* fit in? God helps us grow in virtue by giving us opportunities to practice virtue – just like going to the gym and lifting weights to build muscle. You start with small weights, and when that becomes easy, increase the weight. Do not be surprised when, if you are praying for patience, suddenly you encounter all manner of people and situations that try your patience – these are opportunities to practice the virtue of patience. Find God in these moments, rely on His strength and trust that the Divine Physician is healing your wound.

This is why we include a daily resolution in prayer. The resolution is a concrete way to grow in virtue. When in doubt, remember our first disposition and first principle – Trust in God ("Jesus I trust in You!") and the Primacy of God ("with God all things are possible").

Please spend 15 minutes in meditation either reflecting on today's session or today's Gospel reading.

Let us close in prayer:

Lord Jesus Christ, help me to be ever more aware of Your nearness and Your great love for me. Amen.

Pearls from Day 24: Growing in Virtue and Conquering Your Root Sin

Virtue is how we live a well-ordered life; prioritizing God and neighbor, moderating our passions and turning from sin. We distinguish theological and natural virtues.

The natural virtues (also called acquired or human virtues) are attitudes, dispositions and habits that order our passions and actions. We can acquire these virtues to an extent on our own, but we can only perfect them through God's grace. The four principal natural virtues are the cardinal virtues:

> <u>Prudence</u> is the virtue that disposes practical reason to discern the true good in every circumstance and to choose the right means of achieving it.
>
> <u>Justice</u> is the moral virtue that consists in the constant and firm will to give their due to God and neighbor.
>
> <u>Fortitude</u> is the moral virtue that ensures firmness in difficulties and constancy in the pursuit of the good.
>
> <u>Temperance</u> is the moral virtue that moderates the attraction of pleasures and provides balance in the use of created goods.

There are three *theological* virtues, or infused virtues. They must be infused into our soul by God, we cannot acquire them by any natural means. They are infused into our soul at baptism. We can, however, grow in these virtues by praying for an increase of them and practicing them.

> <u>Faith</u> is the theological virtue by which we believe in God and believe all that he has said and revealed to us.
>
> <u>Hope</u> is the theological virtue by which we desire the kingdom of heaven and eternal life as our happiness.
>
> <u>Charity</u> is the theological virtue by which we love God above

Day 24 (Week 4, Day 2)

all things for his own sake, and our neighbor as ourselves for the love of God.

The challenge we face in growing in virtue comes from our fallen nature and inclination to sin. When we sin, we turn away from God by placing things and ourselves above Him and His plan for our life. Tradition identifies seven capital sins. Each sin is resisted by an opposing virtue.

Capital Sin	Conquering Virtue
Pride	Humility
Greed (Avarice)	Generosity, Trust in God
Lust	Chastity
Anger	Meekness
Gluttony	Temperance as such (e.g. discipline, moderation, sobriety)
Envy	Kindness
Sloth	Diligence, Magnanimity

We all have a root sin, sometimes called a predominant fault. Just like we all have human characteristics that are unique to us such as our fingerprints and unique mix of gifts and talents, we also grapple with our own unique tendencies to sin. Each us of has one or two areas where we are most inclined to fall into sin.

It can be helpful to think of our root sin as a "core wound." Here we recognize that we are all wounded by original sin. It is a like a disease that is passed down to us from our original parents.

For the purposes of this retreat, and as a starting point if this is new to you, we turn to the "two P's" - Pray and Practice. Pray for the grace of self-knowledge of your root sin and the grace to overcome it. And then practice that grace.

Your Pearls from Day 24

DAY 25: GRACE AND GIFTS OF THE SPIRIT

> Grace – what is it? And while we're at it, how, exactly, do we "hear" the Holy Spirit speaking to us? These are profound and subtle questions. It turns out that at our baptism we are given a sort of spiritual hardware by which God communicates with us and acts through us.

Let's open with prayer:

Come Holy Spirit, make of me a fitting dwelling place for the Lord. Amen.

YOUR JUNGLE MISSION

The Savior often talks about His relationship with His Father and His Spirit. He tells you how they are all One. He explains how they have different modes of operation – the Father looking down upon creation and ordering all things, and His Spirit dwelling within the nomads and guiding them, and the Savior Himself, sharing in their humanity. And that seems to make sense. But then he explains that they are always in communion, what One does all Three do.

He says it is exactly that communion, shared by Him, the Father and the Spirit, that is life itself.

The Savior told you that this was why He sought you out in the jungle and saved you. He explained what it means to be *saved*; that it's not so much that He saved you from death as it is that He brought You into Their life.

He explains to you that this is really what your journey through the jungle is all about. To learn to live as the Three of them live. He points out how you are acting more and more like Him with each passing day – He is showing you what it means to be perfectly human, with all the beauty and dignity that the Father intended for humanity. And He points out how you are learning to listen to His Spirit and allow the Spirit to guide you and even work through you to help the other nomads.

He has a word for all of this. Grace.

GRACE AND GOD'S DESIRE FOR COMMUNION

Grace is one of those things often spoken of and invoked, but not well defined. What really is it? A common definition is that grace is a share in the divine life. Fine, but what exactly does that mean? The divine life is the Trinity - living in perfect and eternal self-contemplation and self-love. Great! But what does it mean to have a "share" in that?

Have you ever been around a clique, the "in group," and some part of you had the desire – "I wish I could join them?" In a perfect world we would simply go up to the "in group," be welcomed with open arms and all would be well. In the real world that usually doesn't happen because we're all terribly broken. God, however, is the ultimate "in group" – and He *does* want us to join Him. He *does* welcome us with open arms.

Day 25 (Week 4, Day 3)

But we can't just go up to God and talk with Him on our own. God is infinitely beyond us. In fact, by comparison, it would easier for an earthworm to talk with us than for us to talk with God. God, however, desires us to join Him so much that He gives us supernatural gifts and powers that enable us to do so. Those gifts and powers are grace. Everything God does for us that permits us to draw close to Him are acts of grace. God breathing His Spirit into Adam was grace.

What is Grace?

All of that said, grace remains something beyond our understanding. We can never fully comprehend it nor explain it because it is *super*natural – it is beyond our natural experience. Is it like electricity that makes a lightbulb come to life? Sort of, but not really. Is it like the "Force" in Star Wars? Maybe a little, but there is certainly no "dark side" of grace. Grace defies analogies and comparisons.

Here are some other notable definitions of grace:

"Supernatural life is something (the soul) can receive only as a direct gift from God .... The gulf between non-living and living is not so great as the gulf between natural life and supernatural life" (F. Sheed, *Theology and Sanity*)

"Grace is a reality of the supernatural order, but not a substance, for no created substance could be supernatural.... This quality, according to the forceful expression of St. Peter, makes us 'partakers of the divine nature.'" (A. Tanquerey, *The Spiritual Life*)

What we can say with certainty is that grace is essential for our relationship with God, for our salvation, and for us to function as we were meant to function as spiritual beings, not just flesh and blood.

There are two major types of grace to discuss here – sanctifying grace and actual grace. Sanctifying or habitual grace is the one-time grace that we receive at baptism. With sanctifying grace comes healing of original sin, and the infusion of the Theological Virtues and the Gifts of the Holy Spirit. Sanctifying grace is permanent; there is a change in the actual character of our soul. In fact, we say the virtues and gifts are "inhered" to our soul, not "adhered." They are not simply grafted to our soul, but rather our soul is transformed so that the virtues and gifts are an indelible part of the soul's nature.

Actual Grace can seem a strange name, as if it "*actually is* the real grace" and any other grace is just pretend. But "actual" in this case is meant as a verb not an adjective, as in "acting," "to actualize" or "to make present." Actual graces are temporary graces given to aid us in our spiritual life. Actual grace helps to:

1. Prepare us to receive Sanctifying Grace (e.g. by prompting us to desire baptism)
2. Restore sanctifying grace (if we fall into mortal sin, actual grace from a sincere confession and desire to turn from sin will restore sanctifying grace)
3. Increase sanctifying grace (we should always be praying for an increase in faith, hope and charity)
4. Resist temptation (e.g. by fortitude and good judgement)

GIFTS OF THE HOLY SPIRIT

This brings us to the Gifts of the Holy Spirit. For context let's return to our jungle mission and our three Guides. We have God the Father, and He is looking out over the jungle from the mountain top, watching our every step, understanding how every detail needs to play out and working all things for our good. We have God the Son who has gone before us, blazed the trail and brought countless souls before us to the Father. And we have God the Spirit, our counselor, our interior GPS, guiding us from within. Communicating with our three Guides is critical to succeeding in our mission.

The Gifts of the Holy Spirit are associated with our internal GPS and are a powerful way for God to communicate with us and act through us. Imagine we could set ourselves on autopilot - allowing the internal GPS to control us. This is a very loose analogy to the Gifts. There are seven Gifts. They are mentioned in Isaiah, implied elsewhere in scripture, and were studied and taught by some of the earliest Church Fathers. The seven gifts are tabulated below with their related virtue.

Gifts of the Spirit	Infused and Natural Virtues
Wisdom	Charity
Understanding	Faith
Knowledge	Hope
Counsel	Prudence
Piety	Justice
Fortitude	Fortitude
Fear of the Lord	Temperance

We cannot get into detailed descriptions of each gift here, but we will offer a future retreat on this topic and you can find detailed information on them in the theology references for this retreat. For now, we simply want to understand why the Gifts are important and how they relate to the virtues.

As an example, let's see how the virtue of Faith relates to the gift of Understanding. Just because you possess the supernatural ability to believe in God and His revelation (the virtue of faith), does not mean that you know *what* to believe. How do you acquire the actual *stuff* of your belief? This is more than simple facts. Many people have had the experience of having read parts of scripture and it seemed boring or even hopelessly unrelated to "real life." But after having a faith conversion, suddenly the scripture comes alive, and they say

- "I've heard that a dozen times, but now *I get it*." That is the gift of Understanding in action.

A timeless analogy is that of a sailing ship. A ship without the Gifts is a ship without sails. If a wind comes the ship might move a little, but aimless and slow. But with sails (Gifts) opened and properly aligned the wind propels the ship forward.

Here are some additional descriptions of the distinction of the Virtues and Gifts

> "The motor cause of the infused virtues is human reason – reason illuminated by faith and prompted by an actual grace. The gifts operate under the impetus of the Holy Spirit, who actuates the gift by direct contact. For that reason, the habits of the infused virtues can be used when we wish, presupposing an actual grace, but the gifts of the Holy Spirit operate only when the Holy Spirt so decides." (J. Aumann, *Spiritual Theology*).
>
> "The essential difference between the virtues and the gifts consists in their different mode of action within us. In the practice of virtue, grace lets us act under the influence of prudence. In the use of the gifts, once they have reached their full development, grace demands docility rather than activity." (A. Tanquerey, *The Spiritual Life*).

Put simply (though less accurately), virtues depend on our impetus and exercise, whereas with the Gifts the Holy Spirit works through us and our role is passive – responding to the promptings of the Spirit. Take the virtue of prudence, for example. Let's say we have an important decision coming up, so we take time before hand to deliberate. We pray and turn our deliberations over to God, but it was primarily our initiative and our activity. Let's look at an alternate scenario, in which we abruptly find ourselves in a crisis and God moves us to act. In this case we did not plan for this situation, we didn't have the luxury of time to deliberate options. Here Gifts such as Counsel

Day 25 (Week 4, Day 3)

and Understanding come into action. These are promptings from the Holy Spirit – our role is to be passive and docile and follow the promptings. A classic example of the Gifts in action comes from our Lord – "When they hand you over, do not worry about how you are to speak or what you are to say. You will be given at that moment what you are to say." (Mt 10:19)

The virtues and Gifts work together to help us follow God's will for our lives. God never does violence to us. He never forces His will upon us. He is always gentle. It is like how we interact with children. Children always want to help us, which is wonderful! And we let them, as we should. Some things they are able to do mostly themselves, and this is analogous to us practicing virtue. But often we need to step in and do things for them, and this is analogous to the Gifts of the Spirit. In the same way, God invites us to participate with Him. We primarily bring our activity to bear through the Virtues. In certain circumstances God's will is to take a more immediate action through us – if we are docile He can accomplish this through the Gifts of the Holy Spirit.

This is another reason why we need silence, not just from the noise of the world, but especially from our own interior noise. We need silence so that the Spirit can flow through the gifts.

> "Here it must be noted that these gifts, conferred as they are together with the virtues and habitual grace, do not exert a frequent or an intensive action except in mortified souls who have by a prolonged practice of the moral and theological virtues acquired that supernatural docility and ease that render them completely obedient to the inspiration of the Holy Spirit." (A. Tanquerey, *The Spiritual Life*)

Fr. Tanquerey is speaking of the fruit of spiritual combat. The more we discipline and master ourselves the more disposed we are to hear and respond to the promptings of the Holy Spirit – promptings that we receive through the Gifts of the Spirit.

This is precisely why the Desert Fathers fled the noise and worldliness of Rome for the silence of the desert. While we cannot physically pick up and relocate ourselves and families to the Mohave, we can and must seek an interior desert each day, in our mental prayer.

This should start to fill out the picture of grace and how we share in divine life. By grace our relationship with God is restored and the lines of communication reopened, as it was "in the beginning", in the Garden. By grace we are given the infusion of Virtue and Gifts of the Spirit – our spiritual equipment for participating in God's life; to hear Him and act like Him. Thus, by grace we can continuously be in contact with God and share Him with the world around us.

Please spend 15 minutes in meditation either reflecting on today's session or today's Gospel reading.

Let's close in prayer:

Lord Jesus Christ, help us to be ever more aware of Your nearness and Your great love for us. Amen.

Day 25 (Week 4, Day 3)

Pearls from Day 25: Grace and the Gifts of the Holy Spirit

Grace is "sharing in divine life." Any specific and complete definition of grace beyond this is elusive because grace is essentially supernatural. What we can say with certainty is that grace is essential for our relationship with God, for our salvation, and for us to function as we are meant to - as spiritual beings, not just flesh and blood.

There are two major categories of grace – sanctifying grace and actual grace. Sanctifying, or Habitual Grace, is the one-time grace that we receive at baptism. With Sanctifying Grace comes healing of original sin, the infusion of the Theological Virtues and the Gifts of the Holy Spirit. Sanctifying Grace is permanent; there is a change in the actual character of our soul. In fact, we say the virtues and gifts are "inhered" to our soul, not "adhered." They are not simply grafted upon our soul, but rather our soul is transformed so that the virtues and gifts are an indelible part of the soul's character.

Actual Grace can seem a strange name, as if it "*actually is* the real grace" and any other grace is just pretend. But "actual" in this case is meant as a verb not an adjective, as in "acting" or "to actualize" or "to make present." Actual graces are temporary graces given to aid us in our spiritual life. Actual Grace acts in these ways:

1. Prepares us to receive Sanctifying Grace (e.g. by prompting adults us to desire baptism and enter the Church)
2. Restores sanctifying grace (if we fall into mortal sin, actual grace from a sincere confession and desire to turn from sin will restore sanctifying grace)
3. Increases sanctifying grace (we should always be praying for an increase in faith, hope and charity)
4. Resists temptation (e.g. by fortitude and good judgement)

There are seven Gifts of the Holy Spirit. They are mentioned in Isaiah, implied elsewhere in scripture, and were studied and taught by some of the earliest Church Fathers. The seven gifts are tabulated below with their related virtue.

Gifts of the Spirit	Infused and Natural Virtues
Wisdom	Charity
Understanding	Faith
Knowledge	Hope
Counsel	Prudence
Piety	Justice
Fortitude	Fortitude
Fear of the Lord	Temperance

Whereas virtues depend to a greater extent on our impetus and exercise, with the Gifts the Holy Spirit works through us and our role is passive in that all we must do is receive the promptings of the Spirit. Virtues and Gifts work together to help us follow God's will for our lives. God never does violence to us. He never forces His will upon us. Rather, God invites us to participate with Him. We primarily bring our activity to bear through the Virtues. In certain circumstances God's will is to take a more immediate action through us. And, if we are docile, He can accomplish this through the Gifts of the Holy Spirit.

Thus, we need silence. The more we discipline and master ourselves, the more disposed we are to hear and respond to the promptings of the Holy Spirit – promptings that we receive through the Gifts of the Spirit.

Day 25 (Week 4, Day 3)

Your Pearls from Day 25

DAY 26: DISCERNMENT OF SPIRITS – AN IGNATIAN APPROACH

> Today's reflection includes one of the most important rules of the spiritual life. A rule that can literally save your life.

Let's open with prayer:

Come Holy Spirit, make of me a fitting dwelling place for the Lord.

YOUR JUNGLE MISSION

Evening in the jungle. The twilight brings out the deep blues and greens of the plant life. The cool and calming colors match the evening air and muted chirps and warbles of birds and insects. No longer wild and forbidding, the jungle now seems only peaceful.

You've settled in with your journal and are looking back at the entries of the last few weeks.

You had been coming up to a difficult region of the jungle and the Savior asked you to assist and guide a group of the newest nomads. You were honored and humbled and more than a

Day 26 (Week 4, Day 4)

little nervous to do so. But the Savior thought you were up to it and you trusted in Him and His Spirit.

You gave the very best of yourself to this new level of responsibility and it was going better than you dared hope – not without some ups and downs, but all in all your charges were off to a good start.

But the daily expeditions through the jungle continued to increase in complexity and rigor and you could sense it taking a toll on the new members with problems and complaints increasing each day. You could also sense it taking a toll on you, but your priority was the well-being of your charges.

At about that time you also developed flu-like symptoms; nothing debilitating, but it made the daily exertion that much harder. Not surprisingly you took a few tumbles along the way and were growing quite a collection of bruises, aches and pains.

Between the flu and the aches and fatigue and duties as a guide you hadn't been spending regular time with the Savior. And it was harder and harder to hear His Spirit – He speaks so softly.

You were starting to entertain thoughts of calling it off. Certainly calling off your duties with your charges. And ... maybe calling it *all* off. That mountain was still so far in the distance. Would you ever reach it? Would there really be anything special about it if and when you did? What were you thinking? Who were you to trudge through a jungle?

The voices in your head were telling you to stop. And you certainly felt like stopping. But there was another voice in your head. That voice was telling you "this isn't the time to make any changes – not in this darkness."

That was all weeks ago.

And now here you are in the cool of the evening. And back in the light – in the *spiritual* light, that is. Of course, you hadn't called it all off. The turning point was when you sought out the Savior to tell Him everything you were going through.

He affirmed that you were being greatly tested, and to be confident in the original decisions that you made with Him. He assured you that you were growing in fortitude and many other virtues. And that He and His Spirit would not allow any harm to come to you and your charges.

That all turned out to be so true, and you wouldn't have had the last few weeks play out any other way.

Discernment of Spirits

At the beginning of this week we talked about consolation and desolation. Yesterday we talked about receiving promptings from the Holy Spirit. This is all part of the very real reality of sharing in divine life. Our Lord tells us, "My sheep hear my voice, and I know them, and they follow me." (Jn 10:27) There are many ways we hear the Lord's voice, including prayer and promptings of the Spirit.

This is also part of what we call the discernment of spirits.

To discern something is to come to know what something is. If you see an object far off on the horizon you squint to discern what it is. If someone asks you to do something out of the ordinary you might take a moment to discern their motives – are they serious or is it a prank?

Discernment of spirits, then, is about understanding what is happening at the spiritual level. Great care must be taken because not all voices we hear come from the Lord. Scripture tells us that satan and his demons masquerade as "angels of light." Likewise, we are also quite good at deceiving ourselves and the world is constantly seeding our conscious and subconscious with unhealthy messages.

We turn again to St. Ignatius of Loyola, the leading Christian figure for discernment of spirits. For St. Ignatius the question of discernment distills to "the process by which we seek to distinguish between different kinds of spiritual stirrings in our hearts, identifying those that are of God and those that are not, in order to accept the former and reject the latter." (T. Gallagher, *Discernment of Spirits*)

St. Ignatius' teaching on discernment of spirits is contained in the greater framework of his Spiritual Exercises. The complete teaching is embodied in fourteen brief rules. The first five rules set the stage for discernment and we will limit ourselves to those for this retreat.

St. Ignatius uses the terms "enemy" and "bad spirit" to identify everything that is not of God, which is to say our classic three enemies – satan, the world, and the flesh (our fallen nature). Conversely, "the Good Spirit" references God in the Trinity and includes His action through the angels. In what follows, the writing in italics is St. Ignatius' complete wording of each rule.

First Rule: Moving Away from God

The first Rule: In the persons who go from mortal sin to mortal sin, the enemy is commonly used to propose to them apparent pleasures, making them imagine sensual delights and pleasures in order to hold them more and make them grow in their vices and sins. In these persons the good spirit uses the opposite method, pricking them and biting their consciences through the process of reason.

We see here that the enemy is content to leave in peace those who are moving away from God, and even to entice them further away with worldly allurements. God, in opposition, disturbs these persons through their conscience. Here we see why so many people today seek distraction and deaden their conscience with constant worldly stimulation. It is in quietude and reflection that God works to get our attention and draw us to Him even by "biting and stinging" of our conscience (this is sometimes referred to as "hard consolation" and is somewhat akin to "tough love"). Be aware, though, that even when "biting and stinging," God is always encouraging, never condemning. God provides such thoughts as "you are better than this" and "I desire more for you." It is only the enemy that generates thoughts like "you are a terrible person" and "you'll never be any better than this."

SECOND RULE: MOVING TOWARD GOD

The second: In the persons who are going on intensely cleansing their sins and rising from good to better in the service of God our Lord, it is the method contrary to that in the first Rule, for then it is the way of the evil spirit to bite, sadden and put obstacles, disquieting with false reasons, that one may not go on; and it is proper to the good to give courage and strength, consolations, tears, inspirations and quiet, easing, and putting away all obstacles, that one may go on in well doing.

Here the process is reversed. The Good Spirit now gives consolation and encouragement. The enemies' tactics turn to disquieting, deceptive, condemning thoughts.

THIRD RULE: SPIRITUAL CONSOLATION

The third: Of Spiritual Consolation. I call it consolation when some interior movement in the soul is caused, through which the soul comes to be inflamed with love of its Creator and Lord; and when it can in consequence love no created thing on the face of the earth in itself, but in the Creator of them all.

Likewise, when it sheds tears that move to love of its Lord, whether out of sorrow for one's sins, or for the Passion of Christ our Lord, or because of other things directly connected with His service and praise.

Finally, I call consolation every increase of hope, faith and charity, and all interior joy which calls and attracts to heavenly things and to the salvation of one's soul, quieting it and giving it peace in its Creator and Lord.

This we discussed at the beginning of the week and the reader is encouraged to review that session. Spiritual consolations increase our love for God and increase our faith, hope and charity. Recognition of consolations will lead us to find God during the hours of the day. Here we must remember the golden rule – follow consolation.

Fourth Rule: Spiritual Desolation

The fourth: Of Spiritual Desolation. I call desolation all the contrary of the third rule, such as darkness of soul, disturbance in it, movement to things low and earthly, the unquiet of different agitations and temptations, moving to want of confidence, without hope, without love, when one finds oneself all lazy, tepid, sad, and as if separated from his Creator and Lord. Because, as consolation is contrary to desolation, in the same way the thoughts which come from consolation are contrary to the thoughts which come from desolation.

The reader is again encouraged to review the treatment of desolation from the start of this week. We recall that nonspiritual desolation (psychological or physiological – e.g. fatigue) can lead to, or at least create fertile ground for spiritual desolation. But it is important to note that the response to spiritual desolation is not necessarily the same as for nonspiritual desolation.

In desolation the enemy attempts to redefine our spiritual past and future (e.g. "I never really felt God's love for me, that was my imagination" or, "that was in the past, I'm never going to experience God's presence like that again") The enemy also tries to deceive us with absolute negatives - notice the frequency of the word "never" in the previous examples.

A common tactic of the enemy is to propose "lesser goods." If we are moving toward God the enemy won't try to tempt us with serious sin, but rather lure us toward something less good than what we should be doing (e.g. "I don't have time to pray today because my friend asked me to go shopping"). At the other extreme, the enemy may tempt us with unachievable lofty goals. Let's say we are doing quite well with our 15-minutes of meditation and suddenly we have the "inspiration" to increase to a full hour each day. In truth, this is likely our pride leading us to the sin of presumption ("I'm doing great and God will see me through"), and then to discouragement and desolation when we are not able to maintain an hour of meditation.

Desolation may last for moments, hours, days, weeks or even longer. How we respond to desolation is more important than how we respond to consolation (which is simply to follow consolation). This is because in desolation counsel is from the enemy, whose sole purpose is our destruction.

FIFTH RULE: SPIRITUAL DESOLATION – A TIME FOR FIDELITY

The fifth: In time of desolation never to make a change; but to be firm and constant in the resolutions and determination in which one was the day preceding such desolation, or in the determination in which he was in the preceding consolation. Because, as in consolation it is rather the good spirit who guides and counsels us, so in desolation it is the bad, with whose counsels we cannot take a course to decide rightly.

For many people, Rule #5 is the single most important spiritual guideline in their life. Rule #5 gives us the iron clad directive that we never change our spiritual plans when in desolation. Again, this is because the changes we are considering are proposed by the enemy. This is also where our response to spiritual desolation will be different than our response to ordinary desolation. For example, if we are

Day 26 (Week 4, Day 4)

experiencing ordinary, physical "desolation" because we are getting run down, we probably should change our patterns so that we get more rest.

The two threshold questions we should always be asking if we sense ourselves slipping into desolation:

- Am I in spiritual desolation? (see Rule #4)
- Am I thinking of changing plans that were made when not in desolation?

If we recognize that we're in spiritual desolation and we're thinking of changing plans that we put in place prior to the desolation we should stop right there, discard those thoughts and remain faithful to our spiritual commitments.

Rules #6- #8 continue with specific responses to desolation. First and foremost, we cling to God and we maintain our prayer until the desolation has passed. We should also "console" ourselves with thoughts opposed to desolation. We should remind ourselves that our prior consolation was very real (if you keep a prayer journal, this is a good time to review past entries). We should also reclaim our future and remind ourselves that, as it always has in the past, the desolation will lift. We should also remind ourselves that God *permits* desolation so that we can grow from it (like an athlete lifting weights). God will not permit anything without giving us the grace to overcome it.

Rules #9 - #14 provide additional guidance on consolation and desolation, and how to fortify our interior life in general.

In a sense, all fourteen rules are distilled in St. Ignatius' three-point spiritual assessment plan:

1. *Be aware.* What is happening now? Are you in consolation or desolation? Are you at peace or assaulted by thoughts, feelings, and stirrings of the heart? Are you moving toward God or away?

2. *Understand.* Now that you are aware of your current circumstance, what is the meaning of it? What is the source – is it of the Good Spirit? Is the Holy Spirit giving you an inspiration? Or, are your pride and ego guiding you?
3. *Act.* Now that you understand your current circumstance do not delay in taking the appropriate action. If it is of God, accept it. If not, reject it.

Let's take a hypothetical example. While in consolation, or at least not agitated by desolation, we resolve to increase our prayer time to 20 minutes. The following week we have a couple of difficult days at work. As we become fatigued because of work challenges, our prayer time also becomes dry and tedious. Still we proceed, and even if prayer doesn't "feel" effective, we *choose* to spend time with God because we know it is for our good. At this point we're not in spiritual desolation. But after a few more days our spirit starts to waver, and we start giving in to lowly things. We put off prayer to spend a little more time on the internet. Darker thoughts start entering our mind: "Isn't all of this spiritual stuff just my imagination?" and "Prayer doesn't really change anything" and in the extreme, "Look at me, I'm no different than I ever was." Now we are in desolation. And then it comes – the thought that today we should just skip our prayer time. This is when we must be spiritually aware and stop ourselves. We ask the first question – "Am I in desolation?" Yes! And then, "Am I thinking of changing a spiritual commitment?" Again, yes!

Our response must be threefold:

1. Cling to God. "Lord, come to my assistance. God, make haste to help me!" (Ps 70:2)
2. Keep our commitments.
3. Don't give in to base temptations (internet, food, alcohol, et cetera).

Day 26 (Week 4, Day 4)

If you find yourself thinking, "I don't know if I'm in desolation?"- the answer is "when in doubt, act as if." If some of the indicators are there, and it's also clear that it's not just ordinary desolation from being run down or experiencing a hardship, that is enough to err on the safe side and respond as if you are in spiritual desolation.

St. Ignatius introduced several other powerful aids to the spiritual life. In particular, the Examen prayer and methods for Discernment of the Will of God are invaluable resources. Both are in the retreat reference list and will be part of up-coming *Interior Life* retreats.

The Examen prayer involves reviewing our day in the company of God, so that the Holy Spirit can show us the spiritual movements of the day. When was God trying to get our attention? When were we in danger of succumbing to desolation?

Discernment of the Will of God applies discernment of spirits to specific issues in life, particularly in facing major life decisions. In his characteristic style, St. Ignatius provides a concrete yet spiritually rich and flexible approach for drawing closer to God to determine the path He desires for us.

Please spend 15 minutes in meditation either reflecting on today's session or today's Gospel reading.

Let's close in prayer:

Lord Jesus Christ, help me to become ever more aware of Your nearness and Your love for me.

Pearls from Day 26: Discernment of Spirits – An Ignatian Approach

To discern something is to come to know what something is. If you see an object far off on the horizon you squint to discern what it is.

Discernment of spirits then, is about understanding what is happening at the spiritual level. But care must be taken because not all voices are from our Lord. Scripture tells us that satan and his demons often masquerade as "angels of light." Likewise, we are quite good at deceiving ourselves.

St. Ignatius' teaching on discernment of spirits is contained in the greater framework of his Spiritual Exercises. The complete teaching is embodied in fourteen brief rules. For this retreat we will look at the first five.

For St. Ignatius, the question of discernment distills to "the process by which we seek to distinguish between different kinds of spiritual stirrings in our hearts, identifying those that are of God and those that are not, in order to accept the former and reject the latter."

First Rule – Moving from God. The enemy is content with his progress and leaves us in peace – enticing us further away from God with worldly allurements and preoccupations. God's response is the opposite -he gets our attention and draw us to Him often by "biting and stinging" of our conscience.

Second Rule – Moving Toward God. Here the process is reversed. The Good Spirit now gives consolation and encouragement. The enemy's tactics turn to disquieting and deceptive thoughts.

Third Rule – Spiritual Consolation. Recognition of consolations will lead us to find God during the hours of the day. Here we must remember the golden rule – follow consolation.

Fourth Rule – Spiritual Desolation. Desolation may last for moments, hours, days, weeks or even longer. How we respond to desolation is more important than how we respond to consolation (which is simply to follow consolation). This is because in desolation counsel is from the enemy, whose sole purpose is our destruction.

Fifth Rule – Desolation and Fidelity. The 5th Rule gives us the iron clad directive that we never change our spiritual plans when in desolation. This again, is because the changes we are considering are proposed by the enemy.

In a sense, all fourteen rules are distilled in St. Ignatius' three-point spiritual assessment plan:

1. *Be aware.* What is happening now? Are you in consolation or desolation? Are you at peace or assaulted by thoughts, feelings, and stirrings of the heart? Are you moving toward God or away?

2. *Understand.* Now that you are aware of your current circumstance, what is the meaning of it? What is the source? Is it of the Good Spirit? Is the Holy Spirit giving you an inspiration? Or, are pride and ego guiding you?

3. *Act.* Now that you understand your current circumstance do not delay in taking the appropriate action. If it is of God, accept it. If not, reject it.

Your Pearls from Day 26

DAY 27: SPIRITUAL DIRECTION

> When your new car has a problem, you take it back to the dealership. When you have questions in school you go to the teacher. Health concerns? Visit your doctor. To whom do we turn when we have spiritual questions? Answer - the Creator of our spiritual soul. Ok, but how do we do that?

Let's open with prayer:

Come Holy Spirit, make of me a fitting dwelling place for the Lord.

YOUR JUNGLE MISSION

You helped your charges to successfully navigate the challenging stretch of the jungle, and expected that to be the end of your responsibilities to them.

The Savior, however, has asked you to continue on in your role as a mentor to them. You question why – they've passed through the hard part of the jungle and the going would be much easier for the foreseeable future.

He reminds you that the physically challenging parts of the

jungle aren't necessarily the most perilous. He reminds you of your own challenges with monotony and distraction.

And, He reminds you how some of the experienced nomads helped guide you through those stretches.

He is now asking you to do the same. To help direct the newer members in the same way.

You know your answer should be "yes", but you can't help weigh in your mind whether you're up to this request.

The Savior observes that you have grown proficient and disciplined at spending time with Him and listening to His Spirit. He reassures you that this is the key to helping the other nomads along the Way, because it is actually Him and His Spirit guiding them, through you.

SPIRITUAL DIRECTION

There are many questions that naturally arise along our spiritual journey. *Over time our prayer starts to change, and what once came easily now does not. Is this normal? We have been getting promptings to make significant spiritual changes in life.* Should we follow them? *We have been led to certain scripture passages in our meditation, and they raise more questions than answers.* What does it mean?

What are we to do when such questions arise? First and foremost, we go to our guides in the Trinity. We bring these questions to the Lord. We make these questions part of our prayer session. "Make known to me your ways, Lord; teach me your paths." (Ps 25:4) If there is a persistent question, we might consider dedicating a separate time of prayer to that alone.

This is Spiritual Direction. We seek *direction* on *spiritual* matters. We turn to the Holy Spirit since Jesus gave us His Spirit as our counselor, consoler, and protector. Recall also that the action most appropriate to the Holy Spirit is sanctification – we can trust in the Holy Spirit to guide us to greater holiness.

God also works through the people he places in our life. Sometimes we receive spiritual inspirations and answers through others. We have all experienced the gift of someone saying *just the right thing at just the right moment.* Over time and in prayer we come to recognize that God was speaking to us through that person. That again is spiritual direction.

And sometimes God will call us to formation with a spiritual director.

A spiritual director is someone advanced in the spiritual life and who can be an instrument through which the Lord can guide us. Here again, this is not fancy word smithing. The Holy Spirit is always our Spiritual Director. But, there are times when God will guide us to a human spiritual director. What is happening in that instance is the Holy Spirit working through that person to guide us. An analogy to this is Jesus Christ being the one High Priest, and now He acts through the human priesthood.

We see this form of spiritual direction modeled throughout scripture. Examples from the Old Testament are Moses directing Aaron and Elijah directing Elisha. Christ was, obviously, *the* Spiritual Director. And then we see St. Paul guiding so many people along "the way." A good spiritual director can be a powerful way for God to guide us through our spiritual jungle. Many of the Saints had spiritual directors who were likewise Saints.

SPIRITUAL DIRECTION IN PRACTICE

How does spiritual direction actually play out?

First, we must further clarify what spiritual direction is and what it is not. Spiritual direction entails regular meetings (usually monthly) between the director and the directee. The purpose of the meeting is to receive direction from the Holy Spirit via the director, on how the directee should proceed in his spiritual journey. For example, the director may guide the directee as to making changes to his spiritual commitments such as prayer and service. Likewise, the director may help address issues that arise in the directee's vocation, say, as spouse and parent.

Spiritual direction is a long-term commitment, oriented toward the overall spiritual development of the directee. We say long-term because the major trends and growth in our spiritual life play out over time; we watch for patterns. We also watch for fruit to validate whether we have discerned properly in different circumstances. Direction can also be short-term, focused on addressing a specific issue, but this is best distinguished as *spiritual counseling*.

Spiritual direction is not psychiatric counseling, or any variation thereof. Spiritual direction should be true to its name – spiritual. However, it is reality that human life is complicated. For example, a directee may be going through great struggles with their marriage. This is primarily a spiritual matter if the struggles stem from understanding and living out the sacrament of marriage and staying committed to vocational responsibilities. However, if the struggles are rooted in emotional and psychological trauma, the matter now requires psychiatric intervention. A good spiritual director will know when a directee requires non-spiritual intervention.

FINDING A SPIRITUAL DIRECTOR

The best way to find a spiritual director is with prayer. Discern in prayer whether God desires to lead you to a spiritual director. If the preponderance of prayer is such that you receive repeated inspirations and even validations outside of prayer, then the next step is … more prayer. Pray for the Lord to guide you to a good spiritual director. And then you cooperate with prayer by doing your part to seek out a spiritual director.

Day 27 (Week 4, Day 5)

You can start with people you know who have a well-established spiritual life – do they have suggestions? You can ask your Pastor, someone in your parish administration or at the diocesan level (if you are Catholic). In time your efforts and God's grace will lead you to prospective directors.

As with all important matters, it is essential to test the waters, so to speak. You should start with an informal meeting with your prospective director. The purpose of this is to get to know one another and gage whether the relationship will be a good fit. This is still a human relationship and you must be able to connect on a personal level. There is nothing wrong with deciding that a potential director is not a good fit and politely letting them know that you're not going to proceed with direction. Likewise, the potential director might tell you they do not think they are the right director for you. Here a great deal of emotional maturity is required – both to say "no thank you" to a potential director and to be told "no thank you" by a potential director. If it is not a fit for whatever reason, receive it as God's protection. God is telling you to keep searching.

Regrettably, it needs to be said that there are many poorly formed spiritual directors out there. Being a priest or consecrated religious does not guarantee competence in spiritual direction. Trust your spiritual instincts – if it doesn't feel right there is nothing wrong with making a polite exit. Yes, we are very critical of "feelings" in this retreat, but this is a good use of your feelings. God gave you feelings for a reason, and if you are doing your best to pray and work at finding a spiritual director you can trust that God is guiding your feelings in this matter. More importantly, if the director suggests anything that seems to go against the formal teaching of the Church, you should move on, or seek an independent opinion.

THE LORD WILL ALWAYS PROVIDE THE DIRECTION YOU NEED

If you think you should be in spiritual direction but are having no success finding potential directors, be not discouraged! First, keeping praying and trust in God's providence. Second, there are many other avenues for spiritual direction, and you should avail yourself of these types of resources. There are many good books that provide the type of guidance that you would receive in direction. A classic is *Introduction to the Devout Life* by St. Francis de Sales. *The Twelve Steps to Holiness and Salvation*, a collection of writings by St. Alphonsus Liguori is on par with *Introduction to the Devout Life* and more concise. Any book by Fr. Jacques Philippe will be a wonderful resource. Venerable Fulton Sheen gave hundreds of magnificent talks and wrote dozens of books on very practical matters of the spiritual life, many are available for download. There are several radio programs (such as Relevant Radio) if you have a long commute. And Formed (www.formed.org) has excellent spiritual programming. The *Roman Catholic Spiritual Direction* and *Holy Family School of Faith* websites have numerous resources as well (see the References list). And, *Interior Life* will be providing additional follow-up retreats on specific aspects of the spiritual life. The Holy Spirit can work through all these resources to guide you to His desired ends.

The bottom line is to trust (our first disposition) that you already *are* in Spiritual Direction, with the greatest of all Spiritual Directors. "He will guide you to all truth" (Jn 16:13) and if that includes finding a human spiritual director, He will guide you in that as well!

Please spend 15 minutes in meditation either reflecting on today's session or today's Gospel reading.

Let's close in prayer:

Lord Jesus Christ, help me to become ever more aware of Your nearness and Your love for me. Amen.

Day 27 (Week 4, Day 5)

Pearls from Day 27: Spiritual Direction

There will be many questions that naturally arise along our spiritual journey. When questions arise we go to our guides - the Trinity. We bring these questions to the Lord. We make these questions part of our prayer. "Make known to me your ways, Lord; teach me your paths." (Ps 25:4)

That is Spiritual Direction - seeking direction from God on spiritual matters. We turn to the Holy Spirit since Jesus gave us His Spirit as our counselor, advocate and protector. Recall also that the action most appropriate to the Holy Spirit is sanctification. Put differently, the Holy Spirit is our Spiritual Director.

The Holy Spirit is always our Spiritual Director, but there are times when God will guide us to a human spiritual director. A spiritual director is one advanced in the spiritual life and who can be an instrument for the Holy Spirit. In this instance the Holy Spirit works through that person to guide us.

Spiritual direction entails regular meetings (usually monthly) between the director and the directee. The purpose of the meeting is to receive direction, from the Holy Spirit via the director, on how the directee should proceed in his spiritual journey. This is usually a long-term relationship because the major trends and growth in our spiritual life play out over time; we watch for patterns. We also watch for fruit to validate whether we have discerned properly in different circumstances. Direction can also be short-term, focused on addressing a specific issue, but this is usually distinguished as *spiritual counseling*.

Spiritual direction is not psychiatric counseling, or any variation thereof. Spiritual direction should be true to its name – spiritual. However, human life is complicated and careful discernment can be needed to assess when an issue is spiritual, non-spiritual, or a significant combination of both. A good spiritual director will recognize when a directee requires non-spiritual intervention.

The best way to find a spiritual director is to pray for the Lord to guide you. Cooperate with prayer by doing your part to seek out a spiritual director. You can start with people you know who have a well-established spiritual life – do they have suggestions? Take time to get to know potential directors, it must be a good fit for both parties, and if not, either should be comfortable to say that it isn't a good fit (do not assume just because a director is a priest or religious that they will be a good director for you).

Whether or not you have a spiritual director, you can and should be making use of the nearly endless spiritual resources available to us (see the reference list for this retreat). Great books and of course, Sacred Scripture all provide excellent material for the Holy Spirit to work through to provide the Spiritual Direction that He desires for you.

Day 27 (Week 4, Day 5)

——————— Your Pearls from Day 27 ———————

DAY 28: THE SACRAMENTAL LIFE AND MARY, OUR BLESSED MOTHER

> We have all had the experience of hearing a song on the radio – one we haven't heard for years, yet it takes us right back to a specific point in time that is forever paired with that song in our memory. That song has been *sacramentalized*...

Let's open with prayer:

Come Holy Spirit, make of me a fitting dwelling place for the Lord.

Your Jungle Mission

She was always in the camp looking after everyone. No matter how early you awoke in the morning she was already at the camp stove. No matter how late you turned in she was still attending to the needs of one of the nomads or making preparations for the next day.

She was kind and skillful and attentive to every need. She was also very quiet and slow to speak. Whenever you asked something, she was most likely to respond "That's a fine question. You should ask Him about that."

You noticed that amid whatever she was doing, she would be softly speaking with His Spirit. You could tell because her voice took on a certain tone – light and almost musical.

Early on you asked some of the experienced nomads who she was. They had the most remarkable answer – she was the Savior's mother. At first it seemed the strangest thing in the world to you that the Savior should have a mother. But then, she seemed to be everyone's mother and after a while it came to be so natural you never much thought about it; you just thought how much brighter the camp was because of her loving, motherly presence.

OTHER SOURCES OF GRACE

This week has focused in a particular way on the topic of grace, and how we share in divine life. We receive supernatural equipment to do this at baptism with infused virtues and gifts of the Holy Spirit. It is by grace that we receive this supernatural equipment, and that same equipment then becomes channels of grace in our lives. There are many other ways that we receive grace. The greatest among them are the Sacraments and Mary, our Blessed Mother.

We will spend time with Mary in a moment, let's start with Sacraments by going back to our opening comment about the power of a song. I can recall listening to *American Pie* on a transistor AM radio, very tinny with plenty of AM static. Now, when I hear *American Pie*, I'm a kid in the early 70's all over again. God created this wiring in us. There is something in us that naturally attaches something beautiful and enduring (like a song) to events in our life, so that we can recall that moment.

Sometimes we do not make the best use of this wiring and choose poorly in both the life events and the songs, but God created this wiring for His great and lofty purpose - to guide us to Him.

I recall on one retreat having a powerful experience of the love of God the Father, His plans for me, and His desire for my freedom (real freedom, interior freedom, the freedom to do His will). At that moment there was a large bird soaring overhead, effortlessly on the thermals so that he was barely moving his wings, practically floating over me. To this day, in an uncanny way, when I am feeling the weightiness of life, I will look up and there will be a large bird soaring overhead. I am instantly transported to that time on retreat and I am consoled by the memory of God's revelation. That image of a bird has been *sacramentalized* for me. It is a sign of God's love for me.

THE SACRAMENTS

A Sacrament is a sacred sign of Christ's love and gift of salvation. In Christianity we distinguish Sacrament with large *S* and sacramentals, with a small *s*. Sacraments with a large S are efficacious signs instituted by Christ by which divine life is dispensed to us through the Holy Spirit. By efficacious we mean that the signs accomplish what they signify. If "American Pie" were a Sacrament, if it was an *efficacious* sign, it would literally take me back to the event that is tied to it in my mind – I would literally be a goofy kid on his Huffy bike. The song wouldn't simply be a memory. The Holy Family School of Faith (see References) provides this analogy: "if a stop sign were a Sacrament it would actually cause your car to stop."

Thus, the Sacraments are powerful channels of grace. On Day 14 we spoke about how we plan for our children. We want to leave a legacy, an inheritance for them, not simply money but rather a sense of connectedness to the family of origin. Thus, we put together photo albums. We leave them heirlooms.

Christ desires that for us as well, but even more so. Christ's "heirlooms" are supernatural. He left them to strengthen us in the most important areas of our life, such as our vocations. When we become adults in the Church we receive the Sacrament of Confirmation. If called to religious life, one receives the Sacrament of Holy Orders. If called to family life, the couple receives the Sacrament of Matrimony.

Virtually all Christians agree on this in general, but there are important distinctions to the Catholic embodiment of the Sacraments. The universal starting point is the Sacrament of Baptism. Why did Christ get baptized? He did not need to receive the Holy Spirit because He and the Holy Spirit were of one divine nature. Christ was baptized so that He could sacramentalize the ritual of baptism. Christ sanctified the baptismal water, turning it into a supernatural gift. By His baptism, baptism becomes an efficacious sign for all of us; it accomplishes what it signifies. When we enter into the baptismal water (or have it poured upon us) we are supernaturally present with Christ in the Jordan River, being baptized with and by Christ, and we are purified because Christ made the water pure.

One of the most important facets of our lives is forgiveness. When we sin, we turn away from God, and we need to seek His forgiveness. Thus, Jesus left us a sacramental way to free ourselves from the poisons of sin in the Sacrament of Reconciliation. This Sacrament provides us the fulness of reconciliation with God.

The Sacrament of Reconciliation is supernatural, *super* in that we receive absolution and healing. Only Christ can absolve and heal. The question is often asked – why the need for a formal Sacrament and confessing sins to a priest? Well, if you simply confess your sins to God in your mind, how does that play out? It is human nature (fallen nature) that we are tempted to give ourselves "a pass" or "benefit of the doubt." We might by-pass some sins or become presumptuous of God, that He "gets it and it isn't really any big deal." There may be some things we are doing that we don't even recognize as sins. However, when we articulate something aloud and in front of another, often clarity and insights emerge. Beyond that, the supernatural aspects enter in when we do this before God in the Sacrament of Reconciliation with a priest as the intermediary.

We stress here that if you are Catholic and have committed serious sin you must seek out a priest and receive this Sacrament – it is a gift you can't afford to pass up. Like so many things in life, once we return to the Sacrament of Reconciliation and experience it's healing power, we wonder why we stayed away (the answer is spiritual combat – our threefold enemy does not want us to experience this grace). If you are not Catholic, you should make as complete of a private confession as you are able (we have included an act of perfect contrition at the end of this session) - this is a beautiful offering to God, and please consider seeking out a priest to explore reconciliation further.

The pinnacle of the Sacraments is the Sacrament of Holy Communion. As living beings, we must eat or we die. It is that simple. How much more do we need food for our souls, and that is the Eucharist. Christ gives us the fullness of His divinity under the appearance of bread and wine.

This is known as the "real presence" of Christ, as He is truly present in the Eucharist. This is extraordinary and only by supernatural faith and time with Christ in mediation can we come to truly appreciate the gift of the Eucharist. A common argument against the Eucharist is that were we to genuinely believe that the Eucharist was the real presence of Christ, all Catholics should be on our hands and knees in reverence and awe. But this isn't proof against the Eucharist; it is simply recognition of the weakness of our faith in the supernatural reality that surrounds us. Christ anticipated this - "When the Son of Man comes, will He find faith on earth?" (Lk 18:8) But if you look at Catholics who believe and give their lives over to the Sacraments and mental prayer, it is a different story. They are transformed, and you *will* find them in reverence and awe.

Most people who live out a truly sacramental life aren't sensational about it. They go about life quietly and do great things (often in seemingly small ways like raising their children for Heaven rather than Harvard). You may have to search hard to see this being lived out. It is as if the world doesn't want this secret getting out. A sacramental life is not the sort of thing that makes splashy headlines nor

Day 28 (Week 4, Day 6)

gripping Reality TV. But it is the source of fulfillment in this life and what makes Saints. Without the Sacraments, there would be no Saints. They all had deep devotion to the Sacraments – particularly the Eucharist and Reconciliation.

All Christians recognize Sacraments to one degree or another, most closely in the higher Protestant churches – Anglican, Episcopalian and Lutheran. C.S. Lewis, himself, believed in the real presence of Christ in the Eucharist.

For non-Christians – one way to think of the Sacraments (and grace in general) is as the actuality of the desire we all have for a greater reality. Almost everyone, deep down, has a sense and hope that we can connect with something bigger than ourselves. The Sacraments are just that – very real ways that we encounter the supernatural. To be clear, as always, we are not talking about magic. Magic is man's attempt to bend nature and even the spiritual realm to his will. Sacraments are God working both outside of nature and through nature to accomplish His will for us.

The Saints and spiritual masters are unanimous in the necessity of the Sacrament to advance in the spiritual life. If you find you are having difficulties in prayer or any other aspects of life, it is quite likely that Christ is permitting this challenge and through it calling you to come home to Him in His Sacraments.

Our Blessed Mother

Let's turn to a related topic – the Blessed Virgin Mary.

Not only is there a hunger in society for a greater reality, but we also live in a time when there is great emphasis on the role of women in all spheres of life.

What then of Christianity? Where are women in Christianity? As we have noted previously, God has no gender. God is pure spirit. We give both masculine and feminine attributes to God. God is a father. Wisdom is a woman. But God does not take on gender until he becomes human, when he becomes man. In a theological sense, God becomes all of mankind – perfecting humanity (women and men). But God also becomes specifically and genetically a man – Jesus Christ. He is considered the new Adam. What, then, of Eve? What of Woman? That is the role of Mary. Mary becomes our Spiritual Mother. Jesus appoints her as such.

There can be a great deal of misunderstanding of Mary's role in our spiritual lives. We will touch on only a few points of clarification here. First and foremost, Mary always leads us to her Son. As she told the stewards at the wedding in Cana, "...do whatever He tells you." (Jn 2:5) Christ came to undo the sin of Adam and Eve. Christ became the new Adam. Would he not give us a new Eve? From the earliest days of Christianity, it was understood that Mary's "yes" to archangel Gabriel undid Eve's "no" to God, and this is why Christ repeatedly refers to His mother as "woman" – the same title used for Eve. Why should we need to know Mary? Because Jesus desires it. Among Christ's seven last statements from the Cross, He tells his beloved disciple, who signifies each of us, "Behold your mother." (Jn 19:27)

Most of the great Saints had a strong Marian devotion. C.S. Lewis did as well. Anyone who develops a devotion to Mary finds that she will lead them to her Son, with no distractions. To paraphrase Venerable Fulton Sheen, Christ is not offended by our reverence to His mother any more than we would be if a friend of ours told us that they loved our mother. Fulton Sheen continues, "as the mother knows the needs better than the babe, so the Blessed Mother understands our cries and worries and knows them better than we know ourselves."

A perfect place to begin to get to know Mary is with the Rosary. In the rosary we meditate on the great mysteries of the life of Christ. The rosary is both a vocal prayer and a meditative prayer. We recite one Our Father and ten Hail Mary's as we meditate on a specific mystery from the Gospel. The recitation of repeated prayers (ten Hail

Mary's) is a natural way to focus our mind and avoid distraction. In the East this might be considered a Mantra, but in Christian spirituality it serves not to empty ourselves, but rather to create a closeness to Christ and our Blessed Mother.

Please see the *References* to learn more about Sacraments and Marian devotion.

Closing Comments

Today's session is not intended to "pull a fast one" on non-Catholic retreatants. We've said repeatedly that all that is required to be a world class person of prayer is (1) be yourself (2) spend daily time with God in mental prayer, and (3) make a committed effort to grow in virtue (love of God and neighbor and denial of self).

Again, there are terrible and evil forces working against us, as we discussed with *Spiritual Combat*. The simple fact is that it is virtually impossible to prevail and progress on our own. Christ gave us His Sacraments and His mother. It would be disingenuous and irresponsible to come to the end of this retreat without emphasizing how important these gifts are. They are not optional.

The Sacraments are supernatural expressions of Christ's love for us. And our Blessed Mother is so quick to lead us to Him.

Please spend 15 minutes in meditation either reflecting on today's session or today's Gospel reading.

Let's close in prayer:

Lord Jesus Christ, help me to be ever more aware of Your nearness and Your great love for me. Amen.

Day 28 Post-Script - Act of Perfect Contrition

Forgive me my sins, O Lord, forgive my sins of my youth, the sins of my age, the sins of my soul, the sins of my body, my idle sins, my serious voluntary sins, the sins I know, the sins I do not know: the sins I have concealed so long, and which are now hidden from my memory.

I am truly sorry for every sin, mortal and venial, for all the sins of my childhood up to the present hour.

I know my sins have wounded Thy Tender Heart, O my Savior, let me be freed from the bonds of evil through thy most bitter passion, death and resurrection, Jesus my precious Lord, forget and forgive what I have been.

In the name of the Father, the Son and Holy Spirit. Amen.

Pearls from Day 28: The Sacramental Life and Mary, Our Blessed Mother

A sacrament is a sacred sign. A sacrament draws us to God. All of creation is meant to be a sacrament, "The heavens declare the glory of God; the firmament proclaims the works of his hands." (Ps 19.1)

God can *sacramentalize* anything for us. We are familiar with this idea from songs, which have a way of taking us back to a specific event that we associate with the song.

In Christianity we distinguish Sacrament with large *S* and sacramentals, with a small *s*. Sacraments are efficacious signs instituted by Christ by which divine life is dispensed to us through the Holy Spirit. By efficacious we mean that they accomplish what they signify. If that old song were a Sacrament, if it was an efficacious sign, it would literally take you back to the event that is tied to it in your mind; it wouldn't simply be a memory, you would be physically transported.

Christ instituted the Sacraments to give special graces where we need them most in life - in our vocations (Holy Orders and Matrimony), for forgiveness (Reconciliation), and for spiritual food to sustain our soul (Eucharist).

Mary always leads us to her Son. As she told the stewards at the wedding in Cana, "... do whatever He tells you." (Jn 2:5) Christ gives us Mary as our spiritual mother. Christ came to undo the sin of Adam and Eve. Christ became the new Adam. Would he not give us a new Eve? From the earliest days of Christianity, it was understood that Mary's "yes" to the angel undid Eve's "no" to God, and this is why Christ repeatedly refers to His mother as "woman" – the same title used for Eve.

A perfect place to begin our journey with Mary is praying the Rosary. In the rosary we meditate on the great mysteries of the life of Christ. The rosary is both a vocal prayer and meditative prayer.

We recite one Our Father and ten Hail Mary's as we meditate on each mystery. The recitation of repeated prayers is a natural way to focus our mind and avoid distraction. In the East this might be considered a Mantra, but in Christian spirituality the recitation of prayer brings a closeness to Christ and our Blessed Mother.

The Sacraments and our Blessed Mother are Christ's great gifts to us. And, they are indispensable to our spiritual progress.

Day 28 (Week 4, Day 6)

Your Pearls from Day 28

DAY 29: WEEK 4 – PUTTING IT ALL TOGETHER, FRUITS OF THE HOLY SPIRIT AND BEATITUDE

> Welcome to the end of Week 4 of our retreat. Human beings crave feedback. We don't always *like* the feedback we get – but we hunger for it all the same. How do we receive feedback in our spiritual life? From God, as He never ceases communicating Himself to us. Two of the most powerful and reliable forms of feedback are the Fruits of the Holy Spirit and the Beatitudes. To be sure they are much more than feedback; they are the outcome of the transformation of our very being into something glorious.

Let's begin with opening prayer:

Come Holy Spirit, make of me a fitting dwelling place for the Lord.

YOUR JUNGLE MISSION

You are very encouraged when you look back through your journal.

You can remember your first days in the jungle, trekking along with the other nomads. Everything was new, everything was awkward. None of it came naturally.

Day 29 (Week 4, Day 7)

You watched, listened, and learned from the experienced nomads and, especially, the Savior. Over time it became habit forming. Over even more time it became second nature, to the point that you usually enjoyed the challenges presented by the jungle.

But you've made note of an even deeper area of growth, and that is your ability to follow the promptings of His Spirit. This was much subtler than simply accumulating knowledge and practicing the skills necessary to thrive in the jungle. This was a matter of allowing the Spirit to guide you. First, it took much time and interior silence to come to be able to "hear" the promptings of the Spirit. And then, it took even more time to follow those promptings. It was all too easy to override the Spirit's prompting with your own doubts and desires. But the more you gave yourself over to the Spirit, the easier and more natural it became, and your journey through the jungle took on an entirely new character.

Your growth in ability to emulate the Savior, and your growth in docility to His Spirit – those are threads that weave through each day of the journal. But they're not the only threads. By far the greatest theme that emerges is your growth in relationship with Him. It seems they all developed together.

FRUITS OF THE SPIRIT AND BEATITUDE

This week we looked at how God shares His life with us through grace. We looked at the infused virtues and the gifts of the Holy Spirit, the spiritual equipment we receive as part of the sanctifying grace of baptism. We looked at two other primary channels of grace - the Sacraments which are Christ's gift to us, and Mary, who is always guiding us to her Son. We also looked at how we engage in God's plan for our life through spiritual combat (mastering ourselves) and discernment of spirits (listening and responding to God's voice).

We expect change when we invest in an activity. If we read a book, we expect to grow in knowledge. If we go to the gym, we expect to grow stronger. How exactly does spiritual growth manifest itself? How do prayer, practicing virtue and receiving the Sacraments change us? How do we know if it is "working"?

We have a general idea that we should expect to grow in love and that we will experience peace. And that is right on track. But God always does much better than generalities. God, very deliberately, gave humanity two ways that growth in holiness manifests itself in our lives – the fruits of the Holy Spirit and the Beatitudes.

We discussed earlier this week that the virtues are closely tied to our activity whereas the gifts of the Holy Spirit are more closely tied to the Holy Spirit's activity working through us (our role is to be docile and receptive to the promptings of the Spirit.) There is a direct parallel with the fruits and beatitudes. The fruits of the Holy Spirit are closely aligned with our activity (like virtue) and the beatitudes are closely aligned with the action of the Spirit (like the gifts of the Spirit).

Channel of Grace	Mode of Action	Gives Rise To
Virtue	Our Initiative	Fruits of the Spirit
Gifts of the Spirit	Holy Spirit Acting Through Us	Beatitude

Let us look at our jungle mission. Despite all our preparation and training, there is no substitute for entering the jungle because experience is a great teacher. Inevitably the initial phase of our mission will be difficult. As we begin to use our newfound skills in the actual jungle conditions, we will likely suffer minor accidents, mistakes, and injuries. Hopefully, they will be small and simply part of the learning curve. Over time, closely and diligently following our Guides, our skills will have habituated and the way will become easier. This is equivalent to growing in virtue.

And what happens then? We begin enjoying the adventure of the mission. We thrill at the start of each new day and the challenges it will bring. We become confident that when those challenges come, we will meet them with composure and a sense of peace. This is akin to the fruits of the Holy Spirit. We have grown so far in virtue that practicing virtue becomes easy and is accompanied by joy even amidst challenges.

Now suppose we have discovered a different mode of trekking through the jungle. We have found that we can set our internal GPS (the Holy Spirit) to autopilot, so that it can take over and animate us. This is comparable to the gifts of the Holy Spirit.

Now, we are still aware of what is happening while our GPS is set to autopilot. Our own thoughts and uncertainty can jam the signal and disrupt the control of our GPS (the Holy Spirit). But over time we become so comfortable with our internal GPS that we no longer fight it. We allow it to flow and we grow to be in perfect harmony with it. This is akin to the beatitudes. We are transformed into something new as we become proficient at letting the gifts of the Spirit flow through us.

FRUITS OF THE HOLY SPIRIT

Let's look more closely at the fruits of the Spirit. The fruits are implied throughout scripture and explicitly taught by St. Paul in his letter to the Galatians:

> *I say, then: live by the Spirit and you will certainly not gratify the desire of the flesh. For the flesh has desires against the Spirit, and the Spirit against the flesh; these are opposed to each other, so that you may not do what you want. But if you are guided by the Spirit, you are not under the law. Now the works of the flesh are*

> *obvious: immorality, impurity, licentiousness, idolatry, sorcery, hatreds, rivalry, jealousy, outbursts of fury, acts of selfishness, dissensions, factions, occasions of envy, drinking bouts, orgies, and the like.*
>
> *I warn you, as I warned you before, that those who do such things will not inherit the kingdom of God. In contrast, the fruit of the Spirit is love, joy, peace, patience, kindness, generosity, faithfulness, gentleness, self-control. Against such there is no law. Now those who belong to Christ [Jesus] have crucified their flesh with its passions and desires. If we live in the Spirit, let us also follow the Spirit. Let us not be conceited, provoking one another, envious of one another.*
>
> (Gal 5:22-23)

In the mind of the Church this is not an exhaustive list of the fruits but important nonetheless since St. Paul was inspired to list these nine in particular.

The fruits of the Spirit result from our transformation, and that transformation is a result of our spiritual combat and detachment from worldly allurements. Recall the battle cry for spiritual combat rooted in St. Paul's declaration that "The flesh has desires against the Spirit, and the Spirit against the flesh." (Gal 5:7) The "spoils of war" in this spiritual combat are the fruits of the Spirit.

The fruits are both virtuous acts and the spirit of joy that accompanies those acts. The fruits cannot be feigned because they proceed from the Holy Spirit acting within us. If you have experienced this, you know it. However, the onset of the fruits can be subtle. You may be experiencing them starting to grow in you right now and not realize it.

One way to come at this is in reverse. In that same passage, St. Paul talks of the "works of the flesh." Let's take "outburst of fury" as an example. An outburst of fury is the sin of rage or extreme and unjustified anger. This sort of fury simply wells up in us, unbidden and uncontrolled. Yes, sometimes (Heaven help us) we work ourselves into a boiling little pot of rage when we anticipate some insult coming our way. Most times, however, rage just wells up from deep within. We don't make the rage happen and we can't fake authentic rage. That is the main point – *it wells up from within us*.

The fruits of the Spirit operate in a similar but opposite way.

Let's compare our example of rage with the fruit of peace. This is peace that the world cannot give, nor can the world take it away. This is the peace possessed by Christ even during His passion. If you have ever experienced this peace, then you know what it is. Even amidst trials, the heart is at peace. Obviously, this type of peace is much different than rage, but they have something important in common. Like genuine rage, we can't fake true peace, nor can we conjure it up on our own – *it wells up from within us*. But it wells up from an even deeper place than rage or the other "works of the flesh" because they well up from our disordered passions, whereas the fruits emanate from the Holy Spirit dwelling in our spiritual soul. Furthermore, the fruits are part of, and reveal, the healing of our disordered emotions. The fruits well up from our spiritual soul where the Holy Spirit dwells and eventually envelop our sensitive soul (recall that distinction from Day 4) – healing our disordered passions and emotions.

When our natural state is more given to virtue than vice, we begin experiencing the fruits of the Holy Spirit welling up from within us. We are imitating Christ, by the power of the Holy Spirit, to the point that we derive a spiritual joy from exercising virtue.

However, the fruits of the Holy Spirit are not the end of our transformation journey. There is something greater yet. Christ, in the Sermon on the Mount, tells us that the height of Christian perfection is *beatitude*.

Beatitude

We opened this retreat talking about everyone's desire for happiness. Here again, we distinguish the world's view of happiness from God's plan for our happiness. The world confuses happiness with pleasure and other self-focused outcomes. The paradigm here is that pleasure is the end goal of the flesh. It is in the body. It is fleeting. And most often this pleasure is something we try to arrange for ourselves. God certainly gives us opportunity to enjoy worldly delights as simple consolations along our journey, but this is not true happiness. Happiness and holiness, as always, are synonymous. Happiness is found by living out our destiny of freely loving God and our neighbor for His sake. This type of happiness is everlasting.

Another word for this vision of happiness is beatitude. Even more so than the fruits of the Spirit, beatitude is wholly God's action in us. The beatitudes represent the perfection of Christian life. They are the result of steadily giving ourselves ever more completely over to God and relinquishing our poisonous desire for control.

We will look with some small detail at the first beatitude and in the postscript for today we continue to briefly look at the remaining seven and how they evolve in us with one beatitude leading to the next. Each beatitude is presented in the Gospels in two parts, a perfected action and then the blessing that results from it.

As you reflect on the beatitudes you will find they can be interpreted in two ways – how they apply to your exterior activity in the world and how they apply to your interior life.

Here are the beatitudes as presented in Mathew 3:5-12.

Blessed are the poor in spirit, for theirs is the kingdom of heaven.
Blessed are they who mourn, for they will be comforted.
Blessed are the meek, for they will inherit the land.
Blessed are they who hunger and thirst for righteousness, for they will be satisfied.

Day 29 (Week 4, Day 7)

Blessed are the merciful, for they will be shown mercy.

Blessed are the clean of heart, for they will see God.

Blessed are the peacemakers, for they will be called children of God.

Blessed are they who are persecuted for the sake of righteousness, for theirs is the kingdom of heaven.

Blessed are you when they insult you and persecute you and utter every kind of evil against you [falsely] because of me. Rejoice and be glad, for your reward will be great in heaven. Thus, they persecuted the prophets who were before you.

We'll now look at the first beatitude, *blessed are the Poor of Spirit, for theirs is the kingdom of heaven*. This beatitude can be viewed in terms of exterior poverty, in which case blessed are those who either act as if they were poor (they practice *detachment*) and those who literally are poor. Reliance on God comes by necessity for the poor and to those who do not place their faith in worldly resources. That is why Mother Teresa, when visiting the US, commented that she had never seen such poverty. Not financial, but spiritual.

There is an even deeper interior poverty which comes with detaching ourselves from our pride and vanity. This is when we recognize that we are truly nothing without God. We recognize any good that we do is only because of God. When St. Faustina was near death and thought she had given all that she had to God, the great Saint was told by Jesus that she was still holding one thing back from Him – her suffering. The fullness of poverty is when we hold nothing back from God and desire nothing but Him.

When we start to recognize God as our source of happiness, as opposed to wealth or control or our own abilities, we begin to experience *the kingdom of heaven* on earth.

The other beatitudes can be similarly considered from an exterior and interior perspective, and they bring us full circle. We are back to the three ages of the interior life. As was taught by Augustine and

Aquinas, in the first three beatitudes we are purging ourselves of connectedness to the world and our pride – the Purgative Way. Then, in the next two, *thirsting for righteousness and mercy*, we move to imitating Christ in the active life - the Illuminative Way. And only the pure of heart can enter the Unitive Way and be true bearers of peace and accept persecution and even receive it joyfully for God's glory.

Thus, we grow and advance in beatitude as we grow and advance in our interior life. We cannot make the beatitudes happen within us. The beatitudes are the result of our transformation.

This is not to say that we should not try to live according to the beatitudes. We certainly should! We should detach ourselves from the world and our own pride. We should offer mercy and bring peace to others. But we can't feign the transformation of our interior nature. Let's again take the first beatitude, poverty, as an example. You should live *as if* you were poor. Do you need a fancy new car (maybe you do, some professions like real estate sales, require a nicer vehicle) or will a more modest and reliable model be just fine? Do you need a second helping of dessert or was one helping just the right treat to set your mouth at the end of the meal? And so on. There are two important things that we find when we try to live out the first beatitude:

1. It does not come naturally. It is an effort. It hurts a little to deprive ourselves.
2. It really does not get any easier if this is all that we do.

#2 is the key to the situation. If our sole focus is self-denial, we will not make much progress. Self-denial is important, but it is one piece in the puzzle. What we need first and foremost is to grow in relationship with God, and *everything* that entails – mental prayer, worship, love of neighbor *and* denial of self (the first beatitude). When we grow in love for God and neighbor, we will necessarily become less self-absorbed. Guess what happens then? After a while, self-sacrifice becomes easy. It becomes natural. We welcome sacrifice because we see it as a source of grace for us and the people around us.

Now when we sacrifice and *act as if we are poor*, we are happy – with a true happiness that is not forced. This true happiness is beatitude. And now we understand *Blessed Are the Poor* – it is not something that we are consciously forcing ourselves to do. It has become who we are.

CLOSING COMMENTS

The fruits of the Holy Spirit and beatitudes complete our "spiritual equipment" for sharing in God's life. We'll close with this summary from Fr. Tanquerey (*The Spiritual Life*): "The beatitudes put the final touch to the divine work in us. Like the fruits, they are acts, but possess of such perfection that they seem to flow from the gifts rather than from the virtues; they are fruits, but fruits of such mature perfection that they already furnish us with a foretaste of heavenly happiness; hence, their name, beatitudes."

Please spend 15 minutes in meditation either reflecting on today's session or today's Gospel reading.

Let's close in prayer:

Lord Jesus Christ, help me to be ever more aware of your presence and great love for me. Amen.

DAY 29 POSTSCRIPT: A WALK THROUGH THE BEATITUDES

Blessed are the poor in spirit, for theirs is the kingdom of heaven. What happens when you are truly poor in spirit? You start drawing close to God because you are relying on Him day in and day out for everything. And remarkably, as you draw close to God, you start seeing things as they truly are. You see the world, for example, with the eyes of Mother Teresa who visits the US and sees great spiritual poverty. And you feel sorrow, a deep, genuine sorrow. And then you mourn.

Blessed are they who mourn, for they will be comforted. We mourn everywhere that God is absent. We mourn all the evil, all the injustice in the world. We mourn all the lack of faith and all the wounds we inflict on one another. And most of all we mourn our own sin, our own failings. It makes us weep because we see with the Lord's eyes when He looked down upon Jerusalem, soon to be destroyed. We see with the Lord's eyes when He looked upon the tomb of His friend Lazarus. But, we are comforted because Jesus wept too, and weeps with us. And we are comforted because He promises us that in Heaven "I will wipe every tear from your eyes, and there shall be no more death or mourning, wailing or pain...." (Rev 21:4)

If we are not careful, the enemy will twist and distort our emotions. When we see all the injustice around us and experience injustice ourselves, satan will twist our mourning into anger, self-pity and self-righteous rage. Mourning over our own sinfulness, he will turn it into self-loathing and despair. That is why *Blessed Are the Meek*. We are blessed when we take hardships and mourning to spiritual intercession, heroic patience and, when called for, righteous anger. In our meekness comes a humility that recognizes our own sinfulness, weakness and failings – not in despair but in hope in God's mercy. We bring it all to God and respond accordingly. We neither yield to unbridled anger, nor cower in despair. We accept our circumstances and do whatever God wills for us in each situation.

Thus, meekness and submission to God's will stir us to action. Now we *Hunger and Thirst for Righteousness*. Righteousness is God's justice. The opposite is vengeance – when we take matters into our own hands. We look to God to enter in and make things right in His way. We also look for interior righteousness. We are stirred to take action to root out all sin that separates us from God (because we mourn this as much if not more than we mourn injustice suffered by others).

But even greater than God's justice is God's mercy ("mercy triumphs over judgement"). *Blessed are the merciful.* When we draw close to God and see with His eyes, we see with eyes of mercy. We see how merciful God has been with us. We begin to see the brokenness all around us, even in our persecutors, and especially in ourselves. Yes, everyone needs to be brought into God's righteousness, but our eyes see with great mercy. This is how Jesus could weep over Jerusalem. He knew the people of Jerusalem were going to kill Him, but He wept for them just the same because of His great mercy.

Now we are becoming perfected in love of both God and neighbor. We are freed of attachments to the world, and the attachments to sin. We see our neighbor with eyes of mercy. We are purified. *Blessed are the pure of heart, for they shall see God.* When we learn to see properly, we see God as "all in all." (1 Cor 15:28)

And when we are purified there is no interior struggle. We are single-hearted. We are filled with peace. *Blessed are the peacemakers.* We receive in our hearts Christ's promise that "Peace I leave with you; my peace I give to you. Not as the world gives do I give it to you. Do not let your hearts be troubled or afraid." (Jn 14:27) And, we hear Christ send us forth has He did his disciples, "Into whatever house you enter, first say, 'Peace to this household.' If a peaceful person lives there, your peace will rest on him; but if not, it will return to you." (Lk 10:5-6)

Christ warns that not everyone will receive our peace. When Christ endured His passion, He was the center of peace. All around Him were in chaos, but Christ was at peace. And we know how it played out. *Blessed Are Those Who Are Persecuted.* The world is unwelcoming to prophets. When we come and bring God's peace, there are those who will have none of it. And the persecution will come. And we will experience interior persecution as we grow in self-sacrifice and redemptive suffering. The enemy will continue to attack us from within and without, but we accept and embrace all attacks, unified with Christ on His Cross.

Thus flows beatitude in our life. The descriptions above are just one very simple walk through the beatitudes. Books can, and have, been filled with reflections on their meaning and interaction. It has been said that the Sermon on the Mount is the distillation of the entire Christian life, and the beatitudes the distillation of the Sermon on the Mount.

Pearls from Day 29: Week 4 - Putting It All Together, Fruits of the Holy Spirit and Beatitude

The fruits of the Holy Spirit and the Beatitudes are manifestations of our growth in holiness – they proceed from our growth in virtue and docility to the gifts of the Holy Spirit.

The fruits of the Holy Spirit particularly reveal to us the transformation of growing in virtue. The beatitudes particularly reveal the transformation of growing in the gifts of the Holy Spirit.

St. Paul contrasts the works of the flesh with the fruits of the Spirit in Galatians chapter 5. "Now the works of the flesh are obvious: immorality, impurity, licentiousness, idolatry, sorcery, hatreds, rivalry, jealousy, outbursts of fury, acts of selfishness, dissensions, factions, occasions of envy, drinking bouts, orgies, and the like... In contrast, the fruit of the Spirit is love, joy, peace, patience, kindness, generosity, faithfulness, gentleness, self-control." (Gal 5:19-23)

The fruits result from our transformation. And that transformation is a result of our spiritual combat and detachment from worldly allurements. The fruits are both virtuous acts and the spirit of joy that accompanies those acts. The fruits can't be feigned because they proceed from the Holy Spirit acting within us. If you've experienced it, you know it. Likewise, the onset of the fruits can be subtle. You may be experiencing them starting to grow in you right now, and not realize it.

But the beatitudes are yet greater than the fruits of the Holy Spirit. Christ, in the Sermon on the Mount, shows them to be the height of Christian perfection and as such, the height of human happiness.

There are eight beatitudes. Each beatitude is presented in the Gospels in two parts, a perfected action and then the blessing that results from it. As you reflect on the beatitudes, you will find they can be interpreted in two ways – in how they apply to our interior life and our exterior activity.

Looking at the first beatitude as an example: *Blessed are the poor in spirit, for theirs is the kingdom of heaven.* We are poor in spirit when we conduct ourselves as if we were physically poor – perfectly detached from the world; not seeking wealth and great comforts. But this beatitude can also be applied to our interior life and our need to be spiritually detached from pride and vanity.

The beatitudes are written in the order of our journey through the three ages of the interior life. The start of the Purgative Way is the first beatitude (*blessed are the poor*). The perfection of the Unitive Way is the eighth beatitude *(blessed are they who are persecuted for the sake of righteousness)*.

As with the fruits of the Spirit, we cannot "fake" the beatitudes – they flow from a holy life.

Your Pearls from Day 29

DAY 30: RETREAT CLOSING

Congratulations on completing your 30-day retreat! As is often said, "this really isn't the end, it's the beginning." We have a few final thoughts before waving farewell as you, following your Guides, venture to the mountain top.

Let's open with prayer.

Come Holy Spirit, make of me a fitting dwelling place for the Lord. Amen.

YOUR JUNGLE MISSION

So many years have passed.

Younger nomads have taken on most of your duties and responsibilities. You may not be able to do them, at least the physical activities, but you still have much wisdom to share, particularly with the younger ones as they help you with the harder parts of each day's hike.

They help you get settled in at night as well, as you thank them and bless them and wish them a good night's rest. That has been the routine now for so many nights you can't remember when it wasn't. Each night you feel a little more worn out. In your mind and your spirit you are still the same person, your body however is like a wind-up toy that is quickly slowing down and must soon stop.

But this morning you woke up a little different, at least you supposed it was morning, it was so bright.

He was right there with you.

"I must have over-slept. We'd better get going, there's still so far to go." You think on it a moment and add, "I'm getting so old I don't know if I'll ever make it. I thought we'd have gotten there by now."

The Savior looks at you and explains it was never that sort of destination. The far-off mountain is not actually a place you physically reach on Earth. It is more a vision that keeps you moving and growing closer to Him and His Father and Spirit.

"Oh, I never looked at it that way" you say.

He takes your hand and you get up and start walking. It seems so much easier this morning. You feel fifty years younger.

"Will you tell me that favorite story of mine, one more time? The one about your Father."

He smiles. *You mean the one about how He and your first parents would walk about the garden at the breezy time of day?*

"Yes, that's the one. Please tell me that one while we walk."

Oh, I think you should ask your Father to tell you Himself. He's right up ahead, waiting for you.

Day 30 (Retreat Closing)

THE VIEW FROM THE HEAVENS

Let's begin with a final summary of the terrain you have traveled. The purpose of this is to simply highlight how far you have come in 30 days.

Week 1

- Mental prayer is conversation with the One who we know loves us.
- In meditation our activity is primary. In contemplation God's activity is primary.
- It is the teaching and example of Jesus and testimony of the Saints that mental prayer is indispensable to growing in relationship with God and thus, in happiness.
- We have a soul with sensitive powers (like animals) and spiritual powers (like angels).
- God is three persons sharing one divine nature. God's self-knowledge begets the Son. The Holy Spirit proceeds from the mutual love of the Father and Son.
- Our spiritual soul gives us powers of intellect (knowing) and will (loving) – it is in these that we are made in God's image.
- Mysticism is simply entering into the mystery of God. We accept these mysteries on faith, and we also penetrate them as deeply as we are able with our reason and intellect. We proceed deeper in both our knowing and faithful unknowing, through meditation and contemplation.
- The mystical path leads us through three spiritual ages – purgative, illuminative and unitive.

Week 2

- Mental prayer is a matter of relationship not method, not technique, not skill.

- Certain dispositions and principles help us to progress in mental prayer.
- Dispositions of faith and trust, purity of Intention, humility and fortitude are particularly beneficial to mental prayer.
- Principles guide how we relate to the Triune God. The primacy of God the Father in all things - God is always the initiator and gives us the law of love. Our incarnational faith – it is through the incarnation of Jesus Christ that we are restored to relationship with the Trinity. The indwelling of the Holy Spirit – our spiritual life flows through the gift of the Holy Spirit dwelling within us.
- Asceticism helps us to empty ourselves of our fallen nature ("the flesh") so that we can be filled with God and all the good things He desires for us.

Week 3

- We embark on our journey with an approach to mental prayer taught by many of the spiritual masters.
- We start with discursive meditation. With discursive meditation we flow from topic to topic with each new session of meditation and particularly focus on the life of Christ in the Gospel.
- By meditating on the life of Christ we grow in relationship with Him and learn how to become more perfectly human – more perfectly who God created us to be.
- We follow the five R's – Recollect, Read, Reflect, Relate and Resolve.
- We also have a plan for dealing with different types of distraction, while recognizing that distraction is simply part of the human condition and to some degree unavoidable.
- Preparation for prayer includes *remote preparation* – everything else that we do in life. The more we bring the rest of our life in line with God the better will be our prayer.

Week 4

- We are constantly being affected by movements of spiritual consolation and desolation.
- We are in a state of spiritual combat – the Good Spirit and the enemy at war for our soul.
- Virtues and Gifts of the Holy Spirit are spiritual equipment we receive at baptism to aid us as we enter into the life of the Trinity. This is also known as grace.
- Discernment of spirits is a methodology and art that we use to determine what is of God, and accept it, and what is from the enemy, and reject it.
- Spiritual direction is the guidance we receive from the Holy Spirit. In practice it involves sessions with an experienced spiritual director who is a vehicle for the Holy Spirit.
- Fruits of the Holy Spirit and Beatitude flow from a life of virtue and responding to the gifts of the Spirit.
- Two other powerful channels of grace are the Sacraments (Christ's gifts to us) and our Blessed Mother (who is always leading us to her Son).

That's a tremendous amount of spiritual ground! In fact, it is a great majority of the landscape of mystical theology. By necessity we've only skimmed the surface – with each spiritual concept we could spend hours, days, weeks going deeper.

Here it must be said, as from Day 22, let this not be a burden.

And here it must also be said – the real fruit of this retreat is not how much content you have covered, but how much time you have spent, and how much of your heart you've shared, with the Lord.

Must you know the three ages of the interior life, the distinction of the gifts and fruits of the Spirt, beatitude and infused virtues? No. This is not an intellectual exercise. It is not a matter of stuffing information into our brains.

God gives us these various teachings to help us along our journey and now you are aware of how they fit into your personal relationship with God and neighbor and how to find out more about them when you need them. God always wants us to be able to enter as deeply as possible. Perhaps some years from now one of these topics will become of great importance for you. Perhaps never. Perhaps your path is simply to draw close to God in prayer and virtue and then go and pour out your love to your neighbors.

Do that with all your mind and heart and you will be a great mystic!

This brings us to our next topic....

The Work of a Lifetime

We have also said again and again – "this is the work of a lifetime."

Let this not be a discouragement.

It's natural to have a gut response - "A lifetime? That is too long, I want results now!" But you can appreciate the distinction between making short term progress (which you will) and sustaining that progress for your lifetime (which is even better).

To belabor the point a little, let's look ahead to the next 10 years of your life. At the end of that time you will be 10 years smarter and wiser than you are now. And in 20 years, Lord willing, you will be 20 years smarter and wiser than now. What good is it to object "I don't want to wait 20 years?" The only way to grow into your 20-year-older self, with your 20-year-older wisdom, is to live another 20 years. There's literally *no, other, way* to get to that version of yourself.

And so it is with the spiritual life. We will be growing in our spiritual life for our entire lives. We never get to a point where "we're done."

That is not to say you will not make tremendous progress from the start. I hope and expect you will. In six months or a year you will look back and think "I can't believe how far I've come." And that progress is measured by how your heart grows. Recall that in the end only love remains, and that we can never *know* perfectly but we can *love* perfectly. It is our heart, our willingness to love and sacrifice that is the true measure of our growth. So these are the marks of spiritual progress to watch for: growth in relationship with God and neighbor, growth in virtue, growth in self-mastery, growth in interior peace.

One of the most immediate areas for growth is simply to steadily increase your time of meditation to 30 minutes each day. As you now know, it is important to not let it become a burden, a distraction or, worst of all, a discouragement. Let the Holy Spirit be your guide in this. Do not attempt to rush to 30 minutes. You may stay at 15 minutes for many months or longer before being prompted by the Holy Spirit to increase your time. One way to start that increase is to incorporate longer sessions on the weekends. If you are meditating 15 minutes each day, increase your Sunday meditation to 20 minutes and then extend that to Saturdays and then to weekdays. This is how athletes increase their stamina. A runner training for a marathon does one extra-long run each week – it by that extra-long run that he incrementally pushes himself to greater distances.

We can also encounter negative thoughts that "It's too late for me ... I should have started long ago ... there's so much water under the bridge ...." Not so! Now is the perfect time to grow your prayer life. Thinking it is too late to start in with mental prayer is just as much a deception as thinking a lifetime is too long to work at it. In both instances this is the work of the enemy either taking us into the past ("there's so much water under the bridge") or into the future ("I can't wait that long"). We must recognize that this is spiritual combat. God is always in this present moment, and in this moment, He is so pleased to be with you.

It should also be reassuring to know that we are not supposed to get this over night. Sometimes we grow slowly into each new dimension of our spiritual life. Other times we have sudden flashes of inspiration, or "growth spurts." St. Therese of Lisieux reminds us: "The good God does not need years to accomplish His work of love in a soul; one ray from His Heart can, in an instant, make His flower bloom for eternity."

Most important is that we need to be gentle and patient and allow God to lead us in this process. Because it is not a process, but rather a relationship.

And we never "master" a relationship. We never look to someone we care about and say "OK, we're done. We are maxed out. Nothing new here." We keep growing. And we keep growing together.

In other words...

THERE'S NO STANDING STILL

Sayings, aphorisms, and maxims can be greatly beneficial because they are simple reminders of deep, abiding truths. Conversely, they sabotage truth when they leave us remembering only the simplistic cliché and not the deep, abiding truth.

Let's take "offer it up" for example. As we discussed on Day 20, what has become a catch phrase (when it's even used at all these days) is really a tag line for one of the deepest and most powerful human realities. We can in fact transcend and transform suffering by uniting it with Christ on the Cross. This is a powerful part of the response to pain and suffering[1]. The phrase "offer it up" should remind us and *stir our hearts* with the underlying truth that our suffering is redemptive.

So it is with "there's no standing still in the spiritual life." This truism is repeated time and again. Pope Francis has been known to say it often. You will find it in many books on theology and spirituality. Here is an example from Fr. Garrigou-Lagrange (Three Ages of the Spiritual Life):

---

[1] Yes – people can still ask "why must there be pain and suffering in the first place?" – there are different and equally powerful answers to that question – stay tuned for future retreats that answer these objections to God.

Day 30 (Retreat Closing)

"As soon as the soul's life ceases to descend, it ascends toward God. It cannot remain stationary on earth...."

Very rarely, however, do we ever find an explanation of why this is. On the one hand it seems fairly obvious that we should always strive to keep growing. On the other hand, it isn't at all obvious why we can't just remain stationary or "tread water". And it does not lend itself to a brief explanation. Thus, we are usually left without one.

In some ways this entire retreat is the full answer to this question of why we can't remain stationary in the spiritual life.

Our spiritual life is about relationship. Specifically, it is about relationship with God, which flows into relationships with others. Distinct but related to this is that life is always coming at us. Nonstop. We are bombarded by thousands of experiences, big and small, each day. And those are just the experiences in the physical world that we take in through the sensitive powers of our soul (seeing, hearing, our mental power of perception, and the like). Simultaneously, there is a war constantly raging in the spiritual realm, as we discussed in spiritual combat, and our soul is constantly subjected to those opposing forces even though we do not perceive them through our physical senses. Thus, we are always "expanding" in the sense of being subjected to all these different influences and taking in these new experiences. And whether we like it or not, these influences and experiences are *forming* us.

How do these influences and experiences relate to our human relationships?

Let's take marriage, as an example. Married or not, you are probably familiar with the concept of husband and wife making time for "date night," so that they do not drift apart amid the busyness of daily life. In fact, every night should be date night. Most nights will look less like going out for surf-and-turf and more like tuna casserole at the kitchen table, but date night it should be. What happens when you have date night every night? You talk about little things. And this is critical because, you know what happens if you don't talk about little things? They grow up and become big things. And now they are *too big* to talk about. "I'm not opening *that* pandora's box." My wife and I have an expression that we will only have hardwood floors in our relationship – no carpets. No place where things are swept under and hidden away. Do we do it perfectly? <Insert your chuckling sounds here> But it's a very helpful and necessary goal.

So, we are always expanding with the experiences of life. Either we bring those experiences to our relationships and our relationships grow along with those experiences, or else our relationships shrink in comparison.

(On a side note, this is where I again implore you to rethink social media and secular entertainment in general. Are you connecting with people as human beings? What is the value of peeking into another's life to see "what their spouse look like?" or "if someone has gained weight?" or be tempted to wonder what that vacation cost them? Do you communicate on social media with people the way you would if they were sitting with you face-to-face? Is social media robbing time from your very real relationships with God and the people around you?

Anyone who knows marketing will tell you "don't end on a sour note." I am stepping into that exact puddle by trekking back to the social media hobgoblin, but it is far too important to leave it unsaid. Social media, and secular media in general, is one of the most spiritually damaging forces in the world right now. Only an exceedingly small percentage of social media has any life-giving value and only an exceedingly small percentage of people have the resolve to use that small percentage of social media in a healthy way. It is another sign of the evil of social media that it made me write a sentence as tortured as the one you just read.)

Back to relationships. Our marriage example applies just as well to our relationship with God. Either you are turning to God in each new experience (scripture tells us to "pray always"), or not. Let's say a hundred new things come at you today (and in reality, it's thousands or more). To remain stationary, you would have to turn to God with 50 of them, and not bother with the other 50 (assuming both groups of 50 are experientially equal, and good look trying to figure out how to do that).

That is a cartoonish example, but you get the idea. The more often you turn to God and stay close to Him, the more you will be moving forward. If you are more often not turning to God, then you will slide backward. Furthermore, not all experiences are morally, spiritually and relationally equivalent. I can turn to God 99 out of 100 times, but if I choose not to turn to Him when I have an impulse to tell a big, fat lie – and I go ahead and tell it – I just took a giant step backward. And this is what we do much of the time. We live in that bright shiny place of God's love most of the day until we come to our little pet sin. Then it becomes, "God? God who? Never heard of him."

When we turn to God in every little thing, nothing is little. Everything becomes large because of the love with which we do it. As St. Therese of Lisieux tells us, "Do little things with great love."

And that is why there is no standing still in the spiritual life. We must bring everything to God. The big, the small, the good, the bad and the ugly. All of it.

So that we can hear His response...

I Love You

Prayer is conversation. God responds to us in many ways. God speaks to us in prayer, in scripture and through people and events in our life. We have the indwelling of the Holy Spirit and "spiritual equipment" to help us hear God's voice. We have discernment of spirits to help us distinguish God's voice from imposters.

Here is the simplest method of discerning God's voice – God's message is always "I love you." If you hear anything other than "I love you" it is not of God.

Now, as we noted in Day 26, God practices "tough love" when He must. If we are moving away from God, he will "bite and sting" our conscience to get our attention because God loves us too much to let us fall into sin and chase after things beneath us.

But God's language is always affirming, always encouraging. He will always tell you that you are too good for whatever sin may be tempting you.

The enemy resorts to accusation, criticism and condemnation. When you hear *that* voice in your head, reject it, and turn to God. Again, there's no standing still in the spiritual life. When those voices come, pray to God ("God come quickly, Lord come to my aid," or "Jesus, I trust in You," or "In the name of Jesus, I renounce _____"). Do this a thousand times a day if you must.

The enemy is also the tempter. When you're tempted, pray to God so you can hear Him tell you that you are better than that and that by His grace you can rise above the temptation. Hear God tell you that "you are fearfully and wonderfully made" and "I have great plans for you." And if you do fall into sin, seek His forgiveness, particularly hearing Him say "I love you" in the fullness of the Sacrament of Reconciliation, and move onward and upward.

This brings us to the end of today's session, and thus to the end of our retreat. And with that, a closing comment on the closing comment that I've used each day in the video sessions of this retreat...

"And I Look Forward to Being with You Again Tomorrow"

That is the phrase I say at the close of each daily video session of this retreat. I say in all humility, those are not only my words to you. I'm not in the habit of putting words in the mouth of the Almighty, but as sure as I know His words to you are "I love you," I also know that those closing words are His words to you.

Why do we pray? Because God wants us to. And it is not just that He wants us to pray *because it's good for us,* like a spiritual "eat your vegetables." Although it certainly is good for us. But He also wants us to pray *for His own sake.* Seriously. Think about that for a minute and let the enormity sink in. God tells us that He delights in us. God tells us that He longs for us. Does God *need* us to share our life with Him to make him happy? No. He is perfectly complete and perfectly happy. But, for some mysterious reason, God *desires* us to be in relationship with Him – for Him and for us.

Each time you end your session of mental prayer, with every fiber of my being I assure you, God the Creator of the Universe, God your Loving Father, God Who gave His life for you on the cross, God Who dwells in your soul, says "I look forward to being with you again tomorrow."

Your Pearls from Day 30

APPENDIX
RECOMMENDED RESOURCES
AND REFERENCES

This very brief list provides some starting points on major aspects of developing your interior life.

Catholicism and Mystical and Spiritual Theology

The Catechism of the Catholic Church, 2nd Ed. (CCC)

Aumann, Jordan – *Spiritual Theology*

Garrigou-Lagrange, Reginald – *The Three Ages of the Interior Life*

Martin, Ralph – *The Fulfillment of All Desire*

Tanqueray, Adolphe – *The Spiritual Life: A Treatise on Ascetical and Mystical Theology*

Introductory Theology, Christology and Thomism

Kreeft, Peter – *A Summa of the Summa*

Marshall, Taylor – *Thomas Aquinas in 50 Pages*

Sheed, F. J. – *Map of Life*

Sheed, F. J. – *Theology for Beginners*

Sheed, F. J. – *Theology and Sanity*

Sheed, F. J. – *To Know Christ Jesus*

Carmelite Spirituality

Dubay, Thomas – *Fire Within*

St. John of the Cross – *The Dark Night*

St. John of the Cross – *Spiritual Canticle*

St. Teresa of Avila – *The Interior Castle*

St. Teresa of Avila – *The Story of a Soul*

St. Teresa of Avila – *The Way of Perfection*

Ignatian Spirituality

St. Ignatius of Loyola – *Personal Writings*

Gallagher, Timothy – *The Discernment of Spirits*

Gallagher, Timothy – *Discerning the Will of God*

Gallagher, Timothy – *The Examen Prayer*

Watson, William – *Sacred Story Affirmations, Meditations on Discernment of Spirits*

Eastern (Christian) Mysticism and the Desert Fathers

Anonymous – *The Cloud of Unknowing*

Pseudo-Dionysius – *Mystical Theology*

Ward, Benedicta – *The Desert Fathers – Saying of the Early Christian Monks*

Waddell, Helen – *The Desert Fathers*

General Christian Spirituality

Brother Lawrence – *The Practice of the Presence of God*

Bunson, Matthew – *The 35 Doctors of the Church*

Chautard, Jean-Baptist – *The Soul of the Apostolate*

Kempis, Thomas – *The Imitation of Christ*

Lehodey, Dom Vitalis – *The Ways of Mental Prayer*

Lewis, C. S. – *Mere Christianity*

Philippe, Jacques – *Time for God*

Ratzinger, Joseph Cardinal – *Letter to the Bishops of the Catholic Church on Some Aspects of Christian Meditation*

Scupoli, Lorenzo – *Spiritual Combat*

Sheen, Fulton – *Lift Up Your Heart*

Underhill, Evelyn – *Mysticism*

Sacraments

Flynn, Vinny – *7 Secrets of Confession*

Flynn, Vinny – *7 Secrets of the Eucharist*

Sheen, Fulton – *These are the Sacraments*

Blessed Virgin Mary

Calloway, Donald – Champions of the Rosary

Fradd, Matt – Pocket Guide to the Rosary

Sheen, Fulton – The World's First Love

Spiritual Direction

St. Francis de Sales – *Introduction to the Devout Life*

St. Alphonsus Liguori – *The Twelve Steps to Holiness and Salvation*

Holy Family School of Faith – online resources at www.schoolof-faith.com

Roman Catholic Spiritual Direction – online resources at www.spiritualdirection.com

ABOUT THE AUTHOR

Steve Smith is the founder of *Interior Life*. Steve was born and raised Catholic but, like so many, didn't come to realize the richness and Truth of the faith until later in life. The *Interior Life* apostolate and the *30 Days to Christian Meditation* retreat were borne of Steve's experiences of applying the principles of Christian spirituality (particularly mystical and ascetical theology) to his ordinary life in the world as a husband and father and working in the field of forensic engineering. Through this he learned that living a contemplative life does not have to be at odds with living in the world; in fact the contemplative life elevates and perfects all the other facets of life. Put differently – we're all called to be mystics.

The *Interior Life* apostolate seeks to bring souls closer to Christ through the marvels of Christian spirituality, and hopefully this retreat will do just that for you.